ON YOUR LEFT

GENDERS 24

ON YOUR LEFT
Historical Materialism in the 1990s

Edited by Ann Kibbey, Thomas Foster, Carol Siegel, and Ellen Berry

NEW YORK UNIVERSITY PRESS
NEW YORK AND LONDON

NEW YORK UNIVERSITY PRESS
New York and London

Copyright © 1996 by New York University

ISBN 0-8147-4681-0 cloth
ISBN 0-8147-4682-9 paperback

New York University Press books are printed on acid-free paper, and their binding
materials are chosen for strength and durability.

Manufactured in the United States of America

10 9 8 7 6 5 4 3 2 1

Contents

Foreword

Ann Kibbey

In these spirited and powerfully written essays, a new generation of intellectuals makes its mark, challenging conservatives and liberals alike to chart a new course for a responsible politics in contemporary society. A new intellectual movement on the left emerges here. No longer trapped by the old polarizing antagonism between Marxism and feminism, these authors demonstrate as never before the need for an awareness of gender as it affects every aspect of our society. At the same time, these paradigmatic essays map out a new terrain for feminist thinking, one that fully recognizes the complex workings of gender and leaves any oppositional feminism, organized only around dualistic categories, far behind.

In the keynote essay, "Ambivalence as Alibi," Rosemary Hennessy challenges the most basic assumptions of postmodern sophistication to forge a compelling new synthesis of political, economic, and artistic theory. Betty Joseph, Jennifer Brody, and Poonam Pillai break through the shibboleths of Western Liberal "tolerance" to describe gender inequalities that are intrinsically inter-cultural. Eileen Cleere demonstrates that novels are an important source for understanding how people interpret the economic conditions in which they live, linking social history and literary criticism in a provocative new way. Bridget Elliott uncovers the unusual social and artistic imagination of Marie Laurencin, an artist who was both working-class and avant-garde, and who makes us rethink basic assumptions of artistic form in the visual representation of women. Laura Lyons, analyzing the no-wash protest among IRA prisoners, discovers a new kind of political protest that draws on performance art and the discourse of the body for its political symbolism. And Joseph Litvak, in a highly suggestive critical reading, makes us wonder if the New Historicism may possibly owe its greatest debt to the charming young men of Jane Austen's fictitious world.

ONE

Ambivalence as Alibi: On the Historical Materiality of Late Capitalist Myth in *The Crying Game* and Cultural Theory

Rosemary Hennessy

There has been much talk and writing in the past few years that affirms a new epistemology of the self figured in terms of ambivalent border identities, the in-between subjectivities of postmodern culture that cross and break down boundaries between one apparently distinct racial, national, gendered, sexual category and another. In academic cultural theory, some of the most recent discussion of indeterminate identity has drawn upon the discourse of materialism to make its points. But because many of these formulations ultimately evade the historical materiality of new forms of identity, their cultural politics is, I will argue, limited. My reading of *The Crying Game* as mythic representation is aimed at redressing these limits. In historicizing the relationship between the film's mythic absorption of the transvestite and of neo-imperialism, I offer an instance of how we might begin to understand some of the historical conditions of possibility on which contemporary representations of ambivalent identities depend.

In addressing the representation of ambivalent identities, I aim to do more than provide a reading of one film. *The Crying Game*'s postcolonial drag romance is an occasion to inquire into the larger and more contentious question, what exactly is meant by the materiality of postmodern ambivalence? Neo-idealists posit that ambivalence is the trace of an unrepresentable Real. Neo-culturalists claim that ambivalence is reducible

1

to the indeterminacy of ideology, signification, or discourse. I will argue
that new, ambivalent, desiring subjects need to be read as ideological
effects that are linked to the persistent and contradictory structures of
capitalism. The last part of the chapter pursues the representation of
ambivalence in the work of Slavoj Zizek and Judith Butler, two critics
whose thinking on ideology and desire has profoundly affected current
debates on the materiality of identity. I will show that, far from giving us
strong critical perspectives, the neo-idealist and neo-culturalist tales of
ambivalence they tell offer alibis for the historical and material conditions
out of which new forms of identity arise and in so doing participate in the
mythologizing strategies of a broad-based postmodern imaginary.

WHAT IS SEEN, WHAT HAPPENS, AND WHAT IS SAID

As one of the most pervasive forms of cultural narrative in the late
twentieth century, commercial film is an extremely powerful vehicle of
myth. To some extent, the films that manage to reach the box office get
there because they already articulate the social imaginary—the prevailing
images a society needs to project about itself in order to maintain certain
features of its organization. The social imaginary is not reproduced simply
by the discourses or images encoded "in" a film nor is it merely decoded
by the viewer from the film's formal structures. Rather, the mythic meanings of films are the effect of a dynamic social process in which their
production and reception both participate. Any film text comes to make
sense by means of the historically available modes of intelligibility—a
variety of assumptions about reality—through which the spectator chains
the film's signifiers into a meaningful story.[1]

In constructing what Masu'd Zavarzadeh has called the "tale" of a film,
the viewer fashions a map of reality and as a result situates herself in a
particular set of social relations (Zavarzadeh, 11). The values promoted
by the tales of commercial films offer imaginary representations, allegories by which subjects live, identify, and take up their proper places in
social life. Because the ways of making sense through which films become
meaningful are not homogeneous but rather contestatory sites of social
struggle, the dominant realist or obvious tale of a film is always unstable,
always different from itself. This difference is the site of suppressed but
potential other tellings. What makes it possible for the viewer to see
against the grain of the cultural obvious and renarrate the tale of a film

otherwise is her social and historical position within those knowledges that refuse or refute the dominant culture's myths. A critical reading of a film as myth renarrates the ways of knowing that the film offers as obvious or visible by drawing on those knowledges that contest its commonsense telling. Unlike a resistant reading that simply dismisses the commonsense tale or a formalist reading that searches for a film's hidden meanings in the dynamics of the filmic apparatus, a critical reading considers the historical conditions of possibility by which the visible comes to be see-able—that is, the divisions of labor and accompanying forms of state power and subjectivity this version of reality helps to reinforce or under-mine.

Roland Barthes's assertion that "myth hides nothing; its function is to distort" acknowledges the oblique relation between the visible and the seeable in myth.[2] As myths, films circulate the contradictions under-girding a social community not by hiding them but by parading them right in front of our (unseeing) eyes. In this sense, mythic display operates in the realm of the imaginary. The mythic tale is imaginary not because it is false or untrue but because it resolves social contradictions that remain unsolvable in other areas of lived history. This resolution takes place through a variety of strategies by which the tale is assembled. Chief among them is the tactic of naturalizing social differences as the way things are. "The very principle of myth," Barthes asserts, "is its transfor-mation of history into nature" (129). As a naturalizing, imaginary repre-sentation of a society's values and order, myth is an allegorical narrative that deprives meanings of their history. Its structure, Barthes contends, reproduces that of the alibi: "I am not where you think I am, I am where you think I am not" (123). As an alibi, myth displaces real social relations with naturalized imaginary ones. The effect of this displacement is to encourage meanings that will smooth over and manage the historical contradictions encoded in the narrative tale. In the process, myth helps to reproduce the prevailing social order as the way things naturally should be.

One of the mythic functions of commercial film in late capitalism is to articulate cognitive maps for postmodern subjects whose historical situation—conditions of work and family, community and pleasure—are in a variety of ways distinct from those of social subjects in industrialized countries a generation ago. Two of the most notable features of this new historical situation are the consolidation of neo-imperialism such that capital accumulation is no longer exercised through imperial ownership of land and direct political control as it was through the first half of the twentieth century but through more densely globalized corporate circuits of production and consumption. The proliferation of sexualities increasingly unhinged from kinship alliances, property, and the reproductive couple has accompanied this process. The media has played an enormous role in both, enhancing the invisibility of empire and capital's ability to create and make use of sexuality and the sexualized body as new colonies. To paraphrase F. W. Haug, "the illusion industry" in late capitalism—advertising, television, computer, video, and film—"has populated the spaces left empty by capitalism" in its former phases.[3] While the imaginary medium of myth's displacements is in one sense a matter of "shades and shadows," as Haug contends, in another sense this new colony is profoundly embodied. Indeed, the sexualized body has become the premier commodity and marketing niche of late capitalism; corporeal fashion, engineering, simulation, and management have created a host of new needs and accompanying new modalities of power, knowledge, and control.

The eruption of the discourses of sexuality in the nineteenth-century West and their saturation of everyday life throughout the next century are entangled intimately with shifts in policy and capitalist production that comprise the second and third phases of empire. Yet this history is for the most part a matter of shades and shadows.[4] We have yet to map out very clearly or to explain very well the historical relation between the proliferation of sexual identities and empire. To what extent, for instance, is empire one of the constitutive features of the emergence of homosexual identities in the West? In what ways did the structures of colonialism enable and shape the emergence of a homosexual imaginary in the imperial metropolises? And how, in turn, was the exercise of colonial power affected by new divisions of labor and ensuing changes in kinship alliances that allowed the possibility of metropolitan counter-heterosexual identities? These are still largely unasked and unanswered questions.

Myth works by atomizing, sorting, reducing—robbing images of their history. That sexuality and empire do not connect very well or easily in our cultural archives is perhaps one of the most unattended lingering grand myths of modernity. If this is so, it is both symptomatic and predictable that *The Crying Game*'s two tales—of empire and of sexuality—are not only entangled but also, in the film's various tellings, entirely opaque to one another. If myth robs cultural representations of their history, the transvestite in *The Crying Game* is doubly plundered. For at the same time she is naturalized back into the heterosexual imaginary or construed as an ambivalent hybrid, Dil also serves as a site of mythic displacement for the loss of imperial phallic power. As the switchpoint between *The Crying Game*'s two tales of political and sexual intrigue, she bonds one to the other. However, in the little sustained critical attention the film has received it has not been read this way. Instead, the two tales are usually separated—the sexual one highlighted, the political one backgrounded or reduced to a discussion of race. This sorting and erasure are both crucial to the film's mythic effects and consistent with the ways sexuality often has functioned in representations of empire.

THE THINGS A GIRL HAS TO PUT UP WITH

After the opening of *The Crying Game*, review after review in the popular press reiterated its tale in more or less the following way: an IRA member, Fergus Hennessy (Stephen Rea), befriends his kidnapped prisoner, a black British soldier named Jody (Forest Whitacker). After Jody's death (ironically not by Fergus's or the IRA's doing but by the British saracen sent to rescue him), Fergus pursues his (homoerotic) attachment to Jody by locating and eventually falling for Jody's girlfriend, Dil (Jaye Davidson), a London hairdresser and (perhaps) prostitute. But Dil—whom both Fergus and the audience have assumed is a woman—turns out to be a man. The disclosure of Dil's "true sexual identity" takes place in a very deliberately choreographed scene in which the camera slowly follows the unveiling of her penis. This is the pivotal moment of shock and fascination when an audience unfamiliar with the codes of transvestism and gay male culture learns that they have been mistakenly reading the marks of Dil's gender as an expression of her sex/genitals.

What makes *The Crying Game*'s sexual tale a postmodern myth is the way it confronts the very problem of identity as a confusion of the visible with the seeable by destabilizing the myth of coherent (gender, sexual) identity only to restabilize it. Playing the transvestite's masquerade against the disguises of other characters is one of these restabilizing tactics. "False" identities provide the very texture of terrorist and romantic negotiation and success: Fergus's female IRA comrade, Jude (Miranda Richardson), passes as a floozy in order to entrap a British soldier—although viewers, like Jody, learn this only in retrospect; when Fergus is on the lam, he disguises his Irish identity with a haircut, a new name, and a new nationality; when Jude turns up in England, she has traded her blonde hair and blue jeans for "a tougher look"—black hair and a suit; the burlap hood Jody is made to wear as hostage operates as a double-sided mask—protecting the identities of his captors and veiling his humanity from them.

The dangerous knowledge that sexual identity cannot be reduced to a visible body that speaks for itself, that it is indeed a conventional encoding of the body, and the even more threatening possibility that sexual desire might not be rooted in a natural heterosexual order are the scandalous secrets of *The Crying Game*'s sexual tale. If this knowledge is quickly remythologized, it is in part because the film's promotion helped insure that it would be. Probably this film's most notable feature for U.S. audiences was the hype over its "secret" which Miramax invented and capitalized on.[5] This marketing strategy had a significant effect on the film's tale.[6] By translating the transvestite's masquerade into the rhetoric of disguise, the film's "secret" helped anchor Dil's "true" identity in the disclosure of her penis. In other words, the tactic of asking audiences and reviewers not to reveal the film's "secret" helped redirect the assumed (unwitting) viewer's misreading of Dil away from the discomforting revelation that gender identity is not grounded in biological difference and sexual desire need not be generated by attraction to "the opposite sex" and toward the more acceptable notion that he or she, like Fergus, was merely fooled into mistaking Dil for a woman. In conjunction with a variety of disguises and naturalizing discourses that encourage this conclusion, the "secret" displaces the dangerous suggestion that gender and sexuality have no authentic foundation. In this way, the "secret" collaborates with the heterosexual imaginary that structures the film's sexual tale.

The heterosexual imaginary is the cultural myth that explains male and female sex as naturally asymmetrical biological givens that masculine and feminine gendered traits express.[7] It organizes and legislates sexual identification and desire so that the subject's sexual aim is directed toward a coherently gendered member of the supposedly "opposite" sex. Historically, capitalism has relied on the heterosexual imaginary to engender desire and to justify an exploitative sexual division of labor. By presenting heterogendered differences as fixed and natural opposites, the heterosexual imaginary robs sexuality of its history, erases the social order it helps guarantee, makes invisible the precariousness of its identifications, and obscures the multiplicity of possible other organizations of identification and desire.

From the opening scene of *The Crying Game*, the viewer is invited to draw on a heterosexual imaginary which will provide the basis for "misreading" Dil. Although Jody's entrapment by the IRA takes place at a carnival—that traditional site of bawdy subversion and temporary liberation from prevailing truths—the seduction scene between him and Jude induces the viewer to naturalize gender and heterosexuality. Jude's sexual "pick up" is interrupted by Jody's need to urinate. He dodges into a makeshift latrine, pees standing up, and continues to hold Jude's hand. The visible evidence seems to confirm the obvious conclusion that Jody is both a real man—he has a penis—and, desiring Jude, he is "clearly" heterosexual.

The fascination provoked by media images such as these is a dynamic process whereby human sensuality comes to be incorporated by means of a series of already available cognitive maps a film's reading draws on, reinforces, or disrupts. Viewing *The Crying Game*, particularly its images of sexual ambivalence, takes place through the negotiation of several strategies of incorporation that both filter through and flex the heterosexual imaginary. The first urinating scene and its complement—the scene after Jody's capture when Fergus holds Jody's penis so he can pee even though his hands are tied behind his back—are two instances when bodies seem to insure gender identity. At the same time, both scenes also open up a possible space of difference within this myth by troubling the corporeal guarantees of the heterosexual imaginary: the first retrospectively when we realize that Jody does not neatly fit into a heterosexual identity and the second by the homoerotic charge between the two men that lurks on the edges of the dramatized "proof" of natural male sexual identity.

But the heterosexual imaginary recurs despite and against these disruptive openings. The most striking instance is the recuperation of the transvestite's unveiled penis by Fergus's physical revulsion (he runs to the bathroom, vomits, and then abruptly leaves). In the wake of the disrupted equation between bodies and "opposite" genders, heterosexuality is redeemed and homoerotic desire—for which Dil is after all only the vehicle—is safely secured in the shadows of fantasy.[8] The interpolated moral tale Jody tells Fergus—the fable of the frog and the scorpion—which seems at first only to naturalize the difference between Fergus and his IRA comrades, is readily available to explain Fergus's disgust. Like the scorpion, he can't help himself: "it's in his nature." However, that Dil "remains" a woman rather than becoming a freak indicates that the heterosexual imaginary can accommodate a certain degree of gender flexibility over and against the appeals to authenticity, nature, and instincts it simultaneously depends on.[9] Having followed their courtship, complete with all of the conventional romantic props, the audience remains committed to Fergus and Dil as a straight couple and so can tolerably secure within the heterosexual matrix both Fergus's homoeroticism and Dil's ambivalent femininity.

Of course, the tale of the film I have been delineating is its dominant one, a narrative that circulated in *Newsweek* and *The New York Times*, a version of the film pitched at and in some ways helping to construct its straight target audience. But many viewers did not see or refused to endorse this version. It is significant that *The Village Voice* review of *The Crying Game* opens by addressing such a potentially oppositional viewer, marked as "too poor or resistant to theatre to attend Mamet's *Oleanna*." Yet the tale *The Voice* offers finally is not very different from that of the mainstream press. After celebrating *The Crying Game* for denaturalizing sex and gender, it praises the film for handling race in "a refreshingly natural way"—that is, for not making distinctions according to race at all. Essays on *The Crying Game* from the slightly more academic alternative arena of *Jump Cut* and *Film Quarterly* (both published out of Berkeley) and in the gay press (*The Advocate*) pursue a more critical tack, coming down quite hard on the film's promotion of a sexist and misogynist social order and a transhistorical humanism.[10] But their renarrations also tend to focus primarily on the sexual plot. Moreover, while they read against the grain of the film's mythic representations of sexual, gender, and race identities, these essays are what I would call resistant rather than critical readings, that is, they refuse or negate the dominant tale without explaining its reasons for being.

Other avant-garde reviews play up the film's endorsement of ambivalent, border-crossing identities. In *Jump Cut*, for example, Robert Payne reads Dil by way of Marjorie Garber's notion of the transvestite as a symptomatic "category crisis" in the culture. He contends that social crises around national boundaries and racial anxieties are displaced onto the uncertainty over Dil's ambivalent gender. The primary focus of

Payne's reading is what he sees as the film's endorsement of emergent postmodern and postcolonial identities, its polymorphous eroticism, and its cultural cross-overs between mainstream and margin. However, while such resistant readings may refuse traditional appeals to human nature or denounce racism and misogyny, they finally are unable to explain why these social structures persistently undergird new representations of racial and sexual identity, and they draw no relation between ambivalent sexual identities and class divisions or new forms of patriarchy and imperialism under late capitalism. In failing to historicize the material mythic effects of cultural representations, they help to keep these social arrangements in place.

The modification of patriarchy's gender system under late capitalism has produced what some feminists have called public or postmodern patriarchy.[11] Under postmodern patriarchy, heterosexuality remains the dominant paradigm for sexuality, family, romance, parenting, reproduction, and feminism even as its boundaries have become more permeable. This permeability is allowed most in the form of cultural or state pluralism where homosexuals are added in as part of the "multicultural" mix of lifestyle choices. Clearly, even liberal pluralism is a site of struggle. The debates in Britain over the passage of Section 28 of the Local Government Act in 1988 are one instance of this battleground whose history the mythologized transvestite in *The Crying Game* both displays and obscures. Section 28 proscribed the promotion of homosexuality and "pretended families" in school and local government-funded events.[12] Although the campaign to defeat the bill failed, and the new law has not had wide-ranging repressive effects, the parameters of this legislation indicate the ways a new "multicultural" homosexual difference is being countenanced without eroding the social order heterosexuality helps secure. The discourse of conservative supporters of Section 28 never promoted a purely homogeneous heterosexual Britain, nor did the law set out to eliminate homosexual difference. But it does differentiate "responsible" (private, closeted, discrete) gays from "dangerous" ones.[13] Significantly, this danger is seen to lie not in homosexual difference per se but in what gays make of it: dangerous gayness flaunts, invades, disrupts a social system in which the heterosexual imaginary helps to legitimize a racialized and gendered division of labor. Responsible gays simply assimilate into this order. Like the discourses of the new racism circulating in Britain since the late 1960s, the incorporation of the "good homosexual" casts sexual difference in suitably tolerant cultural terms. Tolerance of homosexuals does not challenge the reasons why heterosexuality is sanctioned, naturalized, and required by the capitalist state, or why resistance to this imperative is simultaneously allowed, policed, and punished.

When *The Crying Game* appeared in the United States, the religious Right had already launched a massive moral crusade against homosexuals, with the muscle of the Republican party already pushing it into legislation in many states. But at the same time the conservative backlash intensified, the love that dared not speak its name had become a major public discourse. In Fall 1992, when the debate over gays in the U.S. military was in full force, the commodification of gay "lifestyles" was also increasingly proving a lucrative new market, and the promotion of ambivalent, performative sexualities had become a signature of the postmodern avant-garde. Celebrations of ambivalent sexualities, however, often ignore the ways symbolic adjustments to the heterosexual imperative are accommodated easily by late capitalism's class structures and new forms of public patriarchy.

The phallus, so central to Lacanian and feminist psychoanalytic theory, is a concept that has been used to map this uneven operation of (hetero)-sexual ambivalence in public patriarchy. As the arbitrary signifier of sexual difference, the phallus functions much like myth. Both are mechanisms by which subjection to the social order takes place through a promise of coherent identity. At the same time, this promise is forever deferred. The status of the phallus as the mark of difference is a fraud; "having" or "being" it is never finally achieved. Like Lacan's, the transvestite's story in *The Crying Game* disrupts the myth of essential sexual difference, flaunting the dangerous knowledge that the phallus as the mark of difference is a sham. Precariously positioned across "having" and "being" the phallus, the transvestite is the outlaw subject who shows up this arbitrary foundation of the phallic economy.

In the long run, of course, the film's sexual tale resecures this ambivalence within the Law of a patriarchal heterosexual imaginary. Both before and after we know Dil is not female, she nonetheless remains a real woman. Even the viewer who all along reads Dil as the transvestite—and so maintains her gender ambivalence—has to confront the narrative's insistence that she be positioned against Jude and the lessons in hetero-gendered femininity this juxtaposition teaches. As Dil's counterpart, Jude is a woman who can "be" the phallus (the female object of desire able to entrap and lure a man through the masquerade of her femininity) but in her gun-wielding authoritative poses she also can "have" the phallus. In the tale's closure, however, Jude's death instructs us that for a woman to be and to have the phallus finally is forbidden. In other words, even after we know Jude is not a "real woman," she is still a woman. Jude is punished for betraying her proper feminine position, while Dil (like Jody and Fergus) is allowed more gender flexibility. Even though being a "real" woman seems to be not necessarily dictated by one's biology, sexual ambivalence nonetheless turns out to be a strictly heterogendered affair.

Indeed, the tale of the transvestite and her nemesis, the phallic woman, can be read as a set of instructions on the limits of being a "real" woman in postmodern patriarchy. It is no accident that ads for the film feature Jude as the gun-wielding vamp, while the most talked about frame is the spectacle of Dil's unveiled penis, nor is it surprising that the tale's shocking inversion of the primal scene culminates in the murder of the phallic woman. Both are intelligible because of the more flexible circulation of phallic power in postmodern patriarchy, and together they map one dimension of its heterogendered construction of the real. In the Freudian primal scene (culled from the late phase of bourgeois patriarchy), the woman/mother who is thought to have a penis is discovered not to have one, and her status as woman is thereby realized. In the cultural logic of postmodern patriarchy enacted here, however, the woman who is thought not to have the phallus is discovered to have it. How the consequent disavowal of this discovery is handled depends on whether or not her womanhood is perceived as "real." When Dil shoots the phallic Jude, she shouts, "I bet you used those tits and that cute little ass to get him." The message is clear: justice is being served against the woman who both is and has the phallus but who betrays the masquerade of "real womanhood" by using it (rather than "being" it)—in other words, by becoming a man. Despite its play with sexual ambivalence, the tale of *The Crying Game* finally endorses a classic and familiar heterogendered script. There is in the end very little irony in the opening and closing tunes. Together, they provide the heterogendered articulating structure for understanding this tale of what it means to be a real woman: "When a Man Loves a Woman" it is because she knows how to "Stand by Her Man."[14]

What social and historical conditions have engendered these symbolic adjustments to the heterogendered "real"? In the Lacanian narrative the instability of phallic power is seen as the effect of an indeterminacy internal to signification, a result of the irreparable loss of presence that follows the subject's passage from need to desire. Because it ascribes the instability of phallic power to the workings of desire in a symbolic order that has no outside, no history, the Lacanian narrative is idealist yet is also frequently appropriated by "neo-culturalists." While feminists, and feminist film theorists especially, have made use of Lacan's theories to denaturalize gender difference and have even challenged his idealist assumptions, their renarrations of subjectivity, much like Lacan's, unlink desire from need and in so doing displace the continuing social relation between them with signification and culture.[15] One of the aims of materialist feminism has been to theorize the phallus as a historically variable effect of contradictory social arrangements that are not reducible to the symbolic, signifying dimension of culture.[16] Rearticulating the concept of the phallus in a historical and materialist framework situates its symbolic function in relation to the structures of social production that include language but are also outside and mediated by language. In so doing, historical materialism connects the production of ambivalent, desiring subjects in the realm of ideology and cultural representation to the uneven satisfaction of human needs under capitalism. As a result, the persistent, variable, and precarious circulation of phallic power and the incoherent, desiring subject it legislates are seen to be no longer simply effects of the indeterminacy of signification, but of a contradictory set of social relations in which the needs of some are satisfied and the desires of a few heightened because of the collective labors of many. In attending only to the desiring subject and to desire as signification, neo-culturalists reify this historical effect and eclipse its relation to the new/persistent patriarchal and imperialist dimensions of late capitalism.

In the professional and managerial sectors of overdeveloped industrial capitalism, the more malleable heterogender system of late bourgeois patriarchy cannot be disconnected from new global divisions of labor. In the past two decades, as increasing numbers of women have been recruited into the formerly masculine public sphere of professional and corporate wage work, normative divisions of labor under capital's monopoly phase have been reformed, reorganizing the taken-for-granted separation between private and public, domestic and market spheres of social life. At the same time, classic bourgeois gender ideology has adjusted to the impact of these modifications. Changes in the working day—to part and variable time schedules—as well as the proliferation of information technologies have made the formerly "separate sphere" of home a site of waged labor for more middle-class men and women. During the economic recession of the past decade, many unemployed middle-class fathers were recruited into child care and unpaid domestic labor out of economic necessity, and more flexible gender ideologies accommodated these changes. Many middle-class white men are allowed to be more vulnerable and sensitive than their fathers and can eschew a militaristic machismo while middle-class women are allowed to "wear the pants" and exercise a degree more phallic authority than their mothers had.

While these revisions to classic bourgeois patriarchy's more rigid gender arrangements are producing a more pliable, postmodern patriarchal heterogender ideology, they have not dramatically undermined the usefulness of patriarchal hierarchies to global capital's divisions of labor. If in postmodern patriarchy the phallus can circulate somewhat more freely among middle-class white men and women, the range of resources and mobility this circulation affords is still more limited for women than for men, even for the minority of professional women. Although women have made some inroads into traditionally male-dominated professions, the sexual division of labor has changed very little; the vast majority of working women remain confined to poorly paid, low-status work.[17] The persistence of the double day, the glass ceiling, rape, and a host of other forms of sexual violence (dieting, plastic surgery, compulsory deference, romance, motherhood) whereby women incorporate femininity at great cost to their social well-being, all indicate continued restrictions on any increased ideological phallic power women may have gained.

The ideological flexibility of postmodern patriarchy is also conditioned by changes in the relations of production under late capitalism's "flexible accumulation."[18] In the past two decades, the linear Fordist model of manufacture on the global assembly line is gradually being restructured and replaced by the emergence of entirely new sectors of production, new ways of providing financial services, new markets, and intensified rates of innovation. These new powers of flexibility and mobility have given rise to rapid shifts in the patterns of uneven development, an intensification of time-space compression, a restructuring of the labor force into more flexible work regimes, and increasing reliance on part-time, temporary, or sub-contracted work (Harvey, 150). Fordism's rigidities are giving way to "systemofacture" in which all elements of the production unit adopt more system-like relationships at the heart of which is increased product innovation and cybernetics.[19] Just-in-time production allows for rapid small batch manufacturing and combines flexible automation with multi-skilled and flexible workers who can be deployed for a variety of tasks to cheaply produce customized products.[20] The requirements of this new system of manufacturing vary, but they all rely on an overall strategy that joins the use of the most advanced technologies with the most ancient and oppressive forms of sweated labor, for which the tacit skills of women are considered the most suitable (Mitter, 196; Nanda, 8). In other words, the bottom line for extracting surplus value under the regime of flexible accumulation is still rigidly gendered: women remain the most desirable source of cheap and malleable labor. That so many women across the globe labor for low wages and minimal overhead, on schedules responsive to part or just-in-time production needs, often in subcontracted domestic-family labor systems, and with minimal opportunity to organize is in part made possible because more rigid patriarchal regimes underlie and sustain the more flexible gender system of postmodern patriarchy.

The transition from Fordism to flexible accumulation which has taken place since the 1970s was accompanied by the emergence of a postmodern imaginary in industrial centers. Even though the relationship between ideology and divisions of labor is not neatly integrated, direct, or mono-causal, the epistemological shift to more ambivalently coded identities is historically linked to the reliance of the more flexible motion of capital on the ephemeral, the fleeting, the fugitive. Multinational corporations such as Coca Cola, Bennetton, Levi-Strauss, and Mattel are among those who have adopted new "multi-local" systems to enhance the accumulation of relative surplus value through production strategies that involve "adapting rapidly and flexibly to local conditions."[21] At the same time, these new structures of work are accompanied by new structures of consciousness, desire, and identity. It is no coincidence that the marketing strategies for these companies' products, which range from soft-drinks to dolls, rely on the ambivalently gendered postmodern imaginary we see reiterated in commercial films like *The Crying Game*.[22] Tales of ambivalent subjects emanating from industrial centers and circulating across the globe offer palatable alibis that mystify the objective historical conditions binding these new identities to the uneven satisfaction of human needs. Mythologizing a more flexible heterogender system in films like *The Crying Game* empties the ambivalent, desiring subject of its history, obscures the contradictory relation between ideology and labor, and forestalls inquiry into why more fluid pleasures and sexualities have become the signature claim of an emerging postmodern common sense.

GETTING RID OF A SHIT-HOT BOWLER

The tale of sexual ambivalence is, of course, only part of the story of *The Crying Game*. That the film's political tale is finally just a backdrop for a story of sexual intrigue is both a familiar convention of Hollywood cinema and an index of one of the ways sexuality functions in late capitalism. However, fascination with transvestism and homoerotic fantasy in the sexual tale does not so much deflect attention from another site of phallic power—imperialism—as it works to confound any relation between them. As myth, the film does not conceal its colonial context; IRA activities comprise its narrative premise. But the avowal of a seemingly more freely circulating phallus in the tale of sexual ambivalence works mythically to disavow the potential threat of anti-colonialist collective affiliation and the persistence of racist phallic power. Renarrating the sexual tale of the film from the vantage point of its colonial context suggests that Fergus's "impossible" sexual relationship with Dil and Jody displaces anxieties and losses specific to the late phase of imperialism. Unlike the film sagas *Out of Africa* or *Passage to India*, *The Crying Game* tells a story of colonial loss from the perspective of the (Irish) colonized subject in the metropolitan center who gradually rejects the dichotomies of imperialism as a viable epistemology.[23] Clearly the opposition between colonizer and colonized provides the foundation for the IRA's actions, loyalties, and sense of national identity; but this is a way of thinking Fergus—and many viewers—eventually disown. In breaking rank with anti-colonialist struggle and with his revolutionary comrades, Fergus maps out a postcolonial position.

The "post" of postcolonialism signifies a reinscription of the historical relation between colonizer and colonized as a structure of knowledge and power. Postcolonialism is not a sign for a period "after" colonialism in a linear model of history, nor a description of a global historical condition, so much as a term for a discourse that disrupts the binary and hierarchical relations of imperialism. In this sense, postcolonialism is distinct from neo-imperialism, and I draw that distinction in the following way: postcolonialism is a discourse that is emerging as the dominant way of making sense of the historical condition of neo-imperialism. It is the system of representations through which the dominant cultures of late capitalism represent or imagine a global political economy in which capital is decentered nationally, its organization more flexible and divisions of labor more systematized, where nation states are splintered and political interests corporate-driven. Like patriarchy, colonialism as a regime of power has not disappeared from these arrangements, but it has been reconfigured into new forms. "Post" marks the trace of that reconfiguration in the social imaginary of late capitalism.

As divisions of labor and sites of production fall less neatly into the three worlds schema and the demands of formerly colonized immigrants redraw the political boundaries of nationhood, one of the anxieties of the late capitalist neo-imperialist state is the specter of resistance erupting "at home" from "formerly" colonized collectivities formed against its exploitative practices and imaginary public sphere. Various mythic strategies serve to keep intact a new multicultural conception of "the people" that will forestall this threat. The ambivalent postcolonial subject is one of them. The postcolonial subject has been touted as a dangerous supplement both to the ideologies of colonial difference and to their pluralist replacements, troubling any neat coordination of national affiliation with colonizer-colonized status. Yet, because this ambivalence erases any objective historical conditions outside the slippery categories of culture and language, it often collaborates with the mythic strategies of the liberal, multicultural center.

The Crying Game's tale coalesces liberal and postcolonial ideologies—fetishizing ambivalence, naturalizing difference, and displacing the possible third terms of collective subjectivity and social transformation with romantic individualism.[24] In many ways, the principle figures of *The Crying Game* are intelligible as subjects whose identities are playfully unbounded, indeterminate, and permeable. Against this postcolonial tale, however, the film's political tale has no trouble demonizing the IRA. As Fergus increasingly sets the moral standard for the viewer, Peter and Jude appear more and more unfeeling and ruthless. We are invited to see only their rough treatment of Jody, their assassination attempt against the British judge, and Jude's retaliation against Fergus and Dil. The film proves Jody's distinction between Fergus and his "people" to be true: the IRA are "all tough, undeluded motherfuckers." Although we know that Fergus does not really betray the cause—he is kept from his appointed post when Dil ties him to the bed—this knowledge makes little difference in the tale's assessment of the IRA. When Dil shoots Jude, the villain has been removed. The limited information we are given on the Irish Republican Army rehearses familiar stereotypes. Like the IRA splinter group in *Patriot Games* who train in the Libyan Desert or the IRA prisoner of *In the Name of the Father*, their objectives and extreme measures seem obviously fanatical because their history and rationale remain entirely opaque.

In *The Crying Game*, the audience is encouraged to demonize the IRA not only because it rehearses already well-known codes for terrorists but because the standards of moral worth gathering around Fergus endorse an Anglo perspective that is naturalized as universal. As the primary focalizer of the film, his values guide the viewer. His turn to England situates him and us less in the position of insurgent colonialist and more in the familiar, dominant liberal way of knowing. It is no accident, then, that the state finally protects Fergus's stance, since his perspective and the state's are much alike. Narrative closure occurs by way of the state's intervention—Fergus is arrested and goes to jail—and as a result, both heterosexual and imperial imaginaries are kept, albeit tenuously, intact. Justice has again been served: Fergus expiates his crime against Jody, the state suppresses one more outlaw, and the impossible romantic couple is safely managed. Above all, any political relation among colonized collectivities has been forestalled. The ideological pressure to forfeit identification with an anti-imperialist position is one of the historical conditions of the postcolonial imaginary.[25]

Sexuality historically has been a site where imperial conquest and policy have been mythologized and colonial anxieties have been played out.[26] From the vantage point of the dominant metropolitan culture, anxieties over the threatened or actual loss of imperial phallic power are often displaced onto diseased or degenerate women and foreigners (Kipnis, 198). *The Crying Game*'s quasi-art film conventions and seeming "political" interest give this myth a slightly different twist, however. Here, postcolonial losses register in "impossible" sexual relationships that purport to suspend binary difference. But within *The Crying Game*'s tale of indeterminate difference, ambivalent genders, and biracial affiliations, a critical viewer also can read the traces of a racially gendered neo-imperialism. Just as the crisis fomented by the staging of the drag romance is smoothed over by a heterogendered imaginary that heals its ruptures, the freely circulating postcolonial phallus also finally is secured along an asymmetrical racial axis.

As I mentioned earlier, in describing the tale of the film, reviewers often fail to mention race or actually assert that the film transcends racial difference.[27] The argument that racial differences do not matter indicates how successfully the most available ways of making sense have naturalized racial hierarchies through the gender system that structures the relationship between Fergus and Dil. As a black "female," Dil's services to Fergus are doubly allowed; at the same time, her transvestism neutralizes the threat of miscegenation that might otherwise be posed by a potentially dangerous black female sexuality.[28] As for Dil the black "male," it is not just the codes of R and X ratings that forbid her an erect penis in the unveiling scene. It is a necessity of postcolonialism that the symbolic effect of a black penis in a white man's face be softened.

The integrity of the tale's already engendered and racialized romance require that the representation of a sexual encounter between a white (anti)hero and the black (wo)man he pursues both reproduce and deny the history of racialized sexuality under colonialism. In this history, the exploitation of slave and sweated labor and the routine rape of black women by white men had to be justified by a symbolic order that both emasculated black men and projected onto them a hypersexuality that mingled desire for an abject other with the fantasy of potential resistance. Within popular narratives and scientific studies since the nineteenth century, myths of sexual excess and perversion are projected onto colonized peoples, men and women both, as a mystification of the real trauma of imperialism and the potential for opposition.[29] On the one hand, in order that the phallus be sutured to the colonizer, the colonized subject had to be castrated/feminized. On the other hand, this suturing and castration were never entirely successful as the irruption of the hypersexual black man in the dominant social imaginary testifies. As Fanon asserts, "in the European imagination the Negro is turned into a penis. He *is* a penis" (170). By embodying the phallus as penis, the hypersexual black man is robbed of the cultural capital of being civilized—that is, of being a "real" man. As penis/flesh (rather than rational mind), he is situated as being rather than having the phallus. Paradoxically, then, the penis becomes the sign of the black man's feminization (Handler, 40).

The circulation of homosocial desire and homophobic resistance within the history of colonialism cannot be read outside these structures of power. While colonial discourses serve as an unstable site for the articulation and negotiation of phallic power in the symbolic domain,

their engendering functions as a symptomatic displacement of the fundamental social contradiction undergirding imperialism—the disparity between communally produced resources and privately allocated wealth.
The climactic sexual encounter between Fergus and Dil may well involve
two formerly colonized subjects, and the prevailing discourses of postcolonialism may invite us to read their relationship through the lens of
indeterminate oppositions between colonizer and colonized, male and
female. But the incongruity of Dil's limp penis insists on a history that
exceeds this playful gaming and directs our attention away from the film's
scandalous disclosure to the history it mystifies through this sexual alibi:
the persistence of a racialized phallic order and the class system it nour-
ishes despite, or rather within, an ambivalently flexible metropolitan gender system.

This hidden history is also mythologized in Jody's emasculation, which
cannot be separated from his position as formerly colonized subject. Jody
is both soldier and cricket player, but he is not the standard masculine
version of either. Like most others in a "volunteer" army, he enlisted
because "it was a job." Hardly the staunch loyalist, he finds himself in
Northern Ireland wondering, "what the fuck am I doing here anyway" in
"the only place in the world they call you nigger to your face." But we see
him exclusively as hostage and cricket player—never in uniform. And it
is as cricketer that he figures in Fergus's homoerotic dreams. There are
several oddities about Jody as dreamy icon, the black cricketer, all of
them, I would argue, the effects of the ways postcolonial homoerotic
fantasy serves as an alibi for a neo-imperialist phallic economy. First of
all, Jody's physique—just shy of fat—is far from the muscular and trim
bodies of the cricket players that people the British national imaginary.
Just as the absent image of the black British soldier references the West
Indian as loyal colonial subject, the fleshy homoerotic sexual charge that
gathers around the image of Jody as cricketer empties out the symbolic
phallic threat West Indian cricket historically has posed to Britain.

Like membership in the British military, during the first half of the
twentieth century playing cricket "proved you were part of the English
design."[30] From 1928 when West India played its first test match against
England until the 1960s when the first black captain led the international
side, that design meant a sport managed from Westminster, one in which
only white men were appointed captains by the West Indian cricket-
ing hierarchy. In *Beyond a Boundary*, the classic statement of the link

between emergent nationalism, anti-colonial struggle, and sporting culture, C. L. R. James documents the Caribbean-wide campaign that led to the appointment of Frank Worrell as first black captain of the West Indian cricket team.[31] During the 1960s, a cricket of resistance erupted in the Caribbean along with nationalist liberation struggles. By the 1980s, this resistance had consolidated into the West Indian domination of world cricket through the batting of Antiguan Viv Richards and others. As the treatment of players like Richards in the British press and playing fields demonstrates, "the prospect of an exceptionally fast Caribbean man with a cricket ball carries the same threat as a rebellious, anti-imperial black man with a gun; they want him suppressed, disarmed" (Searle, 38).

Any symbolic political charge that might gather around the black cricketer in Britain is muted, however, in the relationship between Jody and Fergus. It is significant that cricket seals the bond of friendship between the two soldiers and that its discussion is sparked by one of the film's only explicit acknowledgements of racism. When Jody repeats the racist epithet hurled at him in Ireland, Fergus's reply—"And you play cricket?"—indicates the ways cricket here serves to mediate and neutralize the phallic economies of race and national identity. Playful banter about whether hurling or cricket is the better sport obscures the shared colonial histories of Ireland and Antigua and displaces a potential counter-colonial affiliation onto the homoerotics of sport. It is to a great extent because Jody is more a sportsman than a British soldier that Fergus (and the audience) comes to bond with him. It is only after Jody announces, "So when you come to shoot me, Paddy, remember you're getting rid of a shit-hot bowler," that Fergus tells him his name. Later, interfaced with the "crying game" of his romance with Dil, cricket continues to be the medium for Fergus's connection to Jody and his new identity as a Brit. Fergus even participates vicariously in the game one day by imitating the cricket players across from the construction site where he works. While his boss' reprimand ("As long as you don't think you're at Lords!") is a faint reminder of cricket's role in enforcing an imperial class hierarchy, this history is erased in the dreamy icon of Jody in his white flannels.

Cricket carries, then, a layered mythic and imaginary investment as a discursive field through which colonized subjects are incorporated. In the tale of *The Crying Game*, this other game constitutes a sexual alibi whereby the formerly colonized subject is encrypted into the social imaginary in a way that masks his genealogy. After Dil is disclosed as a transvestite, the cricket field provides the backdrop for her reincorporation into the heterosexual imaginary; the workers' catcalls as she walks across the grass signal their recognition of a "real woman." When the drama is all played out and Fergus looks one final time at the photo of Jody in his flannels, he tells him, "You should have stayed at home." Whether the referent of this ambivalent signifier of national identity is Antigua or Britain seems hardly to matter, for the difference between Antiguan—or Fenian for that matter—and Brit, between old home and new, have all evaporated as the disarming image of a "shit-hot bowler" from Antigua is incorporated into the erotics of a transnational postcolonial imaginary.

While the homosocial discourse of cricket is a field where British colonial and neo-colonial ideologies of race and nation have been played and opposed, my renarration of the image of the black "shit-hot bowler" attends to only one small facet of the history mythologized in this image. For it is not just the history of cricket that is drained from the mythic icon of Jody as cricketer, but the much longer history of British imperialism for which it is a synecdoche. While the tale of the film invites us to read cricket as a metaphor for the homoerotic ties that bind these three postcolonial subjects, what makes them postcolonial in large part is the way the discourses of culture and ambivalence elide the historical reasons why black Britons and Irishmen find themselves living and working in England at all.

The heterosexual and postcolonial imaginaries are two "scattered hegemonies" through which colonial subjects are articulated.[32] This is to say, they both participate in mythologizing the social structures of late capitalism. These mythologies may be differently narrativized and resisted depending on where they circulate, but the fact that a tale like *The Crying Game* is similarly intelligible across national boundaries indicates the transnational availability of certain structures in dominance through which it is read. Reading against this mythology is an effort to make visible the history of these structures and in so doing intervene in one of the major vehicles for the material production of reality in late capitalism—seeing films.

MATERIALIZING REALITY

Theories of sexuality, like film, can also function mythically to the extent that they empty the representation of reality of its history. I want to close by turning to the work of Slavoj Zizek and Judith Butler whose thinking on drag, romance, and the politics of sexual representation reinforces in the domain of cultural theory the mythology of postmodern ambivalence we see in *The Crying Game*. The intersections among these texts and writers are noteworthy. Zizek has written an essay on *The Crying Game* and Butler, who has established an international reputation on the basis of her theories of the discursive materiality of drag, includes in her most recent book a sustained critique of Zizek. Both have been touted as two of the foremost contemporary theorists of desire. Both are known for the range of their readings—drawing as freely on Hegel, Marx, Lacan, Freud, and Irigaray as on popular culture and, in Zizek's case especially, on film. And both, though from different vantage points, are applauded for their conceptions of identity as ambivalent and performative.

In other respects, however, these two may seem an unlikely pair, not the least because Butler has launched a rigorous critique of Zizek in her latest book, *Bodies that Matter.* Zizek's work is of interest to Butler because they are both anti-descriptivists for whom identity is an unstable and performative practice. Like Zizek, Butler frames her performative politics by way of Laclau and Mouffe's post-Marxist radical democracy. But she contends that despite these "democratic" affiliations, Zizek puts forward a way of seeing and knowing (sexual difference, gender, romantic love, nationalist struggles, the Real) that is finally quite conservative. I aim to suggest, however, that while Butler critiques Zizek's idealist notion of the Real—a reading that could by extension apply to his essay on *The Crying Game*—her own understanding of the materiality of ambivalent, performative identities collaborates with his more reactionary standpoint to the extent that both empty history, and the history of late capitalism in particular, from cultural representation.

In his essay "From Courtly Love to *The Crying Game*," Zizek promotes a gender-flexible, performative, and stylized subject that is nonetheless wedded to the myths of contractual individualism and patriarchal hetero-normativity.[33] Zizek reads *The Crying Game* as "the ultimate variation on the motif of courtly love," a form of human interaction, he contends, that has persisted in a fairly undifferentiated way since the thirteenth century and whose "logic still defines the parameters within which the two sexes relate to each other" (CL 95). For Zizek, the perseverance of the matrix of courtly love bears witness to sexual difference as a Real that resists symbolization. By this, he means that in courtly love, sexual relationship is condemned to remain an asymmetrical nonrelationship in which the Lady functions as an inaccessible object—a sort of "black hole" or lack, a traumatic otherness designated by Lacan through the Freudian term *das ding*—the Thing—around which the subject's desire is structured. The "impossible love" between Fergus and Dil, emblematized in the final scene of *The Crying Game*, where Fergus, now in prison for Dil and divided from her by a glass partition, reiterates the economy of the courtly romance in which the object of desire is rendered inaccessible even as the love itself is unconditional. For Zizek, Fergus and Dil's love "is absolute precisely insofar as it transgresses not only the barriers of class, religion, and race (in today's 'permissive' epoch, all these barriers are obsolete) but also the ultimate barrier of sexual orientation" (CL 107). As Zizek sees it, this is the film's charm—that it does not denounce heterosexual love but rather renders the circumstances in which it can retain its unconditional character (CL 107).

Zizek rewrites the Lady in the tradition of courtly love as an emblematic figure for the Real, the fundamental concept in his neo-idealist, Lacanian intervention into historical materialism. In this narrative, the absent cause of the Symbolic is not the objective material contradictions engendered by the capitalist mode of production (accrual of profits and power for the few through the appropriation of collectively produced surplus value) but an impossible *jouissance*, the trauma that cannot be represented yet gives rise to an indelible inconsistency in the symbolic field (*Metastases* 31). Like Lacan, Zizek contends that this founding, almost ontological negativity lingers as a symptom in the formation of the subject and constitutes his ambivalent, never-coherent identification. By unhinging them from the social, Zizek's concept of the Real reifies the contradictions and incoherences traversing subjectivity. Indeed, by reducing the absent cause of the Symbolic to a universal and irrecuperable negativity, he erases any historical connection between the formation of the symbolic order or consciousness and social struggle. Instead of being seen as the effects of socially and historically produced events, contradictions in the domain of culture and consciousness (the categories of racial, gender, and sexual difference) are rendered either "obsolete" or beyond explanation.

Perpetually undermined by the Real, sexual identity, like all identity, is for Zizek inherently ambivalent. But because this ambivalence is the effect of an unexplainable universal difference, it has no history, and through the ahistorical metaphor of courtly love is condensed into a private, queerly heterosexual frame. Elsewhere in his work, Zizek contends that the castration threat establishes oedipal differentiations and the Law of the Father at a prediscursive level. In her chapter of *Bodies that Matter* entitled "Arguing with the Real," Judith Butler takes Zizek to task for using this psychoanalytic narrative in the service of the heteronormativizing law it interrogates. Butler points out that the Law of the Father is premised on a patriarchal gender hierarchy that naturalizes heterosexuality and is ultimately asocial (194). She astutely details the consequences of these presuppositions for men and women and relates them to Zizek's defensive posture against feminism.

Extending Butler's critique to Zizek's reading of *The Crying Game*, we might say that his metaphor of courtly love not only transcends history and social change, but in doing so, much like the myth of sexual ambivalence in the tale of the film, it also naturalizes ambivalence into the familiar asymmetrically gendered heterosexual imaginary. Zizek insists that it would be a mistake to identify the Lady in the courtly love scenario—this unconditional ideal of the woman—with "the everyday 'tamed' woman with whom sexual relationship may seem possible" (CL 96). Keep in mind, he tells us, this is a "man's fantasy" (CL 96). But his essay endorses and indeed celebrates this "man's fantasy" as the authentic, idealized rendering of love. Beginning with the premise that courtly love still defines the parameters within which *"the two sexes relate to each other"* (emphasis mine), Zizek's reading of *The Crying Game* forcefully reiterates and endorses all of the salient features of the heterosexual imaginary that structure the film's romance. The "two sexes" are a given; heterosexuality is naturalized and universalized in the veneration of a timeless sexual difference; the traumatic effects of capitalism and imperialism on the economy of desire are erased; and an underlying misogyny is endorsed.[34]

Even more severely than in mainstream reviews of the film, in Zizek's reading of *The Crying Game* the political tale is almost entirely swallowed up by the romance tale. Consequently, its marginal irruption in his text is especially significant. In one brief paragraph at the end of the essay, Zizek asserts that, much as de Sade does, "the film demands sexual revolution as the consistent accomplishment of political revolution" (CL 107). By this he means that the "vertiginous revolution in his most intimate personal attitudes" Fergus is compelled to confront is also an important site of struggle for Irish republicans (CL 107). But what exactly is revolutionary about this Sadean courtly romance as Zizek sees it? If sexual difference is "that which resists symbolization, the traumatic point which is always missed but nonetheless always returns,"[35] it would seem that this impossible Real would inhibit—and indeed guarantee the failure of—any political revolution. Precisely because Zizek understands the social as fundamentally psychic, his glancing recognitions of the public sphere are, like this one, reabsorbed into psychodynamics. Sexuality and sociality in this schema are fundamentally private, and it is in this sense that the metaphors of courtly love and sadomasochism function as mythic explanations of the radically ambivalent interpersonal sexual relations he celebrates.

For Zizek, sadomasochism is an ahistorical explanatory trope for two dimensions of sexuality that never finally cohere—a public, communal relation and a private, contractual, performative one. Sadism is a figure for the splitting of the law into its ego-ideal—the symbolic order that regulates social life—and its obscene, superego reverse (CL 98). The deepest bond that holds together a community, Zizek argues, is the guilty identification with the law's suspension or transgression. In a footnote, he illustrates this notion through the example of the U.S. military's resistance to lifting the ban on homosexuals; the open acknowledgement of homosexuality would sabotage the perverted underside of heterosexual machismo which forms the very basis of the military community (CL 98). But because both guilty association and community spirit are ahistorical symbolic figures, the question of how—or even if—these relations should or could be changed is moot. Instead, masochism's staged sexual game becomes the idealized, postmodern alternative.

The element of theatricality in the gender reversals of the typical masochistic scenario (man-servant and woman-dominatrix) concedes the fictionality of the identities it enacts and flexes the gender component of the heterosexual matrix. In other words, the masochistic scenario recognizes that the phallus is permanently insecure. Zizek is particularly interested in lesbian S/M because it enacts the circulation of the phallus. So-called lesbian sadomasochism, he argues, is more subversive than "the usual soft lesbianism which elevates tender relationship between women in contrast to the aggressive-phallic male penetration" because the contractual form of lesbian S/M mimics "aggressive phallic heterosexuality" (CL 99). At the same time, however, Zizek's endorsement of the performative phallic lesbian as the new "real" woman is founded on the premise that sexuality is a private/psychic/symbolic ritual traversed by the irrecuperable difference of desire. Consequently, it functions much like the mythic tale of *The Crying Game* to empty the representation of ambivalence of its history. As my earlier argument implies, the history of the recoding of values around the sign "woman"—soft, womanly, weak versus aggressive phallic penetrating—can be read as one effect of the impact of more flexible class divisions on the formation of postmodern patriarchy. The signature lesson of postmodern patriarchy is, however, precisely that a circulating phallus—even among women and especially in "private"—does not necessarily mean that capitalism's oppressive and exploitative use of patriarchal structures against "softies" of all sorts has ended.

An important component of the performative postmodern masochism Zizek endorses is its private contractual dimension. That Zizek values the performative *and* the contractual subject may seem a bit of an anomaly. At the same time, this is precisely the contradictory position of the postmodern bourgeois subject whose relation to property and law require the persistence of private, contractual arrangements at the same time new divisions of labor require more flexible, deprivatized forms of identification and subjectivity. Postmodern sexuality negotiates these contradictions by being mythologized as a private ritual exchange: "our most intimate desires become objects of contract and composed negotiation . . . but once the game is over, the [lover] again adopts the attitude of a respectful bourgeois" (CL 99). Exchange between free and equal subjects can be achieved sexually only in the form of a bargain "in which, paradoxically, the very form of equal contract serves to establish the relationship of inequality and domination" (CL 108). What better paradigm for love in late capitalism?

Butler counters this notion of performativity by recasting Zizek's impossible, psychic materiality as "a specific modality of power as discourse."[36] In so doing, she advances an alternative understanding of the Real as what she calls the "de-symbolized unspeakable." As she conceptualizes it, the foreclosure that remains "outside" symbolic identifications is not a realm prior to discourse but rather consists of signifiers that have been separated off from symbolization. This foreclosure of particular signifiers is a mechanism for policing the borders of intelligibility that occurs in order to avert the trauma with which certain significations have been invested. But what is the history, the materiality, the cause of the trauma coalescing around signifiers like "queer," "gay," "woman"?

In *Bodies that Matter*, historicity and materiality are important "new" concepts through which Butler frames her explanation of performative identities. From the very first page of her essay on Zizek, she announces that performativity is a matter of the "historicity of discourse and, in particular, the historicity of norms" (187). This historicity is comprised of the "'chains' of iteration invoked and dissimulated in the imperative utterance" (187). For example, as Butler sees it, sex is never a given entity—as it sometimes is for Zizek—but a discursive and normative imperative through which subjects are addressed and bodies are materialized (187). Norms materialize bodies through the cumulative effect of cited conventions. Normative imperatives work through reiteration and exclusion by instituting an unspeakable "outside" that "secures and hence fails to secure the very borders of materiality" (188).

Butler's starting point here is certainly not Zizek's. Her conception of identity as performative displaces the contractual subject and any trace of sexual difference as a transcendent entity prior to discourse. In this respect, her theoretical framework is not at all idealist and can seem more compatible with a sexual politics aimed at social change. But there is a troubling circularity to her conception of the materiality of discourse that ultimately limits her "historicizing." If discourse materializes subjects and bodies at the same time it secures the borders of materiality, what exactly is the materiality of discourse? The answer Butler provides takes her to Laclau and Mouffe's project for radical democracy.[37] They, too, argue for a social and material notion of identity. Both Butler and Zizek accept Laclau and Mouffe's starting assumption that the social is founded on a fundamental antagonism. In an effort to rewrite Zizek's asocial notion of the difference internal to identity, Butler returns to Laclau's argument that the constitutive social antagonism forestalling any coherent identity is founded in the sign's indeterminacy. As she sees it, the referent is suspended not because it is essentially impossible (à la Zizek) but because it is a signified in a set of differential relations that is always open to resignification (217). This openness of language in the social practice of discourse is, then, what constitutes for Butler the historicity and materiality of social life. But because this openness is the effect of antagonisms fundamentally rooted in the indeterminacy of signification, history and social struggle for Butler are finally only cultural and discursive.

She posits, for instance, that "if 'women' within political discourse can never fully describe that which it names, that is neither because the category simply refers without describing nor because 'women' are the lost referent, that which 'does not exist,' but because the term marks a dense intersection of social relations that cannot be summarized through the terms of identity" (21). Butler asserts that the materiality of these social relations that "cannot be summarized through the terms of identity" involves exclusions that nonetheless haunt it, the "violences that a partial concept enforces" (221). But in the end, the social relations to which this cultural, discursive violence refers are never outside the domain of ideology. Indeed, culture and ideology have no outside. They do not refer the partial fixing of what "women" means to capital's changing relations of labor which now require (real) women in advanced industrial societies to be professional, soft, *and* phallic-aggressive while other (less real? soft?) women are invisible, affordable, docile workers. Yet surely these material social relations densely intersect the sign "women" and subvert the stability of its meaning.

I have argued that *The Crying Game* can be read as a myth that indulges and closes down the indeterminacy of signs such as "woman," "man," or "black." While the tale of the film both foments and smoothes over a crisis in the culturally dominant meanings of gender and race, we can still read against the texture of this smoothing—in a way that makes visible the dense intersection of social relations fused in the romantic figure of the British West Indian transvestite and her lovers. My reading of the film claims that the materiality of this dense intersection and the more closed phantasmatic investments its tale secures are not merely the effects of signification or chains of iteration but of the social struggle over changing divisions of labor, land, and wealth. The provisional fixing of meaning does indeed take place through cultural signs and practices such as the eroticized discourse of cricket, for example. However, unspeakable signifiers are foreclosed from the symbolic not simply because they qualify to unravel the subject but because they threaten the ensemble of objective material relations of which subjects are a part and on which capitalism continues to rely (relations which include the need for cheap, feminized Irish/black/immigrant labor).

When I argued earlier that *The Crying Game* teaches lessons about being a "real" woman, I used "real" to signify the ways the imaginary operations of myth draw on a symbolic order whose limits are historically fixed by an ensemble of social relations, including most determinately, divisions of labor. If these limits to the "real" promise a unity that is never successfully achieved, this is not, as Zizek argues, because of a universal and irrecuperable lack or "existential void." Nor is the materiality of the exclusions that haunt identity simply a matter of discursive practices, as Butler maintains. To assert that late capitalism's divisions of labor as they are articulated through state policies and patriarchal formations are the absent causes underwriting its mythic formulations is not, however, to argue for a reductive determinism that ignores the invariably dense and multiply mediated textualities of ideology. But it is to say that now more than ever we need modes of reading that make visible these complex mediations without erasing the fundamental structures of capitalist accumulation that undergird them.

Materializing the tales of popular film is an oppositional political practice of disidentification. Because Zizek's disidentifying subject is grounded on an irrecuperable referent and Butler's poststructuralist disidentifying subject is founded on the instability of the chain of citations, the most either critical practice can change is cultural representation. As I understand it, however, disidentification with the cultural obvious—including its new ambivalent forms of identity—takes as its starting point the assumption that the referents for cultural identities and practices remain lodged in capital's drive to accumulate profits through the appropriation of surplus labor, an enterprise that historically continues to rely on various forms of patriarchy and imperialism. To disidentify with the cultural myths of late capitalism's postmodern imaginary is to claim a vantage point that insists that the achievement of full democracy and social equity will require transformations that span the organization of social life. In the face of postmodern celebrations of ambivalent identities, normative reiterations, enjoyment, and gaming, the disidentifying critic asks, "Why this sort of subject here?" "Why these stories now?" More than that, she speculates whether the difference that has been rendered most invisible in postmodern cultural representations—the difference between rich and poor—has indeed disappeared or merely become another one of the shades and shadows of late capitalist myth.

NOTES

1. The "tale" of a film is the viewer's translation of what Neil Jordan describes as the film's essentials—"what is seen, what happens, and what is said"—into historically available frames for knowing (*A Neil Jordan Reader* [New York: Vintage, 1993], xi). The following analysis of the ideological work of film is drawn

from Masu'd Zavarzadeh, *Seeing Films Politically* (Albany: SUNY Press, 1991), chapters one and three especially.

2. Roland Barthes, "Myth Today," in *A Barthes Reader*, ed. Susan Sontag (New York: Hill and Wang, 1982), 116. Further reference to this work will be included parenthetically in the text.

3. F. W. Haug. *Critique of Commodity Aesthetics: Appearance, Sexuality and Advertising in Capitalist Society*, trans. Robert Bock (Minneapolis: University of Minnesota Press, 1971).

4. The separation of empire and sexuality in cultural history has been affected most profoundly in the past two decades by the influence on cultural studies of Foucault's history of sexuality which all but erases empire from the history of nineteenth-century Europe. The role of psychoanalysis in shaping theories of sexuality has been an important factor in this displacement as well. Recently, however, the archive of studies on empire and sexuality has begun to expand. Often drawing on combinations of psychoanalysis, deconstruction, and Foucauldian discourse theory, this body of knowledge tends to be dominated by what I have referred to as neo-culturalism. See for example, Homi K. Bhabha *The Location of Culture* (London: Routledge, 1994); Jonathan Goldberg, *Sodometries: Renaissance Texts, Modern Sexualities* (Stanford: Stanford University Press, 1992); Laura Kipnis, *Ecstasy Unlimited: On Sex, Capital, Gender and Aesthetics* (Minneapolis: University of Minnesota Press, 1993); Kobena Mercer, *Welcome to the Jungle* (London: Routledge, 1994); Kaja Silverman, "White Skins, Brown Masks: The Double Mimesis, or with Lawrence in Arabia," in *Male Subjectivity at the Margins* (New York: Routledge, 1992), 299-338.

While there is an explicit emphasis on power relations, by taking as a starting point the premise that psychic structures or cultural forms are disconnected from social relations "outside" signification or ideology, this work reduces the complex imbrications of sexuality, race, empire, and capital to cultural politics.

5. Miramax's strategy to promote the film by asking reviewers not to reveal its secret proved a profitable marketing gimmick. *The Crying Game*'s record-breaking $50 million plus in box office earnings alone has earned it the status of the most successful art house release in motion picture history. See Steven Goldman, "The Buying Game," *London Sunday Times*, April 4, 1993.

Bob and Harvey Weinstein, Miramax's founders, who purchased distribution rights for one million dollars, stood to earn more than $10 million in profits from the film in 1993 alone. *The Crying Game* received six Oscar nominations that same year and was Academy Award winner for best screenplay. In Britain, the film did less well but was expected to reach an audience of 4 to 5 million when it aired on Britain's Channel 4 in the fall of 1994. See John Dugdale, "Screen Break with Tradition," *London Sunday Times*, April 4, 1993.

6. The effects of marketing and publicity on a film's reception, of course, are not always predictable or direct. For an interesting example of the skewed relationship between promotion and reception, see Hilary Hinds's reading of the BBC production of Jeanette Winterson's lesbian bildungsroman *Oranges Are Not the Only Fruit* (aired in 1990), whose promotion in terms of its "explicitly lesbian"

sex scenes was at odds with its reception within the frame of "high art." "*Oranges Are Not the Only Fruit:* Reaching Audiences Other Lesbian Texts Cannot Reach," in *New Lesbian Criticism: Literary and Cultural Readings,* ed. Sally Munt (New York: Columbia University Press, 1992), 153-72.

7. For a fuller explanation of this concept see Chrys Ingraham, "The Heterosexual Imaginary: Feminist Sociology and Theories of Gender," *Sociological Theory* 12 (1994): 203-20.

8. Carole-Ann Tyler's analysis of the underlying narcissism informing the conventions of gay male drag is an useful complement to the tale of *The Crying Game* as I am outlining it here. Tyler indicates that the theatricality of drag invariably depends on a masquerade that discloses not only the penis but an underlying phallocentric and misogynist logic. Her reading of drag is interesting for its suggestions about the transvestite's (not so) ambivalent relation to the "real" woman and the "real" man. See "Boys Will Be Girls: The Politics of Gay Drag," in *Inside/Out: Lesbian Theories, Gay Theories,* ed. Diana Fuss (New York: Routledge, 1991), 32-70.

9. It is in part for this reason that I refer to Dil as "she." To the extent that Dil continually asserts that she is a "girl" and enacts a feminine identity, the unveiling of her genitals does not successfully disrupt the system of sexual difference.

10. See for example, David Ehrenstein, "Crying Shame," *The Advocate,* January 12, 1993; Kristen Handler, "Sexing *The Crying Game,*" *Film Quarterly* 47, no. 3 (1994): 31-42; Aspasia Kotsopoulos and Josephine Mill, "Gender, Genre, and Post-Feminism: *The Crying Game,*" *Jump Cut* 39 (1994): 15-24.

11. See, for instance, Teresa Ebert, "The 'Difference' of Postmodern Feminism," *College English* 53, no. 8 (1991): 886-904; Ann Ferguson, *Blood at the Root: Motherhood, Sexuality, and Male Dominance* (London: Pandora, 1989); Rosemary Hennessy, "Queer Visibility in Commodity Culture," *Cultural Critique* 29 (Winter 1994-95): 31-76; Sylvia Walby, *Theorizing Patriarchy* (Oxford: Blackwell, 1990).

12. For a detailed description and analysis of the bill, see David T. Evans, *Sexual Citizenship: The Material Construction of Sexualities* (London: Routledge, 1993): 125-46.

13. Ann Marie Smith, "Resisting the Erasure of Lesbian Sexuality: A Challenge for Queer Activism," in *Modern Homosexualities,* ed. Ken Plummer (London: Routledge, 1992): 200-216.

14. It finally makes little difference that a song typically sung by a female vocalist is here performed by Lyle Lovett. Note the ways the multiple performers of the title song punctuate the tale of Dil's sexual ambivalence: we hear Ann Dudley's version when Dil first lip-syncs in the Metro, Dave Berry's version after Fergus sees Dil's penis, and Boy George's version when Dil holds Fergus captive.

15. See, for example, Mary Ann Doane, *Femmes Fatales: Feminism, Film Theory, Psychoanalysis* (New York: Routledge, 1991); Stephen Heath, "Difference," in *The Sexual Subject: A Screen Reader in Sexuality* (London: Routledge, 1992), 47-106; Laura Kipnis, *Ecstasy Unlimited: On Sex, Capital, Gender, and Aesthetics* (Minneapolis: University of Minnesota Press, 1993); Kaja Silverman, "White Skins, Brown

Masks: The Double Mimesis, or with Lawrence in Arabia," in *Male Subjectivity at the Margins* (New York: Routledge, 1992), 299-338.

16. Materialist feminism is itself a terrain of debate and struggle. Much of the work of materialist feminism since the late 1970s falls quite readily into line with neo-culturalism; indeed, some more recent claims to materialist feminism are emphatically post-Marxist. See, for example, Michele Barrett, *The Politics of Truth: From Marx to Foucault* (Stanford: Stanford University Press, 1991); Judith Butler, *Bodies that Matter: On the Discursive Limits of Sex* (New York: Routledge, 1994); Donna J. Haraway, *Simians, Cyborgs, and Women: The Reinvention of Nature* (New York: Routledge, 1991); Donna Landry and Gerald MacLean, *Materialist Feminisms* (Oxford: Blackwell, 1993). At the same time, there persists a historical materialist feminism that does not reduce social life to culture or ideology. See, for example, Christine Delphy, *Close to Home: A Materialist Analysis of Women's Oppression* (London: Hutchinson, 1984); Teresa L. Ebert, *Ludic Feminism and After* (Ann Arbor: University of Michigan Press, 1995); Martha Giminez, "The Oppression of Women: A Structuralist-Marxist View" in *Structural Sociology* (New York: Columbia University Press, 1982), 292-323; Rosemary Hennessy, *Materialist Feminism and the Politics of Discourse* (New York: Routledge, 1993); Maria Mies, *Patriarchy and Accumulation on a World Scale* (London: Zed, 1986).

17. Ruth Milkman, *Gender at Work* (Urbana: University of Illinois Press, 1987).

18. David Harvey, *The Condition of Postmodernity* (Cambridge, Mass.: Blackwell, 1989), 147.

19. Meera Nanda, "New Technologies, New Challenges: Reimagining the Geography of Global Production" (paper presented at Women in the Global Economy Conference, Institute for Research on Women, The University at Albany, SUNY, April 1994), 8.

20. See Swasti Mitter, "What Women Demand of Technology," *New Left Review* 205 (May-June 1994): 100-110; Nanda, 12.

21. Roger Cohen, "For Coke, World Is Its Oyster," *Business Day*, November 21, 1991: D1.

22. In the case of Coca Cola, at least, the connection has been quite direct. In 1991, Coke hired Michael Ovitz, the leading Hollywood agent, as a consultant. Coke's director of global marketing explained the choice: "The cultural agenda of the globe is set by the U.S. film, music and entertainment industry and Mr. Ovitz sits at the apotheosis of that" (Cohen).

23. See Kipnis for a reading of these two films as postcolonial myths.

24. This position is widely held; two well-known British promoters of it are Bhabha and Mercer.

25. The history of affiliations between transported Irish laborers and rebellious slaves in the Caribbean was one of the reasons English planters switched to using exclusively African slave labor. See Bill Rolston, "The Riotous and the Righteous," *The New Internationalist* 255 (May 1994): 20-22. This story is an important counter-narrative that myths like *The Crying Game* make seem impossible.

26. Some useful studies of the place of (hetero)sexuality in imperial policy making include: Rosemary Hennessy and Rajeswari Mohan, "The Construction of Woman in Three Popular Texts of Empire: Towards a Critique of Materialist Feminism," *Textual Practice* 3.3 (1989): 323-59; Lata Mani, "Contentious Traditions: The Debate on *Sati* in Colonial India," *Cultural Critique* 7 (1987); Susan Pedersen, "National Bodies, Unspeakable Acts: The Sexual Politics of Colonial Policy Making," *Journal of Modern History* 63.4 (1991): 647-78; Vron Ware, *Beyond the Pale: White Women, Racism, and History* (London: Verso, 1992).

27. See, for example, Leslie E. Gerber, "The Virtuous Terrorist: Stanley Hauerwas and *The Crying Game*," *Cross Currents* 43, no. 2 (Summer 1993): 230-34; Wendy Lesser, "De Rerum Naturum," *Michigan Quarterly Review* 32, no. 4 (Fall 1993): 622-27. The following analyses of *The Crying Game*, however, emphasize the conservative, even reactionary cultural politics in the film's abandonment of complex readings of identity: Kristen Handler, "Sexing *The Crying Game*," *Film Quarterly* 47.3 (1994): 31-42; bell hooks, "Seduction and Betrayal: *The Crying Game* Meets *The Bodyguard*," in *Outlaw Culture: Resisting Representations* (New York: Routledge, 1994), 53-62.

28. For an interesting analysis of these issues in Neil Jordan's *Mona Lisa*, see Lola Young, "A Nasty Piece of Work: A Psychoanalytic Study of Sexual and Racial Difference in *Mona Lisa*," in *Identity, Community, Culture, Difference*, ed. Jonathan Rutherford (London: Lawrence and Wishart, 1990), 188-206.

29. For elaborations of this point, see Hazel Carby, *Reconstructing Womanhood* (New York: Oxford University Press, 1987); Frantz Fanon, *Black Skins, White Masks*, trans. Charles Lam Markmann (New York: Grove Weidenfeld, 1967); Jacqueline Dowd Hall, "The Mind that Burns in Each Body: Women, Rape, and Racial Violence," in *Powers of Desire: The Politics of Sexuality*, ed. Ann Snitow, Christine Stansell, and Sharon Thompson (New York: Monthly Review Press, 1983): 328-49.

30. Chris Searle, "Race before Wicket: Cricket and the White Rose," *Race and Class* 31, no. 3 (1990): 29.

31. C. L. R. James, *Beyond a Boundary* (Durham, N.C.: Duke University Press, 1993).

32. This phrase from Iderpal Grewal and Caren Kaplan's anthology of the same name conceptualizes the effects of "mobile capital as well as the multiple subjectivities that replace the European unitary subject" as transnational. While their concept of scattered hegemonies is useful for addressing the ways "what gets *theorized* in the West as hybridity remains enmeshed in the gaze of the West" (7), like many appropriations of Gramsci's notion of hegemony in post-Marxist cultural studies, it tends to erase the international division of labor on which late capital relies. See *Scattered Hegemonies: Postmodernity and Transnational Feminist Practices* (Minneapolis: University of Minnesota Press, 1994).

33. Unless otherwise noted, the version of the essay I am reading is from *New Left Review* 202 (Nov.-Dec. 1993): 95-108, and will be cited hereafter as CL. A later revised version appears as the chapter "Courtly Love, or Woman as Thing" in Slavoj Zizek, *Metastases of Enjoyment: Six Essays on Woman and Causality* (Lon-

don: Verso, 1994), 89-94. This book is hereafter cited as *Metastases* in the text.

34. Zizek contends that the perseverance of courtly love in *The Crying Game* and other films "bears witness to a certain deadlock in contemporary feminism" because "by opposing 'patriarchal domination' woman simultaneously undermines the fantasy support of her own 'feminine' identity" (CL 108)—that is, as lack or other. Against feminism's contention that patriarchal regulation of difference is historically constructed and so subject to change, Zizek posits sexual difference— in which the other, our partner, prior to being a subject is a Thing, and therefore sexual relation can never be an encounter between two equal subjects. An inescapable master-slave relation is the bedrock of all identity (CL 108).

35. Slavoj Zizek, *The Sublime Object of Ideology* (London: Verso, 1989).

36. Judith Butler, *Bodies that Matter: On the Discursive Limits of Sex* (New York: Routledge, 1994), 187. Further references to this work will be included parenthetically in the text.

37. Ernesto Laclau and Chantal Mouffe, *Hegemony and Socialist Strategy: Towards a Radical Democratic Politics* (London: Verso, 1985).

Mutations of the Imperial Contract

Betty Joseph

In April 1985, the Indian Supreme Court upheld a lower court's judgment granting Shahbano, a seventy-three-year-old destitute Muslim woman, a small monthly allowance. The court's seemingly minor decision sparked nationwide unrest. Some reports in the popular press compared the crisis to the "great upheaval of 1857," or the mutiny against British rule.[1] The case gained notoriety not as much because of this woman's victory of sorts over the husband who had refused to support her after ending a forty-year marriage, but because of the legal code under which the provisions had become available. Shahbano won her pittance of Rs 179.00 a month (about $6) by appealing under a provision against vagrancy of the Code of Criminal Procedure—the uniform "secular" code first instituted in 1872 during British rule.[2] Before Shahbano's plea became a public debate, it was assumed that most Indian Muslim women had always contested issues about divorce, maintenance, custody, and inheritance under the Muslim *Shariat*—the religious law which governs matters relating to the family.

Seven months later, the debate initiated by this ruling takes a strange turn: amid nationwide campaigns by leaders of the Muslim minority community against what they perceived to be a Hindu attack on their religious and personal freedoms, and the Hindu extremists' use of this situation to call for the abolishment of special constitutional privileges for the minorities, Shahbano denounces the Supreme Court's ruling. In November 1985, an open letter attributed to her appears in an Urdu newspaper. It tells the "Muslims of India" that she had decided to reject the judgment which (though in her favor) was contrary to the Quran and the *hadith*, and was therefore an interference in Muslim personal law.[3] In rejecting the maintenance or annuity granted to her under the "secular" code, and seeking instead the return of her *mehr* (the marriage settlement), Shahbano now reactivates her religious identity to become a Muslim woman seeking justice under her own community's law.

The political ambivalence of this situation cannot escape anyone studying the phenomenon. We have, first of all, a multiplication of effects: a marginalized female subject enters an allotted space in legal discourse and triggers off a national crisis that will be played out in numerous theaters—from parliamentary debates and electoral politics to protest marches organized by women's groups.[4] Shahbano's role in this crisis does not give us an "agent" in any conventional sense. Neither can her rejection of the ruling be read simply as a retreat in the face of cultural and religious opposition from her community—India's Muslim minority; it is significant in other ways.

Just as the journalist's allusion to the Great Mutiny of 1857 reminds a national reading public that they are replaying a legacy from colonial rule, Shahbano exposes the split nature of the woman in post-colonial India as she is simultaneously produced as the subject of law under two competing legal codes. These legal codes, both fictions written by the same history—one British and the other, the codified customary and religious law encouraged by colonial rule and later instituted by the founding fathers of the newly independent nation—create her duality as a subject caught between "traditionalism" and "modernity." Her actions also expose the contradictions implicit in the process of modernization whereby the myth of national consolidation and progress in India was to be serviced by the myth of the evolution of law: the idea that a uniform and homogeneous civil code would be the culmination of the evolving nation-building task.[5]

Shahbano's contradictory positioning also presents problems for Western feminist scholars and post-colonial critics who want to confront in solidarity the female subject in decolonized terrain. How does the feminist in the West approach Shahbano as a subject of knowledge? Can she do this by avoiding two popular gestures: one, validating the nationalist difference of this subject by asserting Shahbano's agency as totally other to the Western subject of feminism, and two, benevolently evaluating the "sister's" evolution towards her own position? The first position (of nativism) denies the historical link shared by these two figures—Shahbano and the Western feminist—while the second reenacts the social mission of imperialism: helping "them" become like "us." However, there is a third alternative, a position whereby the post-colonial feminist critic can acknowledge the radical otherness of Shahbano's positioning and agency, but also attempt to find "common ground" through a study of their shared subjection to the same history. This would mean looking for points of intersection in their separate trajectories, to reach the moment when the history of the female in the West becoming the bearer of rights *is* the history of colonialism for the female subject presently in decolonized space. By running together these histories to find the "common traits," we can begin to imagine a reading practice that will realize the paradigmatic importance of post-coloniality. Measuring the effects of colonialism as it embarks on violent transformations of subjectivity cannot be done by simply looking at Shahbano here and now. To understand why her position is what it is now and to understand how such a position can challenge prevailing notions of agency and subjectivity, the critic has to embark on a meticulous genealogical project.

My choice of the term *genealogy* is deliberate. Michel Foucault's description of the term suggests how closely we can associate the work of the historian with the work of the post-colonial critic: "Genealogy is gray and meticulous, and patiently documentary. It operates on a field of entangled and confused parchments, on documents that have been scratched over and recopied many times."[6] Especially tangled and confused is the text that gives us the relationship of gender to colonialism. Because relations of gender have developed unevenly during the era of colonization (a project widely regarded as masculinist), her story cannot be found by and through female actors. When "woman" is figured in the colonial theater, she does not simply come on center stage, even though her emergence is a sign that forces have gained entry (Foucault's phrasing). It is not simply a leap from the wings to the center stage, from the private to the public, from the sexual to the economic and the political; her presence is a sign that the insurgency of the female figure erases such demarcations and that her uneven traversal over textual spaces breaks the distinctions of chronology, genre, and discipline.[7] In this chapter, I invoke one such moment of chronological insurgency, when an act by an illiterate woman from contemporary India triggers a number of historical (or genealogical) moments (for the critic) and rewrites the present (for herself). For the post-colonial feminist critic, these moments provide not only a history of her own positioning, but also a reevaluation of the distance between her and the space in which her subaltern counterpart exists.[8]

To track the itinerary of the post-colonial female subaltern as she becomes codified into the double bind of Shahbano, my discussion will perform a series of maneuvers. I will read Shahbano in conjunction with the figure of the female as individualist in Daniel Defoe's *Roxana* (1724), and a silenced rape victim in the records of the East-India Company, to produce a genealogy of a problem in the present: the convergence of "woman," "nation," and "empire" in post-colonial discourses of religion, property, and selfhood. I reopen Defoe's *Roxana* as a novel where elements of female selfhood intersect with a larger debate about women's property in Britain and the ongoing national drive to divert wealth to colonial endeavors. When a classic text of the female-as-individualist can be read along with the history of colonialism, the lesson is not simply that the figure of "woman" is more than a literary trope but also that she is a structuration that reorganizes how we imagine the "private" and "public." The second text is an excerpt from the East-India Company's records. This excerpt, the transcribed proceedings of a trial involving the rape of a native woman on the Company's premises (a factory in South India), occasions another strategy of reading. It serves here not only as evidence of the covert exercises of colonial authority as it moves closer to becoming lawgiver and arbiter on alien soil but as a dress rehearsal of the Shahbano crisis as it will be reenacted two hundred and fifty years later.[9]

This globalizing reading strategy, which connects the debate on women's property and rights in eighteenth-century Britain to the full-fledged project of imperialism in India, brings home another lesson: Shahbano and the feminist critic in the West have a common history. By reading the transformations of women's status (here, that of Roxana and the unnamed rape victim) as partial requirements of colonialist processes and capital accumulation at a historical moment, I ask what the relation between imperialism and feminism is today. Finally, these juxtapositions present the need to read for historical *correspondences* rather than separate histories, as a way of measuring the legacy of colonialism and its contribution to securing positions not only for the advocate of feminism in the West but also for the feminist in decolonized space who might see her struggle as incommensurable with the presuppositions of Western liberal rights.[10]

THE MORAL GEOGRAPHY OF THE INDIVIDUALIST

The ideology of liberal rights is unavoidably an ideology of "possessive individualism" because individualism posits an autonomous producer of value: one who subsequently owns both self and property.[11] But such an autonomy must be produced by a sleight of hand for that is how it gets its mythical status. Robinson Crusoe, for instance, can be posited as a *homoeconomicus* and the origin of value, only because he is cast off on a deserted island, shorn of sociality, and unhindered by competing claims for his habitat. In *Roxana*, Defoe tries a similar magical formula to posit the female individualist embarking on the creation of value. In the novel, the protagonist-narrator Roxana is stripped of the security of her household and her means of support by a foolish, squandering husband. Like Crusoe, she is cast onto the world with nothing but her labor-power as a means of improving herself, but instead of the work ethic that has become the hallmark of our solitary exile Crusoe, we are told that Roxana is not "bred to work" (*R* 17).

Having denied Roxana's ability to perform wage-labor and her capacity to support herself through the services characteristic of the lower-class female work force of the time, Defoe can now posit that she is ready to embark on becoming an individualist through the use of sexuality as labor-power.[12] At the same time, in order to establish Roxana as the subject of contractual relations (the primary discourse that produces the individualist), Defoe must present sexual relations as contractual. Roxana reaches this point when in her penury she is forced to imagine the possibility of having to "lie with [her landlord] for bread." Her indigent circumstances are momentarily suspended as the landlord and she debate the possibility of another contract:

> they agreed in several things exactly; for example, that I was abandoned of a husband in the prime of my youth and vigour, and he of a wife in his middle age; how the end of marriage was destroyed by the treatment we had either of us received, and it would be very hard that *we should be tied by the formality of the contract where the essence of it was destroyed.* (*R* 58, emphasis mine)

In tune with the powerful emerging ideology that determined discussions of polity, economy, and sexuality at that time (a thesis now well established by the work of Nancy Armstrong and Carole Pateman),[13] the framework of the social contract is mapped onto marriage and the narrative now paves the way for an evaluation of the heroine's attempts to better herself through the use of her sexuality. However, once the social contract has become the sexual contract for the female as individualist, the narrative is transformed into a moral fable that can be judged by the criteria of nature, decency, and politeness, rather than by questions of women's unequal status as signatories to such contracts. To understand the implications of what it means to make Roxana a signatory to a sexual rather than a social contract, we have to look at the important role this displacement played in the changing social relations of Britain at that time.

Women's proprietary rights, well up to the eighteenth century, had been based on an idea of status—their rights to property as daughters and wives. The discourse of protection had allowed them traditional forms of wealth such as dower or pin-money. (The former, an entitlement to one third of the husband's estate after his death, and the latter, "pocket-money" for the wife in order to maintain herself in a manner that would not compromise her husband's social rank.) In 1833, the Dower Act made what was the core of the wife's entitlement under the old common law system defeasible at the will of the husband. To ask how dower rights disappeared, we will need a historical inquiry not only into the legal profession's devotion to this topic from the end of the seventeenth century to 1833 but also into the social forces that prompted these legal exercises—namely, the rise of the middle class and its consolidation of economic power through the new forms of wealth such as public stock and funds, East-India bonds, annuities, exchequer-annuities, fortunes in Ireland and Holland, and plantations in America. Dower now became seen increasingly as a "clog on alienability," as an outdated system that was no longer in the interests of the "public" or of the new trade-relations coming into existence.[14] The ideology of contract thus served a legal purpose to deprive privileged British women of traditional rights to property. In terms of procedure, it promoted the need to precede marriages with prenuptial agreements or with settlements and jointures that would fix the period and the amount she could claim. It allowed, that is, the husband more freedom to do as he wished with land.

Contractual ideology, coming as it did when individual rights had become the rallying cry for popular movements leading to the two revolutions in the late eighteenth century, produced the sexual contract not only as a paradigm for a discussion of "women's rights," but also as a rhetorical strategy to displace the site at which the discussion takes place. The ideology of possessive individualism is now removed from the market-place and the habitat of the contractual female subject becomes the family. While all activities relating to the production, reproduction, and consumption of wealth are regarded as fundamentally private, but with beneficial social consequences, the private sphere is also given as an alternative to the space where the white bourgeois male is the property-bearing substance. A question emerges at this point: if the supposition of retreat from the public is the criterion by which Nancy Armstrong defines "domestic fiction," or fiction that represents itself as "removed from political history,"[15] what is the status of fictional works such as *Roxana* and *Moll Flanders?* Do discussions of these novels become marginal to Armstrong's work because they do not (like the domestic novel) "conceal the clash between political interests?" Moll Flanders and Roxana use their sexuality as a political tool to play out very contradictory subject positions (often hinging on self-recrimination and self-abuse) and not as a field to displace political conflicts. This leads Armstrong to suggest that we need "something on the order of psychoanalysis to explain away obvious dis-continuities occurring within the female rather than between her and some male."[16] I wish to offer another possibility here: it is because sexuality is always in service of macro-processes (even when it serves as displacement of the same) that we do not always need the service of psychoanalytic frameworks to understand the relationship between the psychic, the sexual, and the politico-economic relations of production.[17]

In Defoe's *Roxana*, we see such a displacement and retreat (from the public to the private) momentarily deferred as the narrative locates the production of value at the site of the female body. The "home" becomes the marketplace instead of an alternative space, as Roxana moves through a spectrum of sexual contracts: wife, common-law wife, mistress, and kept woman. At the end of each of these liaisons, she takes stock of the multiple forms of wealth she has accumulated: portion, pin-money, jointure, gifts, pensions, and even dower. The subject of the sexual contract only be-comes the freelance signatory of the social contract when Roxana refuses the offer of marriage from a Dutch merchant (who offers to keep her property "separate"). Roxana's refusal is couched in the language of indi-vidual autonomy when she asserts that "the very nature of the marriage contract was in short, nothing but giving up of liberty, estate, authority, and everything to the man, and the woman was indeed a mere woman ever after—that is to say a slave" (*R* 224). At this point in Defoe's narrative, Roxana ceases to be a prostitute as such, driven by necessity and the need to sell her services. Using her sexuality, she has now become a woman of means, the dreaded *femme sole*, as well as the figure of real contractual relations. Her encounter with the Dutch merchant, the eighteenth century's figuration of Europe's frenzied drive for the profits of colonialism, leads her to shift her priorities from production to investment: "Now I was," Roxana tells us, "become, from a lady of pleasure, a woman of business, and of great business too, I assure you" (*R* 197). It is also at this juncture that Roxana is brought technically before the law in Defoe's narrative. On refusing his proposal, the Dutchman warns Roxana: "Dear madam, you argue for liberty, at the same time that you restrain yourself from that liberty which God and nature has directed you to take" (*R* 238).

Literary critics have noted how the bourgeois cultural revolution in the eighteenth century debated its new human subject through the literature of the time. Pamela, Clarissa, Charles Grandison, or Roxana for that matter are not only "fictional characters: they are also public mythologies, coordinates of a mighty moral debate, symbolic spaces within which dialogues may be conducted, pacts concluded and ideological battles waged."[18] To these spatializations of the literary text, I want to offer in addition, the space of a trial. *Roxana* performs a standard ideological function—it stages not a space of prohibitive law but what Derrida calls a "fictive institution"—which in principle allows anything to be said.[19] This "freedom of expression" is crucial for instituting new forms of subjectivity because it mystifies the operation of law at other levels. For instance, the novel's judgment about the economic and sexual transgressions of the female subject must seem to originate from Roxana herself, just as juridical discourse must have no other basis but the protection of law itself. As Peter Fitzpatrick explains, "Disorder on law's part cannot . . . be located in law itself. The sources of disorder must exist outside the law—in the eruptions and disruptions of untamed nature or barely contained human passion against which an orderly law is intrinsically set."[20] In *Roxana*, we see the operation of this discourse when bourgeois morality arrives as a Lacanian law or name-of-the-father, a censuring and castrating agency that prohibits the very desire it has brought into being.[21] When law has been internalized as morality and a subject desires to be made over and reformed, what one sees is the successful consolidation of hegemonic power—from prohibition to consent. Later in this chapter,

I will demonstrate how the emergence of the individualist subject is contingent on such a pervasive success of law, by reading a site where such a subject has yet to emerge: in the colony, where the East-India Company begins preliminary exercises to constitute itself as arbiter.

The novel now replaces Roxana's language of necessity and need, employed earlier to justify the use of her sexuality, with the foreboding language of unnatural vice or "vicious liberty, which is neither honourable or religious" (R 238). Dire consequences are foretold when Roxana informs the reader of the contents of the letter written by the disappointed Dutchman before leaving her: "[He] forgave me everything he said, but the cruelty of refusing him, which he owned he could not forgive me . . . because it was an injury to myself, would be an introduction to my ruin, and that I would seriously repent of it. He foretold some fatal things which, he said, he was well-assured I should fall into, and that I would be ruined" (R 243). Roxana is sufficiently mortified, enough indeed to leave her "melancholy" and crying. Her admission of hubris comes soon after this when she enjoins the readers to see her as a "monument of the madness" that women run into when they "follow the dictates of an ambitious mind" (R 244).

Through this confession, Defoe sets the stage for the victory of domesticity. Roxana repents her decision to remain unmarried and proposes marriage to the Dutchman at their subsequent meeting four years later. This time, she goes about everything in the socially acceptable manner. She makes a full disclosure to him about all her effects and insists that their wealth be combined. When the newly married couple get together to do so, another sleight of hand gives us the distinction between capital accumulation through frugality (Roxana's) and capital accumulation through trade in the colonies (the merchant's). The couple discover their wealth to be equal but with a difference. His is the new wealth: "papers and parchments . . . books of accounts and writing," which indicate stock in the East-India Company, shares in ships bound for the Indies and shares in cargo lying at docks in foreign ports. Hers, on the other hand, is a symbol of the traditional attempts at social mobility—mortgages upon land and securities. At this point, Roxana muses: "Unhappy wretch," said I to myself, "shall my ill-got wealth, the product of prosperous lust and of a vile and vicious life of whoredom and adultery be intermingled with the honest well-gotten estate of this innocent gentleman to be a moth and caterpillar among it" (R II, 100). Aggressive individualism in

Defoe's narrative not only serves as a warning to the female entrepreneur and as a demonstration of the need to keep sexuality within the confines of domesticity, but it also provides a paternalistic and ethical justification for colonialism.[22] When Roxana soon desires nothing more than dependence on a man who values her not for her wealth or for her body, but for her love, and when his "honest and virtuous courtship" also prompts her to decide against a previous vanity, separate property for herself, the narrative transforms the exemplary merchant into paterfamilias.

The ideological shoring up of the "family" at a time when its material basis has become weaker and more internally contradictory with the individualist demands of early capitalism is not unusual. Ideology derives its force from its ability to mask such ruptures. The displacement of fears about social disintegration (now given as disorder originating from female excesses) erases the ways through which "an ideology that seems hegemonic and self-justifying unwittingly produces its own negation."[23] The valorization of male mercantile sensibility, best crystallized in what James H. Bunn has called an "aesthetics of British mercantilism," extolled the assimilation of the foreign from the vast expansive regions of "free-trade" to produce a syncretic "Citizen of the World."[24] The Dutchman is naturalized as British through his marriage to Roxana and his control over her assets becomes a transfer of skills for more efficient management. Such phallic entitlement and its manifestation as resource management produces a conjuncture that not only naturalizes paternal dominance over the family, but as my discussion below will indicate, parcels out colonial wealth and power to the one who is above the law. However, for the Dutchman to emerge as a trope of ethics and social order, Roxana must first be exposed and displaced.

For the novel to enact closure when Roxana relinquishes her quest for profit would confirm the ideological imperatives of making the female-as-individualist realize her true nature in "love," but it is to punish her for forgetting "natural instinct" that Defoe's narrative must persist. Roxana's fears about the guiding hand of Providence are soon proven true: "the most secret crimes are, by the most unforeseen accidents, brought to light and discovered" (*R* II, 160). One of her abandoned progeny, a daughter Susan, sets out in pursuit of the woman she suspects is her mother. Subsequently, by exposing her mother's "inhumanity," Susan brings about the now reformed Roxana's downfall. The protagonist-narrator loses the affection of her husband and the use of his immense colonial assets. Disinherited by her spouse, discarded by her children, and unable to go back to her old profession, Roxana now sees her worst fears come true. Her renewed attempts at self-improvement are thwarted when Roxana now fails as a she-merchant; the ships she had invested in go down at sea. The narrative leaves her alone and destitute again, this time thrown into prison on being unable to meet her debts. It is left to her maid, Isabel, to fill in the last page of the novel to tell us of the death of her mistress: "thoroughly repented of every bad action, especially the little value she had for her children . . . made her peace with God etc." (*R* II, 242).

This confessional ending clinches the paradoxical positioning of the female-as-individualist. Roxana is punished by law acting as the negative restraint on her capitalist aspirations even as the juridical power of bourgeois morality is reinforced by her repentance. She confesses to the educative role of law; she admits the little value she placed on her children as the reason why she placed too much value on "vice"; she admits her subjection to the penitentiary as the just due for her unnatural instincts. The social contract reveals, in Defoe's novel, its repression even as it stages its "participatory power." Roxana's movement through Defoe's narrative, as a trope of possessive individualism, is short-circuited when this figure is simultaneously mapped onto the field of affective relations and gendered "natural instinct." When Roxana, as she-merchant, fails at bourgeois love and motherhood, law (repressive law in the service of "natural" law) is momentarily invoked to produce a disciplined and responsible subject.

BRINGING IT HOME: THE DOMESTIC PROJECT OF IMPERIALISM

In Defoe's novel, the colony functions not only "as a reference, a source of invisible wealth" which Roxana can use as an alibi for her "ill-gotten" wealth, but it also serves as a site of alternative wealth.[25] When Roxana and her Dutch husband get together to display their material assets to each other in what Locke termed the "voluntary compact" of marriage, the conjugal nexus between the female-as-individualist and mercantilist capitalism in its colonialist stage is made clear. We do not simply see a moral distinction between prostitution and trade, between feudal privilege and bourgeois enterprise, and between landed interests and capital. The "paper rights" to property, symbolizing the wealth of the Dutchman, hearken the arrival of the law-merchant—the law that installs bourgeois trade and transferable property as "right."

The moral and ideological underpinnings of the new wealth are made apparent when the Dutchman takes over Roxana's rights regarding her property and children. Roxana is punished for her inhumanity towards the children by depriving her of her wealth. The "ill-gotten" wealth of sexuality as labor-power is now deployed to its "proper" use. In a demonstration of paternal power, that invokes the public debates I mentioned earlier about women wasting money that could be better invested in the colonies, Defoe's narrative now transfers Roxana's natural rights as mother to her husband, who now deploys his colonial influence to set the home in order and stage what can be termed a domestic accompaniment (if not a precondition) to the imperial project abroad.

If Roxana's disciplining by Defoe's narrative is facilitated by the nexus between possessive individualism and colonialism, the same network works to the advantage of the Dutchman. Here, the gendered contradictions of possessive individualism are clearly laid bare. Roxana tries to improve herself and gain economic and personal autonomy as she-merchant, but the instinct for profit replaces her "natural instinct" or maternal feelings. The Dutchman, on the other hand, manifests no such contradiction between paternity and the instinct for profit. In fact, it serves to sharpen his qualities as a parent. What creates base instincts in Roxana now produce paternity par excellence. The Dutchman not only takes care of his own but also children who are not naturally his! He marries off Roxana's daughter with a sizeable dowry to a factor in the Dutch East-India Company on the Malabar coast, and her son Thomas is given a large plantation in Virginia. The Dutchman's own children from his previous marriage also become beneficiaries of Roxana's assets. They are given, before his death, five thousand pounds each in East-India stock. Capital accumulated through prostitution and avarice is morally transformed into "inheritance" by inserting it into the political economy of colonialism.

The minute constructions of bourgeois affective relations have other resonances besides representing colonial wealth as the basis of establishing domestic order. The Dutchman is not simply a figuration of "fatherhood" needing overseas sustenance and Roxana is not merely the female claiming rights that finally deny her "humanity"—but together they establish the allegory of the English-Dutch struggle in the colonial sphere. Just as the sexual contract is often an allegorical displacement of class conflicts and resolutions, Roxana's marriage to the Dutch merchant has important resonances for the contemporaneous reader who is aware of events taking place at this time in the East Indies.

The continuing presence of the Dutch on the Malabar coast in south India and their subsequent success in securing the timber and spice trade along this coast since 1679, had prevented the English from gaining a foothold in Southern India to trade in these prized commodities. Despite numerous attempts by the British East India Company to influence and coerce the smaller kingdoms to grant them favors (these also included some armed conflicts with rulers supported by the Dutch), this situation only ended in 1792 when Malabar came to the British under the terms of the treaty of Srirangapatnam. In the mid-eighteenth century, it would not have been an exaggeration to say that the Dutch were the only major obstacle between the British and the monopoly of the spice trade on the Malabar coast. Thus, Roxana's marriage to the Dutchman and her temporary retirement to Holland have an important function in producing a cultural representation of a possible European coalition in mercantilism (a trope which is replayed when Roxana's daughter marries a factor in the Dutch East-India Company). This is the final instance in a set of narrative strategies by which colonialism is represented and justified by building it into the fabric of the private sphere—love, marriage, and private property—not only as the right channel for wealth that should be kept away from women, and as the source of wealth that will restore social order in the bourgeois family, but also as the referent of the conjugal allegory.

In the preceding discussion, I have not only tried to establish an entry point for the discussion of "women's rights" within the rubric of colonialism but have argued for the necessity of exploring the complicity of the history of feminism in the West with the history of conquest and domination. By doing what Edward Said has called a "contrapuntal reading," the historical connections and parameters that govern the alleged dissonance between "feminism" and "rights of woman" today can be understood by contextualizing the female subject of the social contract and property relations in eighteenth-century Britain within the framework of Britain as empire. This dissonance also establishes another important point: the contradiction central to Western democracy—here, the compatibility of British liberal discourse with a despotic colonialism. While I have read incompatibility so far as the contradictions that lie at the heart of the discourse of individual rights, where affective relations and possessive relations short-circuit each other to disallow women a central place in this narrative, there is also another hermeneutic tool for exposing despotism: an exploration of the compatibility of contradictory positionings within the same discourse when it travels to an alien context. Peter Fitzpatrick explains this procedural export of the law thus:

> The amnesiac quality of modern law's origins avoids a momentous paradox. An advanced Occidental law, wedded in its apotheosis to freedom and a certain equality becomes thoroughly despotic when shipped to the rest of the world in the formal colonizations from the late eighteenth to the early twentieth centuries. . . . This law was a prime justification and instrument of imperialism, one which, in the assessments of [a] great practitioner-theorist of imperialism [was] a gift which should "deserve the gratitude of the silent and ignorant millions."[26]

Reading in the colony the caricature of the theories of liberal rights, and the premises on which they are founded will undeniably expose the limits of what is still a very powerful discourse. It is to that end that I read the record of the colonizer as he unpacks the gift on Indian soil. At the very instance that the discourse of possessive individualism, in its unguarded and illegitimate existence as alien rule rears up as despotism, the tracks of ideology become clearer. In some archival fragments of the East-India Company we can clarify better, perhaps, what the literary text of Defoe relinquishes reluctantly. Defoe's fictional work, it would seem, ends momentarily to be taken up by one of the writers in the numerous factories established under the auspices of the East-India Company. Here, even as Defoe's narrative leaves us with Roxana who is reduced to a transmitter of wealth from one generation to another, halfway across the world, British law is summoned in its nakedly apparent form, no longer to even stage women as owners of their selves or of property, but as property to be owned by someone else.

EXPORTING THE LAW: THE EAST-INDIA COMPANY AS JUDGE

On February 23, 1721, the Diary and Consultation Book of Fort St. George, at Madras in South India, records the arrival of a petition to the President Francis Hastings and the Council, from Venketrauze, "an inhabitant of this place of the Rashboot [sic] cast":

> The import of the said petition being as complaint against Devaroy the Warehouse Conicoply [sic] for seducing his sister from her Lawfull Husband, debauching her and forcibly detaining her when she was demanded by himself and her said husband . . . the Complainant being very pressing and Importunate for Justice and being so much exasperated at the Shame and disgrace which their family was like to Suffer on ye occasion that they could scarcely be restrained

from murdering themselves as well as the Woman, the Cast or tribe to which they belong being so nicely strict in their rules with regard to matters that Concern their honour that they chuse much rather to suffer death than Ignominy or reproach. (*Records* 31)

Normal company proceedings about the arrival and departure of ships, outstanding bills and receipt of revenues, consignments of goods and despatches are interrupted by this petition for "justice." The case is a native affair: a local employee of the company, the warehouse conicopoly (clerk) named Devaroy, has been accused of "seducing" and "forcibly detaining" the wife of a local upper-caste man. The victim appears in the record not as the appellant but as a referent. It is not from her that the petition for justice originates; she is not only spoken for by her brother but is also left unnamed in the entire proceedings. Appearing variously as "the Bashwar woman," "wife," and as "sister of the plaintiff," her anonymity precludes her from being the willed and individuated speaking subject in the liberal tradition of juridico-legal discourse. The erasing of her proper name (all the other male players are named), has a function that will only emerge as the case unfolds. The proper name is the title deed of a legal subject and by being written out of these records her inaccessibility to legal security is guaranteed. It refuses to define her "property-in-person" as bourgeois ideology guarantees it to men: "the self-presence of the subject, that truth which the proper name embodies and which the civil code verifies." [27] Unnamed, she is already placed outside the law.

In addition to this refusal to extend legality to the female colonial subject in the Company's records, we also have the staging of a *collective* victimization, that further disperses the availability of an "individualist" subject. The records tell us that the "Complainant being very pressing and Importunate for Justice and being so much exasperated at the Shame and disgrace which their family was like to Suffer on ye occasion that they could scarcely be restrained from murdering themselves as well as the Woman" (*Records* 31). The threat from the native is not directed towards the company but against themselves—the threat of mass suicide. The point I am trying to emphasize here is a simple one: we cannot easily read here for a Roxana or a Pamela. The difficulty of extricating the female colonial subject, the victim of an alleged rape, from these records of the colonial power as a subject of "possessive individualism"—one who claims a violation of her self and her body—is made difficult by the public staging of rape as a violence against a community. Even if this publicity draws the Company's attention and urges it to act without delay, the records show the Company's inability to conceive social violence in "larger" terms. Instead, attempts are made by the Company Councillors to psychologize the rape as originating from within the person. They acknowledge the conicopoly Devaroy's prehistory of "vile behaviour" even as they show reluctance in accepting the victim's oath on the grounds that she is "wicked," "lewd," and exhibits "loose behaviour." It is in the paradox of *consensual* rape that this unnamed woman comes closest to becoming a deliberate will or an individualized subject in a narrow sense.

That this paradox represents not only a general disbelief in women's testimony but also the inherent contradictions of possessive individualism is borne out by Frances Ferguson's provocative discussion of legal debates about rape in eighteenth-century Britain. In her article "Rape and the Rise of the Novel," Ferguson articulates the relationship between consent, will, and testamentary capacity as they were formulated by two influential works of the time: Sir Mathew Hale's *History of the Pleas of the Crown* and Sir Robert Chambers's *A Course of Lectures on the English Law, 1767-1773.*[28] The notion of consent when extended to women establishes rape through an evaluation of the "mental states" of both parties involved. It thus puts women within the discourse of possessive individualism because consent presupposes a deliberating will and inalienable property-in-person (rights). However, as Ferguson points out, Sir Mathew Hale's legal definition of rape had an inbuilt warning. While he acknowledges that rape was a crime that violated the woman's will and showed the perpetrator's disregard for his victim's consent, rape was also (for him) "an accusation easily to be made and hard to be proved, and harder to be defended by the party accused, tho never so innocent."[29] In one stroke, women, though subjects of will, are disallowed credibility in the eyes of the law. Now it is not a question of the defendant being innocent until proven guilty, but the prosecution is guilty of lying unless proved innocent of perjury.

In order to manage the work of this double standard, Ferguson goes on to show how rape was statutorily defined so that consent or the woman's mental state became immaterial. These statutory definitions were all dependent on situations when the woman was not the willed, self-present, speaking subject that the law in general states that she is. Rape, therefore, was inescapably the verdict when the victim was under twelve years of age (a legal infant), was physically weak or helpless, or was unconscious or mentally deranged. Nonconsent was read as consent in the following situations: if the woman later married the accused (all sexual intercourse in marriage was consensual) or if she was later found to be pregnant (Ferguson believes the explanation for this lies in eighteenth-century medical accounts that linked female orgasm with conception).[30] Finally, the fundamental disbelief in the woman's testimony also drew in the need for extra-individual narratives or circumstantial evidence. (This last point is evident in the case we are discussing here. It is because members of the Company disbelieve the Bashwar woman's testimony that they resort to histories of virtue or debauchery—to establish Devaroy's intention or nonintention to rape and the Bashwar woman's consent or nonconsent to the act.)

In direct contrast to the British legal framework of rape as an act that involves penetration of one body by another and assault of one will by another, rape is presented in the case proceedings here as a transgression that has affected and thrown into disarray a social body (the woman's kin and caste members). Rape is a caste transgression more than it is an individual assault. The social rather than individual nature of this violence (as endangering caste purity rather than individual property-in-person) is explained thus in the ancient legal institutes (the Laws of Manu from the second century A.D.): "For by (adultery) is caused a mixture of the castes (*varna*) among men; thence (follows) sin, which cuts up even the roots and causes the destruction."[31] In setting up this different paradigm for "rape," I am not insisting that the woman's rape must justifiably be read as a violence against a community (the caste's honor) for such metaphoric displacements erase the materiality of her body. Rather, my aim is to show how the persistence to read one way rather than another will expose the constructedness of the bourgeois legal subject's claim to self-presence and originary meaning. We are faced with the difficult task of making the colony perform its own deconstructive task, as the limits of Western discourse. The East-India Company's Records show us not the priority of a legal subject, as individualist; it is a caricature invented at the site of the law's illegitimate address.[32]

Let us go back to the records now as they summarize the accused clerk's testimony:

he reply'd that Vinketrauze came about ten days ago to him and told him that his sister had returned from the place to which he sent her up in the country but that he could not find her, Devaroy added that thereupon he sent to one Eyarnoi-Villevochum a Washerman's wife and bid her look for the Girl and when she had found her, she told her her brother desired she might be carryed to Devaroy's

house, Devaroy added that when the Girl was brought thither t'was very late and
. . . [he] bid her go away but yet they desired to lodge in the house that night for
fear of being taken up by the Rounds, that in ye morning just before he went to
the Fort he enquired which was ye Rashboot Woman who when she saw him
desired his Protection from her friends who she said would use her ill whenever
she returned to them. He affirmed that he bid her go away a second time but she
reply'd she was afraid and could not go. (*Records* 32)

The accused's summary is the longest one in the records and this is
followed immediately by the brother's testimony. When the victim's time
comes to take her place in the records, we are told that the "the Sister to
the Plaintiff Vinketrauze being brought before the board was asked if
Deveroy *[sic]* was guilty of the several particulars wherewith he now stood
Charg'd in answer to whereto the woman declared in the affirmative and
offered her Oath to the same" (*Records* 32).

The Bashwar woman's testimony not only appears last in the string of
testimonies, but it is the one that merits the least attention in the records.
There is no summary of the woman's testimony. Instead, we have to read
her testimony simply as "affirmation" or "denial" and her narrative has to
be read as a differentiated "voice": as the discrepancy between her brother's and Devaroy's testimony. Though the company's policy of summariz-
ing and privileging the "written" over the oral petition is apparent in its
records, how do we counter this textual stifling of the woman's testimony?
We must read, instead, in the interstices of the opposed testimonies her
peculiar agency: it is after all *her* spatial, social, and caste transgressions—
in refusing to go her brother's house; in refusing to forgo the company of
a low-caste washerwoman and in entering company space—that have
"caused" this crisis. Her presence in the records attests to the considerable
danger posed by this "incident," to the interests of the company and its
relations with the locals around the fort. Yet, the Bashwar woman also
functions as a sign that is exchanged to create a new level of relations
between the colonizer and colonized, a function that precludes any reading of her as the juridico-legal subject of possessive individualism. By
entering the company's legal space, her status is now carefully parcelled
out into two alternatives: as an object of protection (Devaroy's claim that
he was protecting her from her relatives) and as an object of coercion (the
relatives' claim about her forcible detention). Here, a woman becomes
the "catalyst" of a political crisis without bearing the deliberate will of the
usual social agent, that is, without intention.

In such instances, the role of the critic as arbiter becomes crucial. Much has been made of the task of the critic in locating historical examples of resistance, in Third-World studies, whether it is in Gayatri Spivak's reading for the subaltern as textual silence in the official account of the Rani of Sirmur, or in Bhabha's repeated formulations of the mimic man.[33] To the question about the strategy by which the critic makes her analysis an intervention—of making visible agency not easily available even to the sympathetic reader—Spivak proposes the reading for subaltern subject-effect. Here, the account of stifled voices is replaced by a meticulous reading for the predication of another will to which the powers-that-be are in fact reacting.[34] For instance, we cannot judge in these summarized transcripts, which leave out the testimony of the victim, the truth of the matter. But we can (and must) read here the terms under which a native woman who is not yet the juridico-legal subject of rights (under British law) has her fate decided by the representatives of a pseudo-legal institution—the East-India Company. We can also read here that she effects the crisis; it is produced by her transgression of social boundaries determined by status and consanguinity. Thus, it is not only an agent that gets displayed but a revelation of a certain totality. We see how gender relations are implicitly built into the relations between the alien merchants and the comprador classes (the native upper-caste men). The confrontation becomes symbolic of large-scale transformations that are only beginning to take place. Just as Roxana's story is also an allegory of Dutch-English colonial relations, the case of the "Bashwar woman" is an allegory of the gradual transformation of merchant capital into imperialism, now ushered in with the appearance of law as the authority of the colonizer and a somewhat grotesque staging of the "rights" of the subaltern female subject.

British attempts to codify Indian law will only begin in another sixty years after they begin to amass vast amounts of land and people to govern, but the experiment in seeking to recruit native agents to legitimize the operations of colonial power has already begun. A body of local "caste leaders" is hastily constituted by the Company's board to give their "opinion." The caste leaders' "verdict" is entered soon after in the proceedings of the council's next meeting:

That Devroy [sic] kept in his house the Wife of a Rajah three or four days together and would not deliver her up though he was Required to do it several times by ye said Rajah and we believe as she herself like wise declares and will have her Oath that he lay with her by Force for which transgression We leave to your Honour and company to punish him as ye may think fit. (*Records* 39)

The verdict handed down by the caste leaders is one of "rape" but it is also a multiple violation: of infringing on conjugal privileges (refusing to deliver her up) as well as caste offence (abducting the "Wife of a Rajah"). Even though she is the sole witness to what actually took place, the woman's oath is evidently sufficient to establish her rape. One must note, however, that no punishment is prescribed by the native legal body and that the power of sentencing has already been delegated to the company. One can read this in two ways: either that native authorities have already acknowledged that the Company is not subject to its law or that cooperation between the two parties over a common threat (Devaroy) is seen as more conducive than unilateral decisions by one party.

The Company's recognition that a "right" outcome of this trial will allow further consolidation of its power and influence in the area is apparent from the trial records. Since the law-merchant is not yet alien *rule*, the Company still treads carefully. It must show willingness to cooperate with local interests without capitulation in order to keep its trade interests safe but capable of domination. For this reason, the Company must act as judge; but it must seek "advice" from local vested interests without losing the position of dominance. The records tell us about the consensus reached by the factory directors against a formal trial: "the admission of a formal trial and hearing of the several parties before the said castes would have been in a manner firming them [the caste leaders] into a Court of Judicature Superiour to ourselves as they were to judge of a matter they then might reasonably suppose they were better acquainted than our selves" (*Records* 41). So while the Company employed the local juridical institutions (leaders of the castes) to advise them, the Company officials must subordinate, in spirit, the judgment of the native.

Here, then, are the salient points of the verdict from the records as the President of the Board, Francis Hastings, delivers the decision at a hastily arranged meeting of the factory council. It is the closest approximation we have of the "intentions" of the East-India Company:

1. The woman's testimony cannot be disallowed for lack of evidence because of "common rules of Justice in England where the woman is often times allow'd to be a substantial evidence against the man in such a case" (*Records* 35).[35]

2. "The Deveroy [sic] is not being tried for rape but for refusing to return the woman to her husband when demanded by her husband. . . . We think he ought to suffer because *the crime is in itself of a very heinous nature and no less than the invading of another man's right and property as well as the possessing and detaining it from him which is in effect a Robbery* and is always punished with severity by the laws of our country" (*Records* 40, emphasis mine).

It is important to note that it is British law that has been invoked to justify the acceptance of the woman's testimony and the caste leaders' acceptance of the same is not mentioned.[36] British law is also invoked here to change the nature of the crime from *rape* to *robbery*—a change obviously made to accommodate the dissenting Company members who agreed that the woman had been restrained but could not concede that she had been raped—and to avoid a harsher sentence (prescribed by customary law). Now, the question of protecting the woman's "rights" (the ownership over her own person) is momentarily suspended as the Company comes forward to safeguard the "property" of the husband and the other male caste-members. In a fascinating reversal of Rousseau's fiction about the unsocialized individual submitting to the law to become the social body, here the native male as social body (upholding caste honor) submits to the law to become property-bearing-substance (he *owns women*). This public gesture of respecting private property is not a new phenomenon; it has served the colonial establishment to protect its monopoly over local markets from unlicensed British traders and pirates (often punished with death). More importantly, it marks the installment of a paradigm that will help future imperial policies, especially in the case of appropriation of communal property and property where no proprietorship can be legally established.[37]

The Company is also aware that this case presents an opportunity to consolidate its standing among the natives. Hastings rationalizes the verdict for the council in these terms: "*we think ourselves under an indispensable obligation to make a very publick example,* that by such an open piece of Justice the Inhabitants may be convinced that we will not suffer such persons to be thereby screened and protected from having due punishment inflicted on them when they commit unwarrantable actions" (*Records* 35, emphasis mine). Reflecting the council's feelings that this is not a case about "rape" but about wrongful possession of another man's property, Devaroy is sentenced: "he should be dismissed from the honourable company's service . . . he should stand in the Pillory and he should pay to the Injur'd husband such a sum of money as should be sufficient for the procuring another wife in the room of her whom he debauched" (*Records* 35).[38] Devaroy is ordered to pay four hundred pagodas to the husband on the recommendation of the caste leaders. He is also ordered to pay a fine of five hundred pagodas to the company on the receipt of which he is to be released (*Records* 101). The Bashwar woman has become an object of exchange—she is property which has been temporarily displaced spatially and in ownership, an error to be rectified by actual monetary transactions to determine her value. The woman's husband is richer by four hundred pagodas and the company's treasury by five hundred pagodas.

A popular argument that the selective imposition of British laws in the colonial situation left women's status for the most part untransformed is proven false.[39] Our archival material provides a different reading of the place of gender in the theater of colonialism and this is that "kinship and marriage are part of total social systems and are always tied into economic and political arrangements."[40] Gayle Rubin's formulations hold true here as the law of the colonizer emerges as an invention at the site of its address to forge a momentary alliance between the colonial power and the upper caste male hierarchy. The "woman" exists metonymically (for us) not only as an instance of patriarchal oppression but as a signifier of the success of the law of the colonizer—as "publick example." It is not colonial transformation of the economic and political that affects the structures of kinship and marriage in the trickle-down manner. In both Roxana's and the Bashwar woman's case we also have seen it work the other way. The affective relations that structure the place of "woman" determine large-scale transactions of imperialism. If we have made little success in measuring those effects, it is because the reading practices that we often employ to study the relationship between feminism and imperialism are complicit with reading for females-as-individualists (as historical agents in their own right) rather than as subject-effects, whose actions often allow very different players to perform symbolic exchange rituals over their bodies.

The modern subject is not an autonomous agent or the distinct starting point from which power flows. The case of Roxana shows us how human beings are made subjects through a variety of forms and modalities, how she recognizes herself as a product of disciplinary administration. If Defoe's novel shows us how bourgeois morality as law effectively acts at the micro-level to produce the individual at its most private site, the trial of the Bashwar woman reveals the large-scale macro-levels of law's interest. As the East-India Company records have shown us, restoring domestic harmony and order in the case of the Bashwar woman is the simultaneous staging of an explicitly political ritual—establishing relations of domination under the guise of free trade between different peoples, races, and nations. To chart the itinerary of this deployment of law no longer as familial concern but as a technology that brings a nation under the order of colonial rule, we have to move from these two sites of transactions (Roxana and the Bashwar woman) to another: where the "Indian" woman's rights becomes a highly contested issue in itself. We have to move from the law of the merchant to the law of imperialism, a difference that is manifested by a shift from impromptu invention to codification. Fifty years after Defoe's novel stages "women's rights," the debate about the native woman's rights will begin in earnest when the Company scrutinizes the law of the native.

WRITING AS CODIFICATION, READING AS ARBITRATION

It is now commonplace to point out that British attempts to codify Indian law were not exercises to bring the colonial subjects under the citizenry of the British rule of law but in fact served to maintain the distinction between the two in order to consolidate the establishment of empire. Soon after the acquisition of Bengal in 1772, Governor General Warren Hastings commissioned Nathaniel Halhed to investigate the ancient Hindu texts of legal commentary. As a glance at the introduction to Halhed's *Code of Gentoo Laws* (1776) will show, nowhere was there an attempt to pass this project off as British largesse in respecting native custom:

The importance of the commerce of India, and the advantages of a territorial establishment in Bengal, have at length awakened the attention of the British Legislature to every circumstance that may conciliate the affections of the natives, or ensure stability to the acquisition. Nothing can conduce to these two points as a well-timed toleration in matters of religion and an adoption of such original institutes of the country, as do not immediately clash with the laws or interests of the conquerors.[41]

Two important consequences followed the British decision to adopt "original institutes" grounded in religious law: first, the point of reference became an idealized body of law rather than an actual one and, second, the interference of a colonial power with a system not built on similar principles led to the privileging of the written. The immobility and petrification of what might actually be termed customary law, into the dictates of a legal commentary written by Manu in the second century A.D., indicates the functioning of the orientalist argument that the native still lived bound to the laws handed down as "divine revelations," unchanged for over sixteen centuries! The colonial situation not only created something that had not existed but, in a process of codification, that enlisted the help of eleven pandits, ensured that the legal statutes remained the expression of the dominant power group in Indian society, the Brahmins. As collaborators in deploying the administrative rule, the power interests of the upper castes were allied to colonial power just as they relinquished their role as arbiters to the centralized administration of the new colonial power. This is the framework in which the "rights" of the female colonial subject become available.

Women's rights became a category of serious intellectual discussion with the imperialist power adopting the civilizing mission in India—when the colonial administrators began a series of social reforms to abolish unacceptable practices. By the end of the nineteenth century, legal philosopher Sir Henry Maine tied the political fate of the Indian empire to the fate of its native women: "The degree in which the personal immunity and proprietary capacity of women are recognized in a particular state or community is a test of the degree of advance of its civilization . . . and the degree in which the dependence [of women] has voluntarily been modified and relaxed *serves undoubtedly as a rough measure of tribal, social, national capacity for self-control*" (brackets and emphasis mine).[42]

The political argument about Asiatic despotism ("the natives are happier under our rule") ran concurrently with "they are barbaric" and therefore incapable of being granted the postulates of bourgeois liberalism. Thus, even at the time when British law was finally conceding proprietary rights to British women, India remained a space of petrification.[43] The Indian woman became the signifier of Indian cultural immobility—its uncivilized status. The Indian Nationalist response to these representations emerged out of the terrain created by colonialist discourse. The Indian social reformers of the nineteenth century will respond to charges of "barbarism" by advocating change, while the nativist will rediscover "rights" for women in the ancient texts. Dwarka Nath Mitter's *The Position of Women in Hindu Law* (1913) is one such nativist project. Not only does he reread the ancient sources to prove that women under Hindu law had more proprietary rights than British women prior to the Married Women's Property Act of 1870, but he also asserts that women's rights were taken away by the Muslim invaders who ruled India prior to British rule. The nativist project's slide into communalism and religious nationalism shows how conditions created for anti-imperialist struggles can also define the limits of such retroactive mythmaking.

This retroactive mythmaking, however, is not unlike the colonizer's project of codifying law; both are attempts to arrest textuality. To "fictionalize" the law, to provide its genealogy, is therefore to never assure its duration: "It seems that the law as such should never give rise to any story. To be invested with its categorical authority, the law must be without history, genesis, or any possible derivation."[44] Not only does a story about the law establish the legal process as an act of reading and interpretation, it also suggests the importance of asserting what Spivak has called the "power of the script." The field of law like the field of the literary is fraught with countersignatures. Just as the critic appears before a text and displaces its pastness with her reading, the subject before the law in applying herself to it creates something new. The text of legal commentary is in that sense like the text of literary criticism—both display the sociality and production that go on at the scene of the text.[45]

Such an undoing of the distinction between the literary and the legal can help us address other questions about "rereading" the past, or for that matter questions about "rewriting" the social text. For instance, there can be no nativist claim to women's rights as always available from the ancient legal text, for that discussion is itself a response to colonial rule. It is in this sense that "rights" and individualism are secured by the history of imperialism, and not in the simplistic sense as a "legacy" of Western social missionaries whether orientalists, administrators, or legal historians. Our reading of the case of the Bashwar woman and Nathaniel Halhed makes that clear. At the level of the social text, it also makes clear how spatial demarcations such as the "public" and "private" do not preexist the law but are set in place by and through the power of legal discourse. The politics of domestication that circumscribed the Englishwoman in the "private sphere" went hand in hand with the large-scale transformations required by mercantilism speedily on its way to imperialism. The scrupulous protection of "personal" law by the British in India was a strategic deployment of similar categories to service colonialist rule. By separating "personal" (or "woman") from the law of colonial governance (the common Criminal and Civil Procedure), the illusion of noninterference was maintained. As the ruling in the case of the Bashwar woman indicates, women and the traditions associated with them are promoted as the separate property of the indigenous patriarchy at one historical moment, while at another moment they become objects for Western transformation and liberation.

The final irony of course is this: it is in the arbitrary divisions created by legal discourse that the agency of the female subaltern realizes its far-reaching implications. The "personal" and the "public" are undone as Shahbano, the subject before law, ignites the contradictions of her dual-positioning. Unlike Roxana, whose possessive individualism was short-circuited by defining the female-as-individualist simultaneously as the subject of affective relations (bourgeois love and motherhood), the Bashwar woman and Shahbano manage to accomplish something else: denied representation through the "I-slot" (Foucault's term), they show instead how "agency" is often an activation of relations that seem to be outside the subjects' domain. The Bashwar woman incites her community to action; Shahbano provokes a national crisis. Neither would have been possible if their subject status was purely "private."

In Shahbano's ability to move between two competing and parallel discourses, the bourgeois discourse of liberal rights and the Muslim *shariat*, we trace a historically available form of agency that cannot be explained by dichotomizing liberal rights (as Western) and a feminism that springs wholly from indigenous soil. To put it differently, the agency of the subject split between two legal codes does not lie in a choice between traditionalism and Westernization. This is not to say, however, that sometimes deploying or foregrounding the notion of the "indigenous" cannot become a radical questioning of the assumed superiority of the latter. But in Shahbano's case, her resort to what was seen as the traditional solution exposed one of the contradictions that underlie the liberal rights definition of "maintenance." In rejecting the annuity available under Western legal discourse and opting for her proprietary right over the *mehr* (dower), she effectively exposed the discourse of protection to which the former implicitly subscribes.[46] She now claims what is "properly" hers rather than the "compensation" dispensed by a divorcing husband. (The discourse of property still remains paramount but it subverts the accompanying patriarchal notion of "protection.")

By paying attention to such slippages and disjunctures, when acceding to unavoidable structures also creates something new, one sees how the position of the subaltern performs a "politics" of interruption (Spivak's phrasing). Shahbano not only interrupts intellectual projects that construct her as totally other (she shares the same history with the woman in the West), but she also destabilizes attempts to diminish her agency (the illiterate woman "rewrites" law as it effects a national crisis). It is by exploring this historical link that has simultaneously produced them, and acknowledging the differential privilege that history has finally accorded them, that the feminist in the West learns from the subaltern in decolonized space.

NOTES

For comments and criticism at various stages, I am grateful to the reviewers at *Genders*, Carol Mason, Monika Mehta, John Mowitt, Paula Rabinowitz, Charlie Sugnet, and Asha Varadharajan. Don Johnson has my thanks for help with locating elusive materials.

1. Quoted in Zakia Pathak and Rajeswari Sunder Rajan, "Shahbano," in *Feminist Theory in Practice and Process*, ed. Micheleine R. Malson et al (Chicago: University of Chicago Press), 249. This essay has been invaluable in helping me formulate notions of agency that are not limited to the realm of individualist intention and will. See especially pp. 261-73. For the text of the Court's ruling, see "The Judgement," in *The Shah Bano Controversy*, ed. Asghar Ali Engineer (Bombay: Orient Longman, 1987), 23-34; hereafter cited as *Controversy*.

2. The Code of Criminal Procedure was piloted by Sir James Fitzjames in 1872. This code, first used by the British government in India, and later by the Indian State, for uniform dispensation of criminal law, has a legal provision intended to prevent vagrancy and destitution. The reason why many divorced women (of all religions) appealed under this provision in order to get a quicker and more effective ruling is indicated in the Supreme Court's ruling on the Shahbano case: " 'wife' includes a divorced woman who has not remarried. These provisions are too clear and precise to admit of any doubt or refinement. The religion professed by a spouse or by the spouses has no place in the scheme of these provisions. [It] . . . is wholly irrelevant in the application of these provisions. The reason for this is axiomatic, in the sense that section 125 is a part of the Code of Criminal Procedure, not of the civil laws which define and govern the rights and obligations of the parties belonging to particular religions. . . . Section 125 was enacted in order to provide a quick and summary remedy to a class of persons unable to maintain themselves" (*Controversy* 25-26, 41-44).

3. "Open Letter to Muslims," *Inquilab* (November 13, 1985). Reprinted in *Controversy* 211-12.

4. For representative positions in the Hindu-Muslim communalism debate see Janak Raj Jai, *Shah Bano* (New Delhi: Rajiv Publications, 1986). For a detailed argument that the ruling is an interference in the religious rights of minorities see Mohammed Shihabuddin, *The Battle of the Shariah in India* (Bangalore: Furqania Academy Trust, 1986); and for the transnational ramifications of the debate, see Mohammad Farogh Naseem, *The Shah Bano Case X-Rayed* (Karachi: Legal Research Center, 1988). For the multiple perspectives from Indian feminists, both Hindu and Muslim, see the following: Madhu Kishwar, "Pro-Women or Anti-Muslim?" 52-57; Seema Mustafa, "An Old Woman Deprived in the Name of God," 63-70; and Zarina Bhatty, "Muslim Women Bill Evades Issues," 107-10 (all in *Controversy*).

5. The divisions in the legal codes were consolidated under colonial rule. In India today, there are a number of codes of "Personal Law" under which issues of marriage, divorce, custody, property, inheritance, and so forth are to be judged. Under colonial rule, the British aimed several legislative measures, such as the Muslim Shariat Law (1937), at appeasing local strongholds of potential resistance. By demarcating a category called "Personal Law," the British not only created the illusion that colonialism had not interfered with local customs and religious practices but in fact effectively created a potentially exploitative situation for a vulnerable part of the population: women, whose legal statuses were now almost wholly determined by outdated and stringent laws, newly codified for the colonial authority. A "private" sphere had been created by the legal discourse deployed by the British to allow native patriarchal structures "self-government."

6. Michel Foucault, "Nietzsche, Genealogy and History," in *The Foucault Reader*, ed. Paul Rabinow (New York: Pantheon Books, 1984), 76.

7. See Hélène Cixous's "Laugh of the Medusa," *Signs* 1:4 (1976): 875-94, for the best formulation of this insurgency as a "shattering entry into history": "Because she arrives, vibrant over and again, we are at the beginning of a new history, or rather the process of becoming in which several histories intersect with each other. As subject for history, woman always occurs simultaneously in several places" (882).

8. I use *subaltern* here not as a term to designate subordinate classes and groups (i.e., in the Gramscian sense) but as Gayatri Spivak uses it in her own discussions of the work of Subaltern Studies scholars: as a relationship of difference that is produced by scrupulous readings of elite knowledges, histories, and frameworks. The subaltern cannot speak but her "consciousness" has an agency because it exposes the limitations of the discourse that tries to know and include her. The responsibility of the critic is to maintain her "irreducibility" and "irretrievability" even as she attempts to speak to her. See Gayatri Chakravorty Spivak, "Can the Subaltern Speak?" in *Marxism and the Interpretation of Culture*, ed. Cary Nelson and Lawrence Grossberg (Urbana: University of Illinois Press, 1988), 271-313.

9. Daniel Defoe, *The Fortunate Mistress; or, a History of the Life of Mademoiselle De Beleau, Known by the Name of Roxana* (Boston: Dana Estes, 1904). Subsequent citations in the text will be indicated by the abbreviation *R* and page numbers; and

Records of Fort St. George, Diary and Consultation Book of 1721 (reprint, Madras: Government Press, 1930). Subsequent citations in the text will be indicated by *Records* and page numbers.

10. In a recent interview published in the *Oxford Literary Review*, Gayatri Spivak takes to task the "nativist" feminist's attempt to argue an opposition between "feminism" and "rights of woman": "I think it is also important that you recognize that the concept of human rights, individual rights, has a deep complicity with the culture of imperialism. If you say this then some anthropological search will isolate and find some native text where something can be translated as 'right.' . . . Again this is a very politically important gesture to say, 'no, we had it all along.' But none the less gesture politics and the production of knowledge are not the same thing. You cannot fight something if you do not acknowledge that what is poison has also historically been medicine" ("Neocolonialism and the Secret Agent of Knowledge," *Oxford Literary Review* 13.1 and 2 [1991]: 220-51). Spivak clearly is arguing the impossibility of a separate history for the Indian feminist who speaks up for rights while rejecting the conceptual framework of Western feminism. Ignorance of the history that "secures one's position" and creates the law under which one is making one's claim cannot for Spivak be equated with self-determination in knowledge-production. For a well-publicized example of elite nativist attempts to maintain an "independent self-view" see Madhu Kishwar, "Why I Do Not Call Myself a Feminist," *Manushi* 61 (Nov.-Dec. 1990): 2-8.

11. For a thoughtful discussion of the evolution of these concepts, see C. B. Macpherson, *The Political Theory of Possessive Individualism* (London: Oxford University Press, 1962).

12. See Gayatri Spivak's argument to this effect in "Theory in the Margin: Coetzee's Foe Reading Defoe's Crusoe/Roxana," in *Consequences of Theory: Selected Papers from the English Institute, 1987-88*, ed. Jonathan Arac and Barbara Johnson (Baltimore: Johns Hopkins Press, 1991), 154-80.

13. Nancy Armstrong, *Desire and Domestic Fiction: A Political History of the Novel* (New York: Oxford University Press, 1987), and Carole Pateman, *The Sexual Contract* (Stanford: Stanford University Press, 1988).

14. See Susan Staves, *Married Women's Separate Property in England 1660-1833* (Cambridge, Mass.: Harvard University Press, 1990), for an excellent historical analysis of the legal changes instituted during this period. Staves demonstrates how increasing amounts of land under mortgage created the need for fluid finances for trade even as dower effectively controlled the possibility of alienation of land rights. Legal discourses that emphasized evolution and progress, therefore, effectively worked against dower both on the grounds that it had no place in the changing society and that women must become parties of contracts rather than be given "forced" entitlements by virtue of their status. Contract thus became a means of paving the way for increased exchange value in land by offering wives by means of prenuptial agreements and jointures, fixed claims to a particular amount of land, or sums of money to compensate for the abrogation of their right to land after the husband's death.

15. *Desire and Domestic Fiction* 48.

16. Ibid. 49.

17. We can, for instance, see *Roxana* as situated within these debates by looking at some of the organs of publicity such as *The Spectator* or *The Rambler.* In 1712, a letter in *The Spectator* responds to another letter in which a man complains about the misuse of his money and status by a wife who enforces the common-law custom of pin-money, to support her lavish habits and immoral practices: "Separate Purses, between man and Wife, are, in my Opinion, as unnatural as separate beds" (*The Spectator,* ed. Donald F. Bond, 5 vols. [Oxford: Clarendon Press, 1987], 53). This connection between sexuality and separate property is made even more forcefully in Samuel Johnson's letter to *The Rambler* in 1751: "Two thousand pounds in the last age, with a domestick wife, would go farther than ten thousand in this. Yet settlements are expected, that often, to a mercantile man especially, sink a fortune into uselessness; and pin-money is stipulated for, which makes a wife independent and destroys love, by putting it out of a man's power to lay any obligation upon her, that might engage gratitude, and kindle affection" (Samuel Johnson, *Rambler* no. 97, in *The Yale Edition of the Works of Samuel Johnson: The Rambler,* ed. W. J. Bate and Albrecht Strauss, 3 vols. (New Haven: Yale University Press: 1969), 158. The letter establishes the connection I have addressed in the discussion above—the further consolidation of mercantilism and trade in the colonies (as national activity) is seen as commensurate with women's willingness to relinquish "unnecessary" rights and embrace an ideology of domestic existence free from attachments to property.

18. Terry Eagleton, *The Rape of Clarissa: Writing, Sexuality and Class Struggle in Samuel Richardson* (Minneapolis: University of Minnesota Press, 1982), 4-5.

19. Jacques Derrida, *Acts of Literature,* ed. Derek Attridge (London: Routledge, 1992), 36.

20. Peter Fitzpatrick, *The Mythology of Modern Law* (London: Routledge, 1992), 81.

21. This argument is an extrapolation of Eagleton's reading of Clarissa in *Rape,* 60.

22. In a recent study, *Ends of Empire: Women and Ideology in Early Eighteenth-Century English Literature* (Ithaca: Cornell University Press, 1993), Laura Brown traces the profusion of narrative conjunctures of the figure of woman and empire in eighteenth-century British literature. Her argument that the "logical conclusion of the extension of the ideal of mercantilist capitalist profit to women is a brutal and uncontrollable violence, a violation of the supposedly natural and benevolent forces of trade" (154) asks that we see Roxana's hatred and cruelty towards her children as a displacement of the violence that originates within and permeates male, mercantilist, colonialist trade practices. Brown's reading of "displacement" is useful to show how female subjects are often proxies for power, but it cannot adequately explain the narrative logic of the conjuncture of mothering and paternalism as stand-ins for female individualism and colonial trade.

23. *Ends of Empire* 168.

24. James H. Bunn, "The Aesthetics of British Mercantilism," *New Literary History* 11 (1980): 303-21.

25. See Edward Said, *Culture and Imperialism* (New York: Columbia University Press, 1993), for a discussion of the literary tradition in which the colony functions as a source of invisible wealth and self-improvement.

26. *Mythology of Modern Law* 107.

27. Michael Ryan, "Self-Evidence," *Diacritics* (June 1980): 7.

28. Frances Ferguson, "Rape and the Rise of the Novel," *Representations* 20 (1987): 88-112; Sir Matthew Hale, *The History of Pleas of the Crown*, 2 vols. (1678; reprint, London: Professional Books, 1971), and Sir Robert Chambers, *A Course of Lectures on the English Law, 1767-1773*, 2 vols., ed. Thomas M. Curley (Madison: University of Wisconsin Press, 1986).

29. Ferguson, "Novel" 89.

30. Ibid. 111 n. 29.

31. See *The Laws of Manu*, trans. Georg Buhler (New York: Dover Publications, 1969), VIII: 352. For this reason (maintaining caste purity), a number of "adulterous" acts that caused "defilement" and "mixture" were seen as synonymous with rape: speaking with female members of another caste, touching, offering ornaments, etc. While the punishments levied for these crimes were also higher if there was no consent from the victim, they were highest when the act neared the greatest levels of caste transgressions. In some of these inter-caste rapes, for instance, statutorily, consent was immaterial because the caste rules against cohabitation forbade anything nearing consensual intercourse.

32. See Arthur Berriedale Keith, *A Constitutional History of India 1600-1935* (New York: Barnes and Noble, 1969). Unlike the relationship between the Crown and the North American colonies before the American Revolution, the East-India Company for the first hundred years of its existence could only make and ordain laws that were in keeping with its character as a municipal and commercial body. The power to legislate for and to govern territory was not contemplated in the case of the East-India Company because even by the first quarter of the eighteenth century, the Company had very little territorial control in India. Moreover, the presence of established local trade markets and native governments with military capability ensured that India was not imagined as a colony of settlement until the end of the eighteenth century. Meanwhile, relatively successful military exploits against small local suzerains had already kindled the Company's aspirations. By 1683, the British Crown had given the Company permission to wage wars to acquire more property and by 1686 the renewed charter acknowledged that the Company had become a sovereign state in India (Keith, 89).

Leading up to this declaration had been two recent acquisitions: the island of Bombay in 1661 and Madras in 1683. (Calcutta was ceded in 1698.) These ceded colonies were the only spaces where the East-India Company had the absolute prerogative to govern and subject Indians to the jurisdiction of British law, a fact recognized by the 1726 charter which established Mayor's courts at Madras, Bombay, and Calcutta with prescriptions for the involvement of local panchayats and caste councils in "inter-caste" disputes and inferior courts with Indian merchants and local leaders (for other cases involving trade disputes). By the time of the case under discussion here (1721), some complications were beginning to emerge. The growing alliance between the Company and local trade interests and comprador classes resulted in disputes between British subjects and natives as well as between native traders and native agents employed by the Company. The handling of these needed more delicate applications of law. (The Company Records show that the petitioner or the brother of the rape victim is a peon in the employ of the tobacco farmers who supply goods to the Company.) Fort St. George, where the rape trial was held, was an area of partial sovereignty. The larger province (Surat) was not under British territorial authority, thus explaining the need to deal with autonomous caste-councils (unlike the incorporated ones in Bombay) and competing systems of law. In the absence of absolute territorial control and the pressure to keep the climate conducive for trade, the Company was still negotiating ways to "respect" local customary and criminal law even when the offender was one of its employees. (See Keith, 1-52.)

33. See Gayatri Spivak, "The Rani of Sirmur" in *Europe and Its Others*, 2 vols., ed. Francis Barker et al. (Colchester: University of Essex, 1985), and Homi Bhabha, "Of Mimicry and Man: The Ambivalence of Colonial Discourse," *October* 28 (1984): 125-33.

34. Gayatri Spivak, "Subaltern Studies: Deconstructing Historiography" in *In Other Worlds: Essays in Cultural Politics* (New York: Routledge, 1988), 197-221.

35. This is clearly a rebuttal to a number of board-members who gave it in writing that they were not willing to consider the woman's testimony over that of a loyal employee of the Company (*Records* 37-41).

36. Even ancient Hindu texts do not show evidence that women were disallowed testimony on the grounds of incredulity. Women were to testify in all cases involving women and in those cases (even inter-caste disputes involving men) where they had "personal knowledge" (of an act committed) in the interior apartments of a house or in a forest, or of (a crime causing) loss of life. Testimony was disallowed on grounds of incredulity to these categories of people: infants, aged men, and the mentally deranged. See Dwarka Nath Mitter, *The Position of Women in Hindu Law* (1913; reprint, New Delhi: Inter-India Publications, 1984), 174-76; and *Laws of Manu* VIII: 75.

37. The social contract is an abstraction put in place of another abstraction—the notion that people at some point in time live outside social relations (or precontractual relations). This logic then becomes a measure of the extent to which a culture has entered modernity and a sure way of erasing all claims to land or property that may have existed prior to the stage of "private property." Just as women must be figured literarily in Defoe's texts as participants in the fabric of liberal rights, so that the narrative can effectively consign them to appropriate places (rather than simply banish them), in colonial India a similar gesture was undertaken to install relations of private property. Land holdings over which peasants had customary cultivation rights were transformed wholesale into "private property," then appropriated by the British for tax revenue with the help of "contracts" with the supportive newly installed landlords. See Ranajit Guha, *A Rule of Property for Bengal: An Essay on the Idea of Permanent Settlement* (Paris: Mouton, 1963). In the above case, in lieu of land, the colonial power delegates the

female colonial subject as property to the male subject. Later, she will be appropriated as a sign of the need for continuing colonial rule. Applying the precepts of bourgeois individualism, her status as the property of the despotic Asiatic male will parallel the understanding that unused land is the property of the despotic Asiatic rulers. And once nineteenth-century legal historians declare that the measure of a society's advancement is the status enjoyed by its women, the concept of "women's rights" will be used to prolong colonial rule. The native woman will reappear as the oppressed Hindu woman in imperialist discourses of development, enlightenment, and civilization, just as imprisoned land needed liberation for profits and advancement. For instances of such debates, I mention here two relevant works that could be seen as book-ends of the corpus: Montesquieu's *Spirit of the Laws* and Henry Maine's *Ancient Law*.

38. These fines can be seen as resulting from the judgment of "robbery"— compensation or restitution of stolen goods. What is up for speculation is the extent to which the fines were invented out of this particular situation. *The Laws of Manu*, for instance, never names the recipient of the fines imposed for sexual crimes and adultery. The understanding is that if unnamed, the recipient is the king. While loss of property is compensated by a fine imposed on the thief, the only named recipient of a fine for rape is the father of a "maiden," who may accept a "nuptial fee" if he is willing to let his daughter marry the accused. The Company, by accepting a part of the fine, is already taking the place of the higher overseers—the displaced authority of the king.

39. See for instance Farida Shaheed's "The Cultural Articulation of Patriarchy: Legal Systems, Islam, and Women," *South Asia Bulletin* 6:1 (1986): 38-44. Her argument that Islam has been mobilized as an instrument in maintaining patriarchy (in modern-day Pakistan) depends on the assumption that colonialism and capitalism for the large part left the private sphere alone because inter-family conflicts and women were not seen as expedient to the macro-processes of alien rule.

40. Gayle Rubin, "The Traffic in Women: Notes on the 'Political Economy' of Sex" in *Toward an Anthropology of Women*, ed. Rayna Reiter (New York: Monthly Press, 1975), 177.

41. Nathaniel Halhed, "The Translator's Preface" in *The British Discovery of Hinduism in the Eighteenth Century*, ed. P. J. Marshall (Cambridge: Cambridge University Press, 1970), 142.

42. Quoted in Mitter, 54.

43. See Lee Holcombe, *Wives and Property: Reform of the Married Women's Property Law in Nineteenth-Century England* (Toronto: University of Toronto Press, 1983), 5-6, 186, for an account of Maine's active participation as public speaker and scholar for the cause of progressive legal reforms for women during the latter half of the nineteenth century.

44. Derrida, *Acts of Literature* 191.

45. See Bram Dijkstra's *Defoe and Economics: The Fortunes of Roxana in the History of Interpretation* (New York: St. Martin's, 1987) for an account of how Defoe's *Roxana* was transformed by literary critics wanting to establish a dominant

concern over other possibilities. Even the law of the text (its authorship, its wording) did not remain in place. *Roxana* underwent a number of literal rephrasings as self-appointed co-authors changed the text to make the heroine more palatable or more "pleasing." On the other side, of course, is our nativist scholar Mitter, who succeeded in making the ancient Hindu texts surrender "rights for women" where it was previously believed none were to be got.

46. Pathak and Sunder Rajan, "Shahbano" 256-61.

THREE

The "Strength of the Weak" as Portrayed by Marie Laurencin

Bridget Elliott

Everything about Marie Laurencin—her artistic practices, her temperament, her appearance, and even her voice—has been saturated with signs of femininity: grace and charm rather than genius, narcissistic self-absorption, surface without substance. Critical discourses on the artist have endlessly echoed Guillaume Apollinaire's early comments on her work during the opening decades of the century when he portrayed her as France's leading exponent of a new feminine aesthetic characterized by joy, purity, and naïveté, as well as by the expression of emotion and a sense of decorative surfaces. In his words, "[g]race is the thoroughly French artistic quality that women like . . . Mlle. Marie Laurencin have maintained in art, even when, as in the last few years, art became severe, and painters, engrossed in new technical experiments that involved mathematics, chemistry, and cinematography no longer cared about charming their admirers."[1]

If Apollinaire found Laurencin charmingly anachronistic, the art critic Roger Allard found her charmingly narcissistic. Discussing Laurencin in the 1920s as a painter of portraits, including numerous self-portraits, Allard conflated the identity of the artist with that of her sitters and models, remarking, "[a]n egotistical and charming art hers . . . which relates everything to the self. She had scarcely any subject other than herself, nor any curiosity than to know herself better. . . . the whole of nature for Marie Laurencin, is but a cabinet of mirrors."[2] Similar sentiments characterized reviews of the artist's work from the 1930s and 1940s which typically started with strategically engendering titles such as "The Capricious Feminine Charm of Marie Laurencin," "The Elfin Maidens of Marie Laurencin," or "A Famous Exponent of Femininity."[3] More recent monographs and exhibition catalogues on the artist have followed suit, often sporting pink covers and titles that stress Laurencin's "undividedly feminine psyche."[4]

On the face of it, such feminine indicators seem to have had a predictable effect on Laurencin's critical stock: in the long term, her success has been rather more popular than avant-garde or academic. During her life, she was generally considered the most famous woman artist of the early twentieth-century French avant-garde. A typical illustration of such fame was a celebratory banquet lunch organized by the writer Albert Flament in 1930 for the four "queens" of French culture: Colette in literature, Valentine Tessier in theatre, Coco Chanel in fashion, and Marie Laurencin in painting. Another instance from the same year was an article in the French society magazine *Vu*, which published photographs of Laurencin, Colette, and Anna de Noailles, who were identified as "The Three Most Famous Women in France."[5] Such success was more than simple media hype. By 1925, Laurencin had sold enough work to be able to purchase not only a large, comfortable, and well-appointed Paris apartment on the rue Savoran but also a country house at Champrosay. Since she had started out in life as the illegitimate daughter of a seamstress with little in the way of financial resources, this was no mean achievement. Her works sold extremely well. Between the years of 1913 and 1940, she maintained a contract with Paul Rosenberg, a leading Parisian dealer who also handled Matisse, Picasso, and Braque. Through Rosenberg, her works were regularly exhibited not only in Paris but also in London, Dusseldorf, and New York.[6]

With few exceptions, recent scholarship on the artist has taken the form of sponsored exhibition catalogues or glossy coffee-table art books. At the same time that a museum devoted to the artist opened outside Tokyo in 1983, there were numerous criticisms of the inflated prices Japanese investors spent in European and North American art markets—the implication being that Laurencin's work was inferior to that of her avant-garde counterparts such as Rodin or Picasso who had museums devoted to them in Paris.[7] In this respect, Laurencin and her work have been figured as the feminized bodies of commodified mass culture—bodies that are highly visible, easily accessible, attractively packaged, and available at (relatively) affordable prices.[8] To be more precise, as Apollinaire pointed out, Laurencin was perceived as occupying the soft and saleable margins of the French avant-garde, working in ways that seemed more appealing than the technical and scientific experiments of other painters. Not surprisingly, this image has been a liability in modernist and revisionist accounts of the period where the worth of the avant-garde has been measured by the "purity" of either its formal innovations or its critical project (depending upon whether one subscribes to the paradigms of Clement Greenberg or Peter Bürger), and in both instances, its distance from the contamination of the marketplace.[9]

Rather more puzzling is that fact that Laurencin has received little attention in recent feminist analyses of the modernist avant-garde.[10] To date, the few major studies of her work focus on reviving her reputation as a serious painter and advocating her inclusion within the avant-garde canon. For instance, an article by Julia Fagen-King demonstrates that Laurencin was an integral member of the Bateau Lavoir circle and analyzes her group portrait, *Réunion à la campagne (Apollinaire et ses amis)*, suggesting it wittily parodied Picasso's *Les Demoiselles*.[11] In a similar vein, recent catalogue essays by Daniel Marchesseau and Heather McPherson reassess a number of Laurencin's paintings and stress that, although she is a difficult artist to categorize, her work should be considered part of the School of Paris along with that of Chagall, Modigliani, Rousseau, Soutine, Pascin, and Utrillo.[12]

I will take a different tack. Instead of arguing that Laurencin be considered a member of the avant-garde, I want to examine how her case reveals certain limitations in feminist theories of avant-gardism—whether, as in the example of Alice A. Jardine, one wants to celebrate it as a transgressive *"écriture/peinture féminine,"* or as in the examples of Griselda Pollock and Carol Duncan, one wants to criticize it as a canonical modernist construction that works to exclude women.[13] The case of Laurencin fits into neither paradigm: on the one hand, the hybrid nature of her work, which often bordered on the commercial and formulaic, cannot consistently qualify as transgressive, while on the other, she was hailed by virtually everyone of her generation as an important *female* member of the French avant-garde. Although on some occasions her femininity was mobilized as an exception to prove the rule that women were not serious avant-garde painters, on others her femininity was considered disconcertingly feminist. These latter charges are worth exploring, not only because they have been largely overlooked but because they indicate a need for more nuanced feminist frameworks.

Susan Suleiman's *Subversive Intent* provides a useful starting point. As Briony Fer points out in a perceptive review of the book, Suleiman attempts to marry French and Anglo-American perspectives, celebrating a transgressive avant-garde tradition of *écriture féminine* which she traces from the historical example of the surrealist movement through to contemporary feminist literary and artistic production of the 1980s and 1990s, at the same time exploring questions of authorship, agency, and women's cultural marginality.[14] Although she insists on the need for historically grounded readings, Suleiman sets up a curiously artificial temporal disjuncture by claiming that women in earlier modernist avant-garde movements had less agency and were more marginalized than women of the postmodern period who, according to Suleiman, are in the totally new situation of having achieved a critical mass of innovative and outstanding work. While this line of reasoning has a certain pragmatic appeal, I think we should be wary about its implied narrative of liberation. It is worth recalling Michel Foucault's discussion of the ways in which a rather dubious notion of Victorian sexual repression functioned as rod for measuring twentieth-century sexual liberation.[15] Indeed, Suleiman worries about this issue in a series of cautionary footnotes explaining that recent research on women artists involved with modernist avant-garde movements of the early twentieth century will have to reshape not only our sense of literary and cultural history but also our theories of avant-gardism.[16]

This study of Laurencin contributes to that reshaping by suggesting that she experienced a constantly shifting and ambivalent relationship to the cubist avant-garde that was both enabling and alienating. By exploring how the signs of Laurencin's femininity were mobilized by the artist as well as by her colleagues, critics, and patrons, I want to question the value of metaphorically gendering avant-garde cultural production as feminine in the case of Jardine or as masculine in the case of Huyssen. Instead, I want to argue that the gendered rhetoric surrounding cultural production was as unstable in the early twentieth century as it is today, leaving even relatively disadvantaged practitioners such as Marie Laurencin a certain room to maneuver. Of course, considering how Laurencin and others manipulated the signs of her femininity necessarily means addressing the ways in which these signs intersected with those of class, occupation, generation, and nationality. As Biddy Martin usefully reminds us, any centering of something called *sexuality* should make us wary of what is being "relegated to the margins or out of sight."[17]

Here, I am using the clichéd notion of "weak sex" counterdiscursively not only to undermine traditional assessments of Laurencin's art, which was generally characterized as feminine, weak, and impure, but also to emphasize the permeability and instability of sexual signifiers. By appropriating Gianni Vattimo's notion of weak thought, I suggest that a certain notion of "weak sex" can describe those forms of poststructuralist feminism that, like Vattimo, reject traditional truth claims in favour of a postmetaphysical experience of truth which is based on a combination of common sense and rhetorical and aesthetic experience, and which is constantly traversed by other sorts of positions.[18] Instead of denigrating the notions of weakness often associated with femininity, I want to explore their unexpected powers of resistance or, to borrow Jean-François Lyotard's expression, the "*force des faibles*" (the strength of the weak).[19] Utilizing ideas from Michel de Certeau's account of the oppositional practices in everyday life, I explore how Laurencin found maneuvering room in and outside avant-garde circles.[20] By making some of her tactical resistances historically visible, I want to further complicate our understanding of the way early twentieth-century culture has been configured

FEMININE AND FEMINIST SPACES OF MODERNITY

Unlike many women artists who adopted avant-garde art practices, Laurencin was *not* seduced by what Griselda Pollock has characterized as cultural modernism's prevailing rhetoric of gender indifference which seemed to offer women artists an escape from the limiting nineteenth-century sphere of feminine art.[21] By playing with the title of Pollock's well-known essay, "Modernity and the Spaces of Femininity," I want to explore not only how traditional notions of "respectable" femininity often diverged from the avant-gardism first espoused by critics such as Baudelaire but also how certain artists such as Laurencin (with varying degrees of success) deliberately tried to manipulate these discrepancies.[22] Evidently, Laurencin harboured few illusions about the freedoms of the modernist community, as she bitterly pointed out in an interview: "Cubism has poisoned three years of my life, preventing me from doing any work. I never understood it. I get from cubism the same feeling that a book on philosophy or mathematics gives me. Aesthetic problems always make me shiver. As long as I was influenced by the great men surrounding me I could do nothing."[23]

Instead, she repeatedly asserted that her painting practices were thoroughly modern *and* completely feminine. Press interviews stressed that she painted in an apartment with all of the latest conveniences. Moreover, she was carefully represented as a modern woman who preferred movies to the theatre and sports clothes and short hair to long skirts and long hair. Reviewers also commented on her passionate support of women's right to work as part of the larger cause of women's emancipation.[24] Over and over, Laurencin insisted on her femininity with a series of remarks which evidently seemed extreme to a number of her contemporaries. For instance, in some autobiographical fragments she pointed out that if the genius of men intimidated her, she felt "perfectly at ease with everything that is feminine."[25]

On another occasion, responding to the comment that she seldom painted men, Laurencin observed that "I am deaf—actually, physically deaf, . . . to the voices of men, my ear is not attuned."[26] She was also quite explicit about how gender related to the practice of painting:

> I conceive of a woman's rôle to be of a different nature: painting to be essentially a "job" for a woman (one who sits so long quiet on a chair); and a painter's inspiration to be life and that of a natural sensibility rather than the outcome of intellect or reason. There is something incongruous to me in the vision of a strong man sitting all day . . . manipulating small paint brushes, something essentially effeminate.

Dorothy Todd, Laurencin's interviewer, seems to have worried that Laurencin's comments needed explaining to the magazine's readers. The ellipsis marks Todd's interjection: "Marie Laurencin always sits to paint— the majority of men painters, as a matter of fact, mostly prefer to stand."[27] It is of course tempting to read this episode as an instance where Laurencin's naïve gender essentialism (after all, she even uses the curiously contradictory phrase "essentially effeminate") led her to justify her presence in the studio by turning the world upside down. But such a reading misses Laurencin's intentional humour or absurdist parody—after all, she was highly aware of her anomalous position as one of very few women painters with a significant public profile.

Laurencin's insistence on the female body of the painter presents an interesting contradiction which upsets what Andreas Huyssen has identified as modernism's cultural divide between a mass culture that typically offers up fetishised female bodies and is represented in devalued, feminine terms and a high modernist culture that is valued as masculine— in terms of its heroic practitioners as well as of the difficulty of making critical art forms. But staking a claim to the body of the painter is a project that presents women artists with an impossible choice: denying the importance of gender effaces the particularity of various historical and systemic discriminations women experience, while insisting upon their femininity leads to marginalization. Instead, as Griselda Pollock points out, feminist practices must work toward changing the ways in which the spaces of representation have been configured: "Feminist practices cannot simply abandon either of these bodies, but whatever constitutes the feminism of the practice results from the necessity to signify a relation to this complex. That is not the same as desiring somehow to have a share in the painter's body while producing new meanings for the feminine body."[28] Given the complexity of the terrain, how are we to read Laurencin's remarks? Was she simply laying claim to the body of the painter by reinscribing it as feminine or was she trying to create a more interesting critical space to maneuver?

Again, Dorothy Todd sheds light on this issue when she notes that Laurencin appeared to be playing a role which should not be taken at face value: "To sit on a cushion and sew a fine seam might, it would almost appear, represent the complete ideal of life to this hundred per cent enthusiast of the feminine, but there is another side to the character of Marie Laurencin who is in many respects a typically twentieth-century woman."[29] According to Todd, the issue of Laurencin's femininity was actually quite complicated. As the English editor of *Vogue*, Todd was well aware that nineteenth-century notions of gender difference still had currency, particularly in the pages of the popular press, and that, at least in part, Laurencin's signs of femininity were shaped by conventional expectations which associated women with beauty, nature, and domesticity. Yet, in spite (or perhaps because) of this, Todd felt obliged to point out to her readers: "To Marie Laurencin all the activities of everyday life, all political or economic movements are listed under the general heading of "masculine affairs"—and yet she is a feminist, probably the strangest feminist the world has ever seen."[30]

The shift from feminine to feminist is particularly interesting given the fact that Todd was writing in 1928, well into the modernist period when, as Pollock explained, many women artists tended to distance themselves from and denounce nineteenth-century femininity (and in some cases feminism) in order to escape the limiting sphere of feminine art. But was it only a limiting sphere? Or is that how it has been retrospectively constructed? Is there something problematic about the assertion in a recent feminist survey of women artists that Florine Stettheimer and Marie Laurencin "embraced the decorative and the fanciful in their work, and both fashioned a myth of the feminine that allowed them to be heard, but that insured they would never be taken as seriously as their male colleagues"?[31] The question I want to explore in Laurencin's case is: taken as seriously by whom? Evidently, even as late as 1928, Todd felt there might be some political purchase in Laurencin's feminine positioning, strange as it seemed.

For the moment leaving aside such questions of intentionality and agency, it cannot be denied that the signs of Laurencin's seemingly inexhaustible femininity were indeed mobilized by many writers who, perpetuating a tradition of nineteenth-century gendered discourse, wanted to reaffirm that women's art—even when produced within twentieth-century avant-garde circles—belonged to a separate (and marginal) artistic sphere.[32] At the start of Laurencin's career, in an exhibition review of 1908, Apollinaire praised the artist for "the greatest possible number of feminine qualities" and freedom from "all masculine short-comings," concluding: "Perhaps the greatest error of most women artists is that they want to surpass their male colleagues, and in attempting to do so, they lose their feminine taste and gracefulness."[33] Or, as John Quinn, the American collector of her work, later put it more crudely: "The thing I like about Marie Laurencin is that she paints like a woman, whereas most women artists seem to want to paint like men and they only succeed in painting like hell."[34]

Frank Crowninshield, another American admirer and the editor of *Vanity Fair*, went even further, emphasizing that Laurencin's femininity distanced her not only from men but also from other famous women painters: "she is the only considerable figure in the annals of art who has painted like a woman; who has, following instinctively the impulses of an undividedly feminine psyche, refused to join that prodigious army of epicene painters—talents that are neither male nor female—headed by such amorphous figures as Vigée Lebrun, Rosa Bonheur, Berthe Morisot and Mary Cassatt."[35] The reference by this conservative critic to Rosa

Bonheur as an amorphous figure was probably based on the intensity of Bonheur's professional commitment, her ambitious animal subjects and scale of painting, as well as a reputation for cross-dressing. However, the inclusion of Vigée Lebrun, Morisot, and Cassatt seems rather surprising, since Vigée Lebrun had made her reputation painting portraits of beautiful women and, by the late nineteenth century, impressionist styles of painting were considered appropriate for women painters whose natures were deemed spontaneous, impressionable, and nervous. Morisot in particular was praised widely as an example to be emulated.[36]

This construction of Laurencin as even more feminine than women painters of preceding generations is part of the writer's hyperbolic strategy: he claims Laurencin's femininity is so marked that it overshadows even her most famous eighteenth- and nineteenth-century female predecessors. While one suspects that writers like Crowninshield wanted to gloss over the fundamental changes generated by a growing women's movement, their attitudes also seem to have been shaped, at least in part, by their strong sense of Laurencin's physical presence. Access to the bodies, living spaces, and studios of earlier women was only indirectly available through reminiscences, historical documents, and various sorts of visual representations. In contrast, Laurencin could be visited, scrutinized, and directly questioned. Although writers on art had long been fascinated by the physical appearances of female artists, by the turn-of-the-century, the growing popularity of journalistic interviews with celebrities provided many more opportunities for observing the intimate details of artistic everyday life. Such interviews were usually accompanied by photographs. Encounters with the artist were no longer confined to professional occasions such as exhibition openings and staged studio displays. The journalistic eye and camera could now enter the artist's home or studio on a more casual basis. In essence, because Laurencin extensively participated in such media interviews—for reasons that will be examined further in a moment—she was more visible than preceding generations of women artists. Of course, important for our purposes is the fact that her perceived femininity (as opposed to masculinity or some form of "deviance") was tirelessly stressed on these occasions.

For instance, a 1925 interview with the *L'Art Vivant* journalist Françoise, entitled "Chez Marie Laurencin," published two photographs of Laurencin's apartment. One of the photographs (see fig. 1) showed the artist seated amidst her ornaments and paintings. Throughout the inter-

FIG. 1. Marc Vaux, *Chez Marie Laurencin.* Photograph, *L'Art Vivant* 3 (February 1, 1925): 9. York University Library, Toronto.

view, the artist's living and working space was described as a vision from one of her paintings:

> On a small blue divan in a corner, a model. A graceful blond girl who herself seems to be a part of the decor poses sitting with a tiny guitar in her long white hands. . . . The room is a poem by Francis Jammes. It has the same freshness, the same purity with all the peaceful and assured naïveté of Marie Laurencin's Art. . . . Two pink ceramic deer lying down on the drawing room mantle seem like the graceful symbol of their mistress. . . . I leave Marie Laurencin filled with a peace which makes me apprehensive of the many noises of Parisian life which will soon darken and then efface the pretty dream of an hour.[37]

In this case, the artist, her model, and her variously displayed paintings and furnishings are all woven into an amazingly consistent image of femininity. The sense of escape into a dreamy and timeless arcadia filled with women playing musical instruments, flowers, pink deer, and other magical animals was characteristic of her work during the 1920s, 1930s, and 1940s (e.g., fig. 5).[38] Even the tools of her trade were described in terms which made them seem like organic outgrowths of her paintings.

Another journalist noted that she wore a little bonnet which made her resemble one of La Tour's eighteenth-century personages and held a palette where several colours were spread like "large petals of flowers."[39]

Much was made of the fact that Laurencin painted at home, mostly in her drawing room filled with "gay chintzes and bowls of flowers on every table," rather than in a separate professional studio.[40] Another source of fascination for reviewers was her meticulous working habits. As one interviewer explained: "above all she hates dirt. That is why she goes on wiping her palette with a rag dipped in gasoline while she talks. 'I am the only painter in Paris who cleans her palette. You can say that. I also hate dust which I can date to within a day.' The fact is that the furniture is polished and shiny and the study in impeccable order."[41]

References to Laurencin's cultivation and extensive library were mixed with visions of a more cozy domesticity by interviewers who elicited such remarks as: "I should have loved to have had many children, so that I could comb their hair and tie it up with ribbons." Of course these sentiments were hypothetical in this case of a divorced and childless working woman. At various points, Laurencin's remarks made such strategies of rhetorical domestication seem slightly absurd. For instance, during one interview, the artist elaborately evoked a domestic scene which was deliberately viewed from a painter's perspective·

I was never asked to set up a house, but I could do it well. My house would have a "lived in" look and a refreshing atmosphere. I would serve burning hot coffee in dark blue cups. There would be Kate Greenaway pictures, with clipped gardens and wooden balustrades, and little ladies clad in pink and blue with great big bonnets and muffs. There would be cats and dogs.[42]

Such impressions of a feminine subjectivity which was inwardly domestic and narcissistically self-absorbed were reinforced by photographs of the 1920s (e.g., fig. 2) showing the artist sitting at her easel in the middle of her drawing room. A later photograph (fig. 3) taken in the 1950s by the artist and photographer Alexander Liberman, who did numerous illustrated interviews of French artists for such magazines as *Vogue* and the *New York Times Magazine*, was published with the accompanying commentary: "Only an easel and a few painter's tools intruded on the attractive serenity of her Paris salon."[43] His photograph of Laurencin captures the cabinet of mirrors effect that Roger Allard and many other critics ascribed to her paintings. Liberman offers one view of Laurencin's upper torso in a large square mirror and another of her lower body in a

FIG. 2. Unattributed and untitled photograph of Tylia Perlmutter posing for Marie Laurencin (c. 1920s). From Billy Klüver and Julie Martin, *Kiki's Paris: Artists and Lovers 1900-1930* (New York: Harry N. Abrams, 1989), 117.

smaller round mirror below, both of which are in turn reflected in a larger mirror beyond the picture frame. While the dizzying fracturing and multiplication of Laurencin's image recreates the confusing mirrored space of many famous modernist paintings such as Manet's *Bar at the Folies Bergère*, it also objectifies and fetishises the body of the artist.

AVANT-GARDE IMPURITIES

At this point, it is useful to consider the signs of Laurencin's femininity in the context of more particular historical moments and cultural formations. Although for several decades (from when she first started exhibiting in 1907 until her death in 1956) Laurencin was represented as signifying some sort of timeless femininity, such gendered identities were anything but stable categories in the twentieth-century French cultural field. By 1907, much had changed since the 1880s when members of the Union of Women Painters and Sculptors had mobilized a largely conservative rhet-

FIG. 3. Alexander Liberman, untitled photograph of Marie Laurencin (c. 1950). From Alexander Liberman, *The Artist in His Studio* (New York: Viking, 1961), 110.

oric of femininity (and occasionally feminism) to justify the admission of women into the Ecole des Beaux-Arts as part of a campaign to defend the historic superiority of French art.[44]

As Debora Silverman notes, during the 1890s the emergence of a modern, decorative art nouveau movement meant that modernity and femininity were no longer necessarily cast in mutually exclusive terms. The fact that many art nouveau initiatives were supported by various state agencies also provided opportunities for public recognition and financial support, which were especially vital to women since most private networks remained closed to them.[45] Around the turn-of-the-century, a number of modernist women artists, including Laurencin, established careers which were based upon the decorative aesthetics and practices of art nouveau and art deco as well as on that of other avant-garde painters.[46] Such careers which were pursued by both men and women existed in a curiously hybrid and often contradictory working space: in part allied to the fairly conventional values and institutional networks of official culture and in part working with groups whose members claimed to be critical outsiders.

By 1912, Apollinaire seemed to champion the same sort of artistic hybridity which he claimed Marie Laurencin best illustrated by producing works which were modern, feminine, primitive, and decorative—all at the same time.

It seems to me that it would obviously be in the decorators' interest to study carefully the works of today's female artists, who alone possess the charming secret of the gracefulness that is one of the most original traits of French painting. This is true of the works of the so-called French primitives and of the delightful tasteful marvels that could have been only produced in France and that were painted by Watteau, Fragonard, Corot, Berthe Morisot and Seurat. . . . This new delicacy, which is like an innate sense of Hellenism possessed by the French woman, can be found to a high degree in the works that Mlle. Marie Laurencin is currently exhibiting at the Barbazanges Gallery.[47]

To a large extent, Apollinaire was recycling the rhetoric of art nouveau when he celebrated an eighteenth-century French decorative tradition that he saw as naturally aligned with the innate Hellenism of the French woman.[48] It is also worth stressing that he was not consigning Laurencin to some sort of feminine ghetto but instead urged artists of both sexes to take up the new decorative aesthetic and its commercial opportunities. His interest in exploring "feminine" creative values can be seen as an

FIG. 4. André Groult, *La maison de l'ambassadrice—La chambre de madame* (1925). Photograph of installation which includes Marie Laurencin's *Portrait de Nicole Groult* (c. 1913) on the wall. From Daniel Marchesseau, *Marie Laurencin* (Martigny: Fondation Pierre Gianadda, 1994), 56.

extension of his own poetic practice, just as his desire to reach new publics was something he achieved as an art critic. It is easy to see how Laurencin was seduced by Apollinaire's rosy prospect of a new artistic arena that would particularly welcome women's participation.

Furthermore, Laurencin was lured by the financial prospect of extending her market beyond the rather limited confines of the avant-garde. She was glad to have her paintings exhibited with the work of interior decorators as in the case of her portrait of Madame André Groult (née Nicole Poiret) of 1913 which was included in a woman's bedroom decoration scheme by André Groult at the Exposition des Arts Décoratifs in Paris in 1925 (fig. 4). The installation photograph demonstrates how Laurencin's famous interwoven curvilinear forms and pastel colours (in this case soft pinks, pale blues, and greys) complemented the lines of the furniture and pattern of the wallpaper. Her work for the theatre also proved a means of extending her public, since her costume and set designs were widely perceived as appealingly fashionable rather than austerely

FIG. 5. Marie Laurencin, frontispiece from *Théâtre Serge de Diaghilew: Les Biches,* 2 vols. Illustrations by Marie Laurencin, text by Jean Cocteau and score by Francis Poulenc. (Paris: Éditions des Quatre Chemins, 1924). Music Department, Free Library of Philadelphia. Photograph by Will Brown.

FIG. 6. Unattributed photograph, "L'Atelier du XVIième: Le Cours de Marie Laurencin" (c. 1932). From Sylvain Laboureur, *Catalogue complet de l'oeuvre de Jean-Émile Laboureur*, vols. 3-4 (Neuchâtel: Ides et Calendes, 1991), 290. © 1991 Sylvain Laboureur and Ides et Calends.

shocking. Attending a performance of *Les Biches* by the Ballets Russes for which Laurencin designed the costumes in 1924 (fig. 5), René Gimpel observed: "In the corridor I heard a woman say to a man: 'Look around the house, all the women look as though they were by Marie Laurencin; she has fashioned a type just as Boldini created the eel look fifteen years ago.' "[49] Laurencin revealingly criticized Picasso's ballet designs for *Mercure*, staged at the Cigale the same year, claiming they were too "highbrow" and that Picasso as a Spaniard took himself "too seriously."[50]

Evidently Laurencin was not concerned with defending a reputation for making difficult and challenging art but instead was happy to execute paintings for patrons such as Helena Rubinstein, the beautician, who ordered three canvases from the artist in 1938 to use as reproductions in her salons.[51] Further proof of the fashionable appeal of Laurencin's portraits was the popularity of a painting course she offered with Jean-Émile Laboureur and Philippe de Villeneuve during the 1930s which taught painting, decoration, and drawing to wealthy women. A photograph of Laurencin teaching her section of the course (fig. 6) shows a number of

society women at their easels, all painting portraits of women in Laurencin's distinctive style.[52] Thus, there is certainly some truth to Apollinaire's
assertion that Laurencin wanted to charm her viewers. As early as 1924,
the critic Roger Allard had noted that Laurencin's work appealed not only
to poets but also to bourgeois and popular muses. In the same year,
writing about an exhibition of hers in London, R. H. Wilenski suggested
that Laurencin's art would appeal even to those who normally found
modern art "inscrutable" because it "speaks to us in the pictorial language
of our day."[53]

Of course, there were those who condemned the more popularly accessible aspects of Laurencin's work as facile and faddish. In 1924, the painter
Jean-Louis Forain privately told René Gimpel that he disliked Laurencin's
portraits because "[t]here are thousands of people around who can do that
sort of thing."[54] But such dismissals were surprisingly rare in the critical
literature on the artist from the 1910s and 1920s. The remarks of Allard
and Wilenski were made in a positive context and a number of other
critics voiced the hope that Laurencin's decorative work would not obscure her reputation as a painter. Particularly interesting are 1913 obser-
vations of the writer, poet, and art critic André Salmon:

> It would be unfortunate if Mlle. Marie Laurencin had no other role to play than
> that of adjunct to our decorators. May the public, reassured as to her artistic
> morality, . . . knowing her to be so fragilely associated with wicked demolishers of
> convenient systems, with the terrorists of modern art, deign to take better note of
> her, and, ultimately, to look at her canvases without preconceived ideas.[55]

Yet, despite Laurencin's precarious position—sandwiched between the
frequently contradictory aesthetic demands of decorators and avant-garde
painters—Salmon urged his readers to take her art seriously.

At this point, it seems important to start untangling the notions of
critical and commercial (or popular) success which need not be mutually
exclusive, despite the fact that modernist discourses tend to celebrate
those artists who appear to cultivate the former. For instance, although in
relation to Laurencin, Picasso secured higher prices for his canvases from
their dealer, Rosenberg, he seldom attracted (or encouraged) clients like
Helena Rubinstein whose exhibition venues were too fashionable to be
prestigious. As we have seen, his ballet costumes and stage designs were
perceived as avant-garde and difficult as opposed to Laurencin's, which
were more appealingly *à la mode*. From a modernist perspective, such
comparisons have worked to Laurencin's disadvantage as her work has

frequently been measured against less conspicuously commercial artists such as Picasso. But perhaps if one considers the maneuvering room available to each artist, rather different conclusions may be drawn. While Picasso appeared to exercise greater artistic license in the eyes of the general public, Laurencin criticized how he toadied to dealers like Rosenberg. In 1933, she remarked to René Gimpel, "He [Rosenberg] hasn't got a hold over me as he has over Picasso and Braque. For instance, Ida Rubinstein commissioned me the other day to do a work with Picasso and Braque, and Picasso said to me, confidingly: 'What will Rosenberg say? Rosenberg is in America.' Picasso fills me with pity, he is like a child."[56]

Evidently the popular accessibility of Laurencin's style freed her from totally depending on dealers since she was able to negotiate many of her own portrait and decorative commissions directly with purchasers. Indeed, the artist seems to have possessed a certain business flair according to René Gimpel, who described how she dealt with one of her more famous English patrons.

Lady Cunard commissioned her to do her portrait, which she painted with a horse in it, but a fantastic kind of dream horse, the only sort she'll do, and naturally very far from anything seen in England in the way of horses. The lady, who was not satisfied, sent the portrait back from London to Marie Laurencin, and customs imposed a 12 per cent luxury tax on it. She refused to go to their offices, Armand took care of the formalities, and she didn't have to pay anything. The matter, though settled with the customs, was not settled with Marie Laurencin. Her honor as an artist was offended, and she made Lady Cunard get down from her horse and get on a camel; she told the story and showed the picture to everyone. Lady Cunard heard of it and came in all haste to Paris. Lady Cunard, who for years had been trying to scale the last rungs of the English social ladder, Lady Cunard on a camel! What a fall! Absolute horror of seeing the canvas exhibited or reproduced in the *Burlington* or the *Tatler*. She had Armand sit down and think of something and commissioned a whole ballroom from Marie Laurencin. The artist has long since ripped up the canvas."[57]

It should be stressed that Laurencin's business acumen did not stem from a miserly nature—quite the reverse. In fact, she was widely known for her generosity to neighbours, friends, and other artists who had fallen on hard times and her spending frequently approached the level of her earning.[58] Instead, the artist seems to have wanted artistically and commercially to hedge her bets by working in an accessible and hybrid style which enabled her to move between various constituencies, sometimes playing one off against another.

Having room to maneuver was a priority established early in Laurencin's career, when she chose to continue living at home with her mother
throughout her intense affair with Apollinaire. Such a choice has often
been attributed to Laurencin's fairly conventional morality since, unlike
Fernande Olivier or Jeanne Hébuterne, who were involved with Pablo
Picasso and Amedeo Modigliani, Marie Laurencin did not reject her
family to embrace the avant-garde. Indeed, many writers have commented
on the surprisingly traditional mores of both Apollinaire and Laurencin,
who apparently never moved in together or married because both their
mothers disapproved of the match. For instance, in her reminiscences
published in 1933, Fernande Olivier was especially critical of what she
described as Laurencin's bourgeois behaviour in Bateau Lavoir circles.
After condemning her for being rather silly, affected, and self-absorbed,
Olivier scathingly commented: "She looked like a little girl, and had a
little girl's mixture of naïveté and viciousness, and a good deal too naïve
to be true. Marie Laurencin, a pupil at an art school on the Boulevard de
Clichy, was to become *the* woman painter of the gang."[59]

But Laurencin's decision to live apart from Apollinaire has been read
rather differently by others who have suggested that the artist went home
every night so she could get up early and paint without interruption for
several hours in the mornings.[60] Unlike Olivier and Hébuterne, Laurencin was interested in securing space for an independent professional
career. Ironically, after criticizing Laurencin's bourgeois behaviour, Olivier later wrote to Laurencin in 1951, rather hesitantly asking her to
contribute a frontispiece illustration (depicting herself and Laurencin) to
a proposed second book on her relationship with Picasso which she hoped
would earn some desperately needed money.[61] But perhaps even more
ironic was the fact that during the Bateau Lavoir period (c. 1906-12),
Laurencin, the illegitimate daughter of a seamstress, could hardly be
described as bourgeois. From an early age, Laurencin's mother had emphasized the merits of a practical vocation, first encouraging her to become a teacher, and when that failed, sending her off to learn the skills of
ceramic painting which was a popular career for artistically oriented,
working-class girls. If there was anything bourgeois about Laurencin's
Bateau Lavoir experience, it was her association with the other members
of the group, not her desire to work.[62] One cannot help suspecting that
because Olivier's own background was more bourgeois than Laurencin's,
the aspirations of the latter made the former decidedly uncomfortable.

Because Laurencin refused to play the usual model/lover role allotted to women in the avant-garde, she was dismissively characterized as a young bourgeois girl playing the role of avant-garde painter.[63]

Significantly, Olivier seems to have been more worried about bourgeois forms of femininity (rather than masculinity) infiltrating the avant-garde. By refusing the values of the *petit bourgeois* aunt and uncle who had raised her and personally disdaining the sort of upward social mobility and professional status that Laurencin sought, Olivier made herself responsible for legitimating the countercultural claims of the French avant-garde, whereas Picasso and Braque (also from relatively more prosperous families) were immune from such considerations, neither judged by class criteria nor condemned for ambitious career aspirations.[64] As the assumptions of class and gender difference underpinning Olivier's reminiscences make clear, Laurencin as a working-class woman had much less cultural room to maneuver than most of her male counterparts. This was especially true in the early years of her career when she had not yet established a broader reputation and wider network of social connections. As we have seen, in 1923 she bitterly recalled how cubism had poisoned three years of her life, the great men paralysing her work.

One wonders how Fernande Olivier might have responded to those women painters outside the Bateau Lavoir, who abandoned the notion of "respectable" femininity and adopted the "bohemian" lifestyle that so many male avant-garde painters carefully cultivated. For instance, Suzanne Valadon and Nina Hamnett, neither of whom had any family money, resorted to modelling for other artists in order to make ends meet. Evidently such options did not appeal to Laurencin, at least on a professional level, although numerous friends captured her image. Nina Hamnett, who unlike Laurencin had difficulty producing a large body of salable work, occasionally turned to journalism to supplement her income. Modelling was something which also supported Gwen John, who lived rather meagerly on the margins of various avant-garde communities.[65] Clearly, when compared with these artists, Laurencin was more ambitious for critical recognition and commercial success, but certainly no more so than an artist like Picasso. It seems worth asking whether modelling was any less problematic than producing salable work given that both activities were frequently denigrated as feminine pursuits.

ARTISTIC MANEUVERS AND TACTICAL TRANSGRESSIONS

While it is true that establishing her own cultural and market niches were important to Laurencin, the choice to cultivate a feminine style must also be read (at least early in her career) in terms that Michel de Certeau would call tactical. In *The Practice of Everyday Life*, de Certeau notes that strategies and tactics are differentiated by the position of their users as well as by the types of maneuvers that each involves. Broadly speaking, strategies are formulated by subjects of will and power, or in other words, those who, by virtue of their economic or symbolic capital, can isolate themselves from their environment and secure advantages by deploying their capital over longer periods of time. Typical examples of strategies are the formal systems which govern most Western societies, including political, economic, and scientific rationalities.

In contrast, de Certeau locates tactics "in the place of the other" whose inhabitants do not have the resources to wait: "a tactic depends on time— it is always on the watch for opportunities that must be seized 'on the wing.' Whatever it wins, it does not keep. It must constantly manipulate events in order to turn them into 'opportunities.' "[66] According to de Certeau, the weak resort to seizing tactical opportunities in everyday practices such as shopping, walking, cooking, talking, and reading in order to make room for their meanings, transforming the property of others into a transient space they can occupy like that of a rented apartment. The occupation of such borrowed spaces can constitute resistance (at least temporarily) despite the fact that, by its very nature, such resistance remains "hidden" from those in power as, for example, in the case of workers who divert the time, tools, and material scraps of their employers for their own everyday use. Under the guise of social conformity, all sorts of other activities may be taking place because, as de Certeau explains, the accounting systems of capitalist societies deal with "*what* is used, not the ways of *using*" (35).

Taking up de Certeau's ideas, it seems worth exploring some of the less immediately visible aspects of Laurencin's feminine aesthetic. As André Salmon's previously cited comments indicate, Laurencin's work was more often than not taken seriously in avant-garde circles where early examples of her painting were acquired by Pablo Picasso and Gertrude Stein, to name two of her more discerning collectors. Speculating on Picasso's reasons for acquiring Laurencin's *La Songeuse*, José Pierre suggests that she brought an important critical perspective to the early cubist experiments of the Bateau Lavoir. Certainly, the pose and title of Laurencin's *La Songeuse*, which may have been playfully feminizing Rodin's monumental sculpture of the thinker, insistently stresses the sitter's subjective integrity when compared with many of Picasso and Braque's portraits of women from this period.[67]

Furthermore, as the reminiscences of both René Gimpel and Fernande Olivier repeatedly indicate, Laurencin intensely scrutinized and discussed the work of others. Fagen-King cites the example of Laurencin's etching, *Le Pont de Passy* of 1908, which mockingly reworked Manet's *Déjeuner sur l'herbe* by replacing the clothed men with animals that the naked woman tames. She also explores how Laurencin's famous *Réunion à la campagne (Apollinaire et ses amis)* of 1909 parodied Picasso's *Les Demoiselles d'Avignon* by transforming his figure of Laurencin (at least as the masked and splayed naked body in the lower right had been jokingly identified in cubist circles) into a demurely dressed and unfragmented woman.[68] Similarly, José Pierre has suggested that Laurencin's painting *Dans la forêt* (c. 1915-16) reworked Rousseau's composition of *Le Rêve* by replacing the body of the black male musician with that of the white female painter which considerably alters the dynamics of looking. Instead of emphasizing the power of the painter's exotic vision, in Laurencin's version both the artist and her model (who sits in the foreground with her back towards the artist) are equally subjected to the gaze of the viewer—a fact which is implied by the painting's other title, *Deux Filles*.[69]

Significantly, when read in an avant-garde context, all of these examples mockingly point out the limits of avant-garde radicality when it came to constructions of gender. Despite using a language which openly problematized conventional bourgeois systems of representation and gender, by and large, the horizon structuring the endless puns and the jokes about female sexuality was masculine and heterosexual. In this particular context, many of Laurencin's depictions of active and relatively unfragmented female subjects need not be viewed as naïvely essentialist and compromising, but instead can be seen as tactical incursions into avant-garde space. The notion of a tactic is more appropriate than that of a strategy in this case of a working-class woman who initially had neither the economic nor cultural capital to produce a consistently critical body of work. In order to keep on making art, Laurencin had to regularly sell a substantial number of pictures. Although she occasionally complained about the day-to-day pressures of grinding out commissioned portraits (she could paint about two portraits a month), her resulting financial security not only enabled some measure of independence from dealers like Rosenberg but also conferred a certain immunity from avant-garde orthodoxy and criticism.

As we have seen in the case of interviews with the artist, Laurencin was capable of suddenly uttering remarks that unsettled the image of feminine conformity which writers and readers anticipated. When examined closely, her artistic practice also seems to have taken some unexpected critical turns, particularly when exploring the roles of painter and model. Perhaps irreverently mocking cubist conceptions of the artist-model relationship, Laurencin's ambiguously titled *Les petites filles modèles* (c. 1912) carefully reproduces the major ingredients of a typical Braque or Picasso still life from this period including a tilted and cropped view of a table-top in the foreground, a vase of flowers, a portrait, some text directly transposed onto the canvas, and several decorative arabesques which possibly function as abbreviated symbols of interior furnishings (fig. 7). The title, painted just below the centre of the composition, emphasizes the gender of the models by doubly underlining the word "filles." Are the vase of flowers and the framed female portrait young female models or model young girls? In either case, Laurencin gestures to the objectifying tendencies in cubist painting and collage of the 1910s where the signs of femininity were not only shown to be socially constructed but were also frequently manipulated and rearranged in disconcerting ways. Laurencin leaves the viewer wondering how and why one differentiates between representations of women and those of inanimate objects like vases of flowers.[70]

The relationship between the female painter and model continued to preoccupy Laurencin throughout her career being explored in numerous self-portraits and depictions of women engaged in the act of painting as well as in an article she wrote for the *Listener* in 1937, entitled "My Model." A brief foray into this material suggests that part of Laurencin's interest in feminizing the body of the painter involved rethinking the sorts of modernist attitudes towards the model that she had examined in *Les petites filles modèles.* By insisting on her own femininity as a painter as well as that of her models (Laurencin often asserted that she disliked and almost never painted men), the artist was able to explore new ways of working.[71] As we have seen, interviewers (evidently encouraged by the

FIG. 7. Marie Laurencin, *Les petites filles modèles* (c. 1912). Oil on panel. The A. E. Gallatin Collection, Philadelphia Museum of Art.

artist) tended to wax lyrical on the subject of Laurencin's curiously "femi-nine" manner of painting, dwelling on her attractively domestic painting space, her cleanliness, the small and detailed scale of her work, its fashion-ableness, and her tendency to paint sitting rather than standing.

The last observation, which was made by Laurencin herself in the Todd interview and captured in various photographs of the artist (e.g., fig. 2), seems to be curiously at odds not only with many of Laurencin's own paintings of woman artists at work (e.g., *Dans la forêt* and *Femme peintre et*

FIG. 8. J. E. Laboureur, *Portrait de Marie Laurencin* (1914). Woodcut. Cabinet des Estampes, Bibliothèque Nationale, Paris.

FIG. 9. Marie Laurencin, *Le bal élégant/La danse à la campagne* (1913). Oil on canvas. Musée Marie Laurencin, Tokyo.

son modèle, fig. 10) but also with an engraving by her close friend, Jean-Émile Laboureur (fig. 8), showing Laurencin in the act of painting her *Le bal élégant* (sometimes known as *La danse à la campagne*) which was exhibited at the Salon des Independents in 1913 (fig. 9). At first glance, the engraving accentuates the differences between the painter and the women she paints—the boldness of Laurencin's fashionably up-to-date check skirt and short bobbed hair contrast with the softly floating diaphanous gowns of the arcadian dancers. Yet in spite of these temporal distances, by showing the artist standing to paint, Laboureur draws attention to the long line of the artist's brush and raised arm which connect the artist and her painted subjects. It seems as if Laurencin could step into the picture given both its scale and a number of spatial ambiguities which confuse the divisions between the spaces of the studio and canvas, including the curvilinear line in the bottom right which meanders into the painting, the strangely rounded bottom edge of the canvas, and the curiously suspended flower in the upper left which looks like it belongs to the flatter two-dimensional space of the canvas but actually hangs in what must logically be the space of the painter. While one could attribute these spatial confusions to an accidental or decorative whim on the part of the engraver, this tendency appears in many of Laurencin's own works.

One of the clearest examples of the reduced distance between artist and model appears in *Femme peintre et son modèle* painted in 1921 (fig. 10). It was probably paintings like this one with an artist and model who closely resembled each other that fuelled the repeated charges of narcissism that critics such as Roger Allard levelled at Laurencin's work, claiming that such limited and imitative creative abilities were typical of women's work. Yet one cannot help wondering whether such hostility displaced a certain anxiety about the portrayal of what was clearly a romantic and, possibly, an erotic relationship between two women. The similar size of the two women and the fact that they are shown painted in the same flat style and with an equivalent degree of illusionism creates the impression that both women are equally real. Reinforcing this impression is the strangely ambivalent position of the grey shape (possibly the artist's palette) that floats between them. A close bond between the two women is established by their similar pink scarves, one of which is tied around the painter's arm like some sort of medieval love token and their pose which suggests the possibility of an embrace.[72] Such depictions of women were hardly surprising given Laurencin's involvement with the lesbian circles of Natalie Barney, for whom she produced a series of Sapho engravings. Whether her involvements with women were platonic or physical remains discreetly suggested and ultimately hidden, perhaps to protect the image of bourgeois respectability which Laurencin cultivated after her return to Paris.[73]

A carefully controlled desire that borders on the erotic and voyeuristic also surfaces in an article Laurencin wrote entitled, "My Model," which was translated into English and published in the *Listener* in 1937. Since I have not located an original French version, it is hard to tell whether the chatty journalistic tone of the article was based on a conversation with a translator or whether it accurately captured the tone of an original text. Certainly, there is some evidence suggesting that Laurencin contributed interviews, poems, and other short articles to periodicals in order to

FIG. 10. Marie Laurencin, *Femme peintre et son modèle* (1921). Oil on canvas. Collection Hervé Odermatt, Paris.

supplement her earnings. She often claimed that writing was easier than painting.[74] Accompanied by a specially executed sketch of three entwined dancing women, the article describes Laurencin's relationship with Julia, her model for the past ten years. Laurencin confesses to not really knowing Julia but fantasizing about her domestic life and house. Laurencin describes never being invited to Julia's home but at least three or four times a year going past the house and staring at it intently. Later she laments "Mysterious Julia! I know nothing of where you sleep or of how you spend your days. You come every morning at the same time without question."

She also acknowledges the huge social distances between the two of them noting that her own middle-class neighbours are terrified of Julia and would be even more terrified if they saw Laurencin's paintings of her. Of particular interest to Laurencin is Julia's working-class lifestyle, which includes her Cossack husband, Basil, lots of time squandered drinking in cafés, and the decrepit neighbourhood where she lives. Julia's aging beauty is described at length by Laurencin who claims that it is an essential element of the artist's creative practice. "Her neck is growing thicker, but her hands retain their beauty, and when she takes the pose this commonplace girl becomes a proud sultana. I cannot change my model. She illuminates me like a living lamp which itself only exists in my presence."[75]

Essentially, she describes her role as adorning and complementing the model rather than manipulating and exposing her. While there is, of course, the usual assertion that the artist transforms the commonplace material of everyday life, elsewhere the article critically probes the power relations between artist and model. While Laurencin may have desired her model, this is only indirectly recorded as in the incident of her repeatedly watching Julia's house. Perhaps in an effort to check her imagination, Laurencin insists on the social and cultural distances that separate herself and Julia. Indeed, there are all sorts of silences and reticences between the two of them which, according to Laurencin, indicate the degree of their mutual respect. Perhaps more than anything else it is this description of disconcerting social distances which lends credibility to Laurencin's initial remark that she really knows nothing about her model because, although Julia has come to her house nearly every day for the past ten years, Laurencin knows her only as an employer in a relationship which is "distant and impersonal."

It is a curiously awkward article which both raises and finally shies away from the question of whether the model was the object of the painter's desire. Clearly, Laurencin was treading difficult ground given that artist-model relationships were popularly believed to be fraught with erotic possibilities, at least for those male artists who engaged female models, such as Gauguin, Kirchner, or the characters in best-selling novels such as George Du Maurier's *Trilby*. Was Laurencin merely adopting an artistic convention which poorly served her needs? Or was she suppressing a desire which could not be publicly articulated? The fact that there are no easy answers to these questions makes Laurencin's case an interesting one. In the end, how are we to interpret Laurencin's reticence, good manners, and professionally distant working relationships? Had she simply become a bourgeois woman painter as Fernande Olivier had claimed so many years earlier? Once again straightforward answers prove elusive. Certainly, by 1937 Laurencin's sound business sense had generated a secure income which would have qualified as bourgeois. Nevertheless, as we have seen, it was that income which gave Laurencin at least some degree of control over her working conditions. In many respects, her relationship with her model seems rather more enabling than many—at least from the model's perspective.[76] Laurencin's pragmatic professionalism was hardly the stuff that spawns artistic myth, but perhaps for that very reason she was able to offer some interesting critical insights into the work of some of the more famous, self-consciously mythmaking painters and art dealers of her time.

To return to the questions raised at the outset, it is evident that Laurencin *was* interested in laying claim to the painter's body. But by emphatically (and sometimes even absurdly) feminizing that body she foregrounded women's problematic relationship to modernist artistic production. Her attempt to formulate a feminine visual language was, even during her own day, easily and enthusiastically taken up by those critics and collectors who continued to believe that women's art belonged to a separate sphere. Evidently, Laurencin herself vacillated on this issue—sometimes hiving herself off from male colleagues and sometimes directly taking up their work. She produced pictures in a surprisingly consistent style for patrons with diverse interpretative horizons, ranging from John Quinn to Natalie Barney. Clearly each saw what they wanted, whether an essential femininity or a lesbian eroticism. Certain individuals seem to have had some difficulty deciding whether Laurencin's work was conservative or disruptive. For instance, when the artist and critic Marius de Zayas first encountered Laurencin's work in Paris in 1914, he wrote to Alfred Stieglitz that although her work would be easy to get for an exhibition at the 291 Gallery in New York, it was probably not worth bothering because her work was only a cheap pastiche of modernism. However, de Zayas changed his tune when her work was exhibited at the Modern Gallery in New York in 1917:

Oh, how the wives of the New Hope Group of Artists would disapprove of the work of Marie Laurencin that is now to be seen in the Modern Gallery, . . . Marie would never do at all in New Hope. Fancy her attending the weekly meetings of the "Lapsed and Lost Society!" It wouldn't do. She'd be too disturbing. She knows too much. It's not good form in Good Hope . . . for a lady to know too much. . . . Marie Laurencin is one of the most conspicuous personalities of modern painting. An adventuress of thought, imbued with the essentially modern spirit.[77]

Perhaps, then, Laurencin and her work offer us examples of de Certeau's tactical indeterminacy where alternative meanings slip into the system under the guise of social conformity. Not surprisingly, these are just the sort of resistances which get lost over time. Never highly visible in the first place, they easily fade into the background. What remains is only the shell of social conformity that housed them. Such has been the critical fate of Marie Laurencin who, by and large, has been relegated to history as a woman painter whose feminine style meant she was successful but not serious. In cases like this one, it seems appropriate to conclude with Roland Barthes's comment on "weak myths" which, unlike strong ones, are not depoliticized abruptly. Instead, as Barthes observes, in weak myths "the political quality of the object has *faded* like a colour, but the slightest thing can bring back its strength brutally."[78]

NOTES

I would especially like to thank Lucy Pribas for research assistance. This work has been funded by the Social Sciences and Humanities Research Council of Canada.

1. From his essay "Art News: Women Painters," originally published in *Le Petit Bleu* (April 5, 1912) and reprinted in translation in *Apollinaire on Art: Essays and Reviews 1902-1908*, edited by Leroy Breunig and translated by Susan Suleiman (New York: Da Capo Press, 1972), 229. Apollinaire also discusses these issues in his review of the Salon des Independents for *La Revue des Lettres et des Arts*

(May 1, 1908) and in an essay entitled "Art News: The Decorative Arts and Female Painting" published in *Le Petit Bleu* (March 13, 1912). See *Apollinaire on Art*, 208-10.

2. Roger Allard, *Marie Laurencin* (Paris: Editions de la Nouvelle Revue Française, 1921), 7. This volume was the ninth in a series entitled "Les Peintres Français Nouveaux."

3. Anonymous, "The Capricious Feminine Charm of Marie Laurencin," *Art Digest* (February 1947): 17; Anonymous, *Art Digest* (November 15, 1937): 10; and J. L., "A Famous Exponent of Femininity," *Art News* (November 13, 1937): 18-19.

4. For instance, pink covers were used in the recent paperback editions of Charlotte Gere, *Marie Laurencin* (London: Academy Editions, 1977); Flora Groult, *Marie Laurencin* (Paris: Mercure de France, 1987); and Douglas Hyland and Heather McPherson, *Marie Laurencin: Artist and Muse* (Birmingham, Ala.: Birmingham Museum of Art, 1989), which contains the essay "Marie Laurencin: An Undividedly Feminine Psyche."

5. René Gimpel, *Diary of an Art Dealer*, translated by John Rosenberg (New York: Universe Books, 1987), 399. The lunch organized by Flament (mentioned on December 13, 1929, p. 385) was apparently cancelled because Colette could not attend—see the entry for January 8, 1930, p. 392).

6. For example, in 1939 she had eleven solo exhibitions. According to José Pierre, *Marie Laurencin* (Paris: Editions Aimery Somogy, 1988), 80, Daniel Marchesseau noted that in 1921, shortly after Laurencin's return to Paris, few artists were on such a firm financial footing. She apparently had about 35,000-40,000 francs in Paris from the sale of her paintings and an equal amount in a Zurich bank. To put these amounts into context, the rent on her apartment was between 350-400 francs per month. Gimpel, a close friend of Laurencin, discusses many details of her financial transactions in his *Diary of an Art Dealer*. For instance, he notes that in 1923 her contract with Rosenberg paid her about 60,000 francs a year for a selection of paintings which Rosenberg shared with Hessel, a German dealer. Laurencin was free to take on additional portraits and decorative commissions for which she charged directly. Gimpel noted that Laurencin claimed to spend about 100,000 francs a year in 1923 (243). In 1929, Gimpel noted that "Marie Laurencin is quite well off these days. She must have nearly a million in canvases. She has some good shares, and her two homes which are worth some 800,000 francs" (361). However, Laurencin's relations with Rosenberg were not always harmonious since she felt he paid her too little (and often irritatingly late) considering what he made on her paintings (see for example Gimpel's comments on pp. 243, 261 and 376).

7. For speculations about the Japanese investment in Laurencin, see Joseph Roy, "Laurencin au soleil levant," *L'Express* (May 16-22, 1986): 132, and F. D., "Laurencin la muse du Japon," *Le Quotidien de Paris* (May 3, 1984). On Laurencin's secondary status as an avant-garde painter, see Jean-Jacques Leveque, "Marie Laurencin: L'état de grâce," *Le Quotidien de Paris* (May 8, 1986). Such discourses tend to be tinged with a Eurocentrism that assumes Laurencin's second-rate

feminine and "primitive" style inevitably appeals to "foreigners" who have more money than taste. In Paris, the Musée Rodin was established in 1915 and the Musée Picasso in 1985.

8. See Andreas Huyssen, "Mass Culture as Woman: Modernism's Other," in *After the Great Divide: Modernism, Mass Culture, Postmodernism* (Bloomington: Indiana University Press, 1986), 44-62.

9. I am of course referring to the classic definitions of the modernist avant-garde provided by Clement Greenberg in such essays as "Avant-Garde and Kitsch" (1939) and "Modernist Painting" (1965). The former has since been republished in *Art and Culture* (Boston: Beacon, 1961), 3-21, and the latter in *Modern Art and Modernism*, edited by F. Frascina and C. Harrison (New York: Harper and Row, 1984), 5-10. See Peter Bürger, *Theory of the Avant-Garde*, translated by Michael Shaw (Minneapolis: University of Minnesota Press, 1984).

10. While Laurencin is usually included in catalogues or excavationary surveys of modernist women artists—see, for example, the entries on her in Ann Sutherland Harris and Linda Nochlin, *Women Artists 1550-1950* (Los Angles: Los Angeles County Museum, 1976), 295-96; Elsa Honig Fine, *Women and Art* (Montclair, N.J.: Allanheld and Schram, 1978), 171-73; and Whitney Chadwick, *Women, Art, and Society* (London: Thames and Hudson, 1990), 279, 281, 285—she often is not mentioned in more critical studies such as Griselda Pollock and Rozsika Parker, *Old Mistresses: Women, Art, and Ideology* (London: Routledge, 1981). For a discussion of the ways in which Laurencin has made feminist writers uneasy, see Hyland and McPherson, *Marie Laurencin*, 14.

11. Julia Fagen-King, "United on the Threshold of the Twentieth Century Mystic Ideal: Marie Laurencin's Integral Involvement with Guillaume Apollinaire and the Inmates of the Bateau Lavoir," *Art History* 12 (1988): 88-114. For an earlier article which also calls for a serious consideration of Laurencin, see Renée Sandell, "Marie Laurencin: Cubist Muse or More?" *Woman's Art Journal* 1 (Spring/Summer 1980): 23-27.

12. See, for example, Hyland and McPherson, *Laurencin*, 39-40, who also discuss the views of Marchesseau.

13. See for example, Alice A. Jardine, *Gynesis: Configurations of Woman and Modernity* (Ithaca: Cornell University Press, 1985), and Carol Duncan, "Virility and Domination in Early Twentieth Century Vanguard Painting," *Artforum* (December 1973): 30-39. Griselda Pollock's work is discussed in more detail below—see notes 22 and 23.

14. Briony Fer, "Knowing the Tropes," *Art History* 15:1 (March 1992): 100.

15. Michel Foucault, *The History of Sexuality*, translated by Robert Hurley (New York: Vintage Books, 1980).

16. Suleiman's claim that in the postmodern period women are in a totally new situation is made on p. 190 of *Subversive Intent: Gender, Politics, and the Avant-Garde* (Cambridge, Mass.: Harvard University Press, 1990). See also p. 19 n. 21 and p. 190 n. 23.

17. Biddy Martin, "Sexual Practice and Changing Lesbian Identities," in *Destabilizing Theory: Contemporary Feminist Debates*, edited by Michèle Barrett and Anne Phillips (Stanford: Stanford University Press, 1992), 118.

18. Gianni Vattimo, *The End of Modernity*, translated by Jon R. Synder (Cambridge: Polity Press, 1988), 12-13. Useful poststructuralist discussions of the permanent contest or struggle over the category "women" are provided by Denise Riley, *Am I that Name?* (New York: MacMillan, 1989), and Judith Butler, *Bodies that Matter* (New York: Routledge, 1993). See especially Butler's chapter "Arguing with the Real," 186-222.

19. Jean-François Lyotard, "Sur la force des faibles," *L'Arc* (1976): 4-12, a version of which has been translated as "On the Strength of the Weak," *Sémiotexte* III 2 (1978): 204-12.

20. Michel de Certeau, *The Practice of Everyday Life*, translated by Stephen Rendall (Berkeley: University of California Press, 1984).

21. Griselda Pollock, "Painting, Feminism, History," in *Destabilizing Theory: Contemporary Feminist Debates*, edited by Michèle Barrett and Anne Phillips (Stanford: Stanford University Press, 1992), 161.

22. Griselda Pollock, "Modernity and the Spaces of Femininity," in *Vision and Difference: Femininity, Feminism, and the Histories of Art* (London: Routledge, 1988), 50-90. Building on Janet Wolff's notion of the "invisible flâneuse," Pollock examines how gendered experiences of public and private urban spaces affected the work of artists such as Morisot and Cassatt. While her case study looks at the impact of gender difference at the level of specific paintings and addresses the way certain spaces and spatial configurations have been privileged in traditional modernist discourses, mine considers how Laurencin consciously mobilized her understanding of gender difference in an attempt to secure artistic space and credibility. Janet Wolff's essay "The Invisible Flâneuse: Women and the Literature of Modernity" was first published in *Theory, Culture, and Society* 2.3 (1985): 37-48.

23. Gabrielle Buffet [Picabia], "Marie Laurencin," *Arts* (June 1923): 394.

24. Dorothy Todd, "Exotic Canvases Suited to Modern Decoration," *Arts and Decoration* (January 1928): 64, 92-95. Todd noted a myriad of details signifying Laurencin's modernity, including the "American complexity and efficiency" of her bathroom and the fact that there were at least six vacuum cleaners in her apartment building. She dwelled at some length on Laurencin's support for the women's movement.

25. Marie Laurencin, *Le Carnet des nuits* (1942; reprint Geneva: Pierre Cailler, 1956), 16. "Mais si le génie de l'homme m'intimide, je me sens parfaitement à l'aise avec tout ce qui est féminin."

26. Todd, "Exotic Canvases," 92.

27. Ibid., 92.

28. Pollock, "Painting," 153.

29. Todd, "Exotic Canvases," 92.

30. Ibid.

31. Chadwick, *Women, Art, and Society*, 281.

32. For a useful discussion of the gendered discourses surrounding women's art in the late nineteenth century, see Tamar Garb, *Sisters of the Brush: Women's Artistic Culture in Late Nineteenth-Century Paris* (New Haven: Yale University Press, 1994), 109-112.

33. *Apollinaire on Art*, 44. The review of Laurencin's work was part of his review of the Salon des Indépendents originally published in *La Revue des Lettres et des Arts* (May 1, 1908).

34. B. L. Reid, *The Man from New York: John Quinn and His Friends* (New York: Oxford University Press, 1968), 470.

35. Frank Crowninshield, *Marie Laurencin* (New York: Findlay Galleries, November 1-17, 1937): [2].

36. On the reputation of Vigée Lebrun, see Pollock and Parker, *Old Mistresses*, 96-98. Apparently, however, some contemporaries of Laurencin thought Lebrun painted like a man. For instance, see Georges Aubry's comments in Gimpel, *Diary*, 210. On the subject of impressionism as an appropriate style for women, consult Garb, *Sisters of the Brush*, 124-27, and, in particular on Morisot, see Garb's article, "Berthe Morisot and the Feminizing of Impressionism," in *Perspectives on Morisot*, edited by T. J. Edelstein (New York: Hudson Hills Press, 1990): 57-66. Garb notes that George Moore claimed that Morisot's femininity outstripped that of previous women painters (59). Interestingly, writing almost forty years later, Crowninshield similarly stressed that the femininity of Laurencin's work separated it from that of other women, including Morisot who by then was relegated to the amorphously gendered scrapheap. Rather than offering innovations building from one generation to the next, women's work was considered fashionably disposable, as each new and ever more feminine painter supplanted her predecessors.

37. Françoise, "Chez Marie Laurencin," *L'Art Vivant* 3 (February 1, 1925): 10. "Sur un petit divan bleu, dans un coin, un modèle. Une gracieuse jeune fille blonde, qui semble elle-même faire partie de ce décor, pose, assise, une minuscule guitare entre ses longues mains blanches. . . . La chambre est un poème de Francis Jammes. On y retrouve sa fraîcheur, sa pureté avec toute la naïveté tranquille et sûre de l'Art de Marie Laurencin. . . . Deux biches de céramique rose, couchées sur la cheminée du salon, semblent le gracieux symbole de leur maîtresse. . . . Je quitte Marie Laurencin emplie d'une quiétude, me faisant appréhender les mille bruits de la vie de Paris, qui ne tarderont pas à ternir, puis, à effacer ce joli rêve d'une heure."

38. Guitars, horses, and deer were some of Laurencin's most frequently recurring motifs. In 1923, she executed numerous sketches for the stage set and costume designs for a production of *Les Biches* performed by the Ballets Russes in 1924.

39. Edmond-Marie Dupuis, "A Visit to Marie Laurencin's Studio" [source and date unidentified]: 27-28, press clippings in the Collection of the Bibliothèque Litteraire Jacques Doucet.

40. Todd, "Exotic Canvases," 94. For a discussion of the ways in which the works and artistic spaces of women artists were "domesticated" in late-nineteenth-century critical discourses, see Garb, *Sisters of the Brush*, 108-110.

41. Christiane Fournier, "Marie Laurencin," [source, date and page references unidentified], press clippings in the Collection of the Bibliothèque Litteraire Jacques Doucet: "mais qu'elle a, par dessus toute chose, horreur de la saleté. C'est pourquoi tout en parlent, elle continue à frotter sa palette avec un chiffon enduit

d'essence. 'Je suis le seul peintre de Paris qui nettoie sa palette. Cela vous pourrez le dire. J'ai aussi horreur de la poussière, dont je connais l'age à un jour près.' Le fait est que les meubles sont astiqués et luisants et l'ordre de atelier impeccable." Todd also comments on Laurencin's extremely tidy working habits.

42. Both quotes are from Marie Laurencin, "Art and Life," *Continental Daily Mail* (March 30, 1950). Laurencin's enjoyment of the schools in her neighbourhood is discussed in another unidentified interview with Dominique Clair in the press clippings in the Collection of the Bibliothèque Litteraire Jacques Doucet.

43. Alexander Liberman, *The Artist in His Studio* (New York: Viking, 1968), 62. Liberman started taking photographs of French artists in 1947, many of which were first published during the 1950s. An exhibition of selected photographs was also held at the Museum of Modern Art (October 29, 1959-January 13, 1960). Marie Laurencin and Nathalie Goncharova were the only women among the thirty-nine artists in the book, and Goncharova was photographed with her husband, the artist Michael Larionov.

44. For a detailed discussion of these issues, see Garb, *Sisters of the Brush*, chapter 6.

45. On the French state's involvement in the promotion of art nouveau, see Debora Silverman, *Art Nouveau in Fin-de-Siècle France* (Berkeley: University of California Press, 1989), chapter 10. However, as Silverman notes, those artists who benefitted most from state patronage were Émile Gallé, Auguste Rodin, Albert Besnard, Eugène Carrière, and Louis Falize (172). Other organizations such as the Union of the Decorative Arts directly promoted women artists and women's patronage when they held the first and second Exhibitions of the Arts of Women in 1892 and 1895 (see Silverman, chapter 11). On women's relative exclusion from many influential networking systems ostensibly organized for the private pursuit of leisure, including the *cercles* which were gentlemen's clubs that often housed exhibitions of art, see Garb, *Sisters of the Brush*, 32-41.

46. Many parallels can be drawn between the careers of Marie Laurencin and Hermine David who also cultivated a decidedly feminine artistic identity working as a painter of portraits and miniatures as well as a maker of dolls. She, like Laurencin, continued to live at home with her mother despite being involved with Jules Pascin. She was photographed along with Suzanne Duchamp, Hélène Perdriat, and Marie Laurencin for an article by Florence Guillam, "Paris Women and the Arts," *Charm* 4:2 (March 1925): 15-16.

47. *Apollinaire on Art*, 210. The review was entitled "Art News: The Decorative Arts and Female Painting," and originally published in *Le Petit Bleu* (March 13, 1912).

48. Significantly, the preface to an exhibition catalogue, *Hommage à Marie Laurencin Peintures-Aquarelles* (Paris: Galerie M. Bénézit, 1963), written seven years after the artist's death, was by Claude Roger-Marx, son of Roger Marx, who had been one of the leading exponents of the art nouveau movement. For a discussion of ways in which femininity was configured in the critical discourses of Roger Marx, consult Silverman, *Art Nouveau*, 219-228. Claude Roger-Marx was very familiar with his father's ideas on art, which he discussed in an article he

wrote on his father, "Roger-Marx," *Evidences* 12 no. 88 (March-April 1961): 34-38.

49. Gimpel, *Diary*, 260. Laurencin also illustrated a book on the production which included the text by Jean Cocteau and the score by Francis Poulenc; see *Théâtre Serge de Diaghilew: Les Biches*, 2 vols. (Paris: Editions des Quatres Chemins, 1924).

50. Ibid., 264. She also commented on Picasso's inexplicable use of steel wire. The music for *Mercure*, which opened on June 18, 1924, was written by Erik Satie, and the dance was choreographed by Léonide Massine, although Picasso's scenes, décor, and stage apparently dominated the spectacle. The wire that Laurencin mentioned was actually rattan which was painted black and used to make schematic outline representations of figures. The ballet was original in terms of evoking Mercury's mythological personality through a series of loosely related episodes. It largely abandoned the classical tradition used by Diaghilew and utilized mime and figural groupings. See Douglas Cooper, *Picasso Theatre* (New York: Harry N. Abrams, 1968), 52-61. It was unpopular with the general public, although Picasso's sets were much admired in certain avant-garde quarters, particularly by the Surrealists, who wrote their "Hommage à Picasso," *Paris-Journal* (June 20, 1924).

51. Ibid., 428.

52. Sylvain Laboureur, *Catalogue complet de l'oeuvre de Jean-Émile Laboureur*, vols. 2-4 (Neuchâtel: Ides et Calendes, 1991), 20.

53. Roger Allard, "Marie Laurencin," *L'Art d'Aujourdhui* 2:8 (winter 1925): 49, and R. H. Wilenski, *Marie Laurencin* (London: Leicester Galleries, December 1924), 10-11.

54. Ibid., 251. Such criticisms tended to increase by the 1930s as Laurencin continued painting prolifically in what was by then a passé art deco style. For instance, by 1937 an anonymous critic noted that Laurencin's work was beginning to look dated; see the *Studio* 13 (February 1937): 103.

55. André Salmon, "Marie Laurencin," *L'Art Décoratif* (August/September 1913): 116. "Il serait pénible que Mlle. Marie Laurencin n'eût d'autre rôle à tenir que celui d'auxiliaire de nos décorateurs. Que le public, rassuré sur la moralité artistique, ... la sachant si fragilement associée aux méchants démolisseurs de systèmes commodes, aux terroristes de l'art moderne, daigne prendre mieux garde à elle et regarder, enfin, ses toiles, sans idées préconçues." The point that Laurencin should be seen as more than a decorator is also made in M. Raynal, *Anthologie de la Peinture Francaise* (Paris: Editions Montaigne, 1927), 204.

56. Gimpel, *Diary*, 418. Gimpel discussed Laurencin's own flaunting of Rosenberg's rules (376) when, outraged by what she regarded as his excessive profiteering, she painted a water colour of a woman in the guise of a fury with black hair standing on end which she described as "A woman who isn't afraid of Rosenberg." Gimpel also noted in this same diary reference from 1929 that Laurencin had begun to free herself from Rosenberg by selling to other dealers despite the fact that "Rosenberg, livid, has spoken to her like a warring general: 'You are selling to my enemies' " (376).

57. Armand was Gimpel's nephew and a close friend of Laurencin; see Gimpel, *Diary*, 360-61.

58. On the subject of her spending, see Gimpel, *Diary*, 261-62, and on her loans to others, see the example of her generosity to the wife of Laboureur (279).

59. Fernande Olivier, *Picasso and His Friends*, translated by Jane Miller (London: Heinemann), 43 (italics are in the original).

60. For a further discussion of this, refer to Pierre, *Laurencin*, 66.

61. Her undated letter written to Laurencin in 1951 is in the Bibliothèque Litteraire Jacques Doucet (ms. 3296). The proposed book was to be titled *Picasso et Moi*. By 1951, Olivier was much less disparaging about Laurencin's artistic career, which earlier in 1933 Olivier had characterized as rather more pretentious than serious. Almost twenty years later, in relation to Laurencin's considerable reputation, Olivier's remarks about her own situation seemed rather pathetic: "J'ai toujours hésité à l'écrire [the proposed *Picasso et Moi*] mais maintenant je m'y vois forcée pour essayer de gagner un peu d'argent car à le fin du mois je serai sans travail et comme depuis toujours 'sans le sou.' Depuis deux ans je vis avec moins de 10,000 par mois, tu juges de ma fortune." Olivier's second book was eventually published posthumously over thirty years later under the title *Souvenirs intimes: Écrits pour Picasso* (Paris: Calmann-Lévy, 1988). In the preface, Gilbert Krill notes that in the mid-1950s when Picasso heard of Olivier's financial plight and her intention to publish a book on their life together, the artist sent her about a million francs, which resulted in Olivier returning the manuscript to the privacy of her wicker trunk (9).

62. On Laurencin's early education, see Groult, *Laurencin*, 48-52. In the interview with Dorothy Todd ("Exotic Canvases," 95), Laurencin noted, "I only like people who work, . . . I have no use for idlers."

63. This has also been noted by Groult, *Laurencin*, 92-93.

64. Olivier seems to have quite self-consciously constructed an image of herself as a *declassé* bourgeois from an early age, at least according to her second set of memoirs, *Souvenirs intimes*, where she stresses both her illegitimacy and the fact that she found herself more comfortable with the maids than the family of the *petit bourgeois*, half sister of her father who raised her. She also mentions not wanting to pursue her aunt's educational plans and instead, much to her aunt's horror, passionately wanting to become an actress. Gilbert Krill notes in the preface that Olivier lived in a state of bohemian chaos until the end of her life, her apartment in Neuilly with all its bric-à-brac unconsciously recreating the atmosphere of the Bateau Lavoir (8).

65. For further information about Suzanne Valadon, see Rosemary Betterton, "How Do Women Look? The Female Nude in the Work of Suzanne Valadon," *Feminist Review* 19 (March 1985): 3-24, and Patricia Mathews "Returning the Gaze: Diverse Representations of the Nude in the Art of Suzanne Valadon," *Art Bulletin* 73 (September 1991): 415-30; on Nina Hamnett, see Denise Hooker, *Nina Hamnett: Queen of Bohemia* (London: Constable, 1987) and chapter 5 in Bridget Elliott and Jo-Ann Wallace, *Women Artists and Writers: Modernist (Im)positionings* (London: Routledge, 1994); and for a useful review of the literature on

Gwen John by Deborah Cherry and Jane Beckett, see *Art History* 11 (September 1988): 456-62.

66. de Certeau, *Practice*, xix. A summary of these ideas is presented in the "General Introduction," xi-xxiv.

67. Pierre, *Laurencin*, 61-62, remarks "c'est ce que lui [Picasso] ne pouvait pas ou ne voulait pas faire: quelque chose d'intinmiste (et, bien entendu, de féminine) de l'ordre de la confidence, là où, avec des moyens semblables, il entreprenait, lui, d'accéder à une généralité, à une impersonnalité, à un absolu." He further suggests that *La Songeuse* may well be a self-portrait. Picasso and Braque typically rendered female subjects in a monochromatic and highly fractured style which has frequently been described as analytical cubism. See, for example, Picasso's *Woman with a Mandolin (Fanny Tellier)* of 1910 and his *Ma Jolie (Woman with a Guitar)* of 1911-12 as well as Braque's *Woman with a Mandolin* of 1910 and his *Woman with Guitar* of 1913.

68. See the similarly positioned figure of the woman in the lower right of both paintings. Fagen-King, "United on the Threshold," 105-7.

69. Pierre, *Laurencin*, chapter 6, "Marie Laurencin entre Picasso et le 'douanier' Rousseau," 44-51, 76. The second title is listed in Hyland and McPherson, *Laurencin*, 50.

70. For a recent feminist discussion of the differences between painting female models and bowls of fruit, see April F. Masten, "Model into Artist: The Changing Face of Art Historical Biography," *Women Studies* 21:1 (1992): 17-41.

71. See, for example her comment to Todd on this subject, which was cited above. Laurencin had also made this point in earlier interviews; see, for example, Buffet [Picabia] "Marie Laurencin," 396.

72. Women embracing was a recurring motif for Laurencin, see for example, *La Danse* (1919), which is reproduced in Daniel Marchesseau, *Marie Laurencin 1883-1956: Catalogue raisonné de l'oeuvre peint* (Tokyo: Editions du Musée Marie Laurencin, 1986), no. 153.

73. It is worth noting that Laurencin had been much more interested in flamboyantly flouting social convention during the prewar period of her involvement with the Bateau Lavoir—ironically, just when Olivier had been so dismissive. While various writers have either hinted or openly suggested that Laurencin had lesbian affairs, those parts of her correspondence and papers that have gone to public collections have been carefully sorted.

74. See, for example, René Gimpel's observation that Laurencin had told her dealer that to raise money quickly she only had to sign an article or two on fashion (*Diary*, 419).

75. Marie Laurencin, "My Model," [translated by V. B. Holland] *Listener* (September 8, 1937): 511-12.

76. Writing about *Femme peintre*, Douglas Hyland and Heather McPherson (*Laurencin*, 30) note that Laurencin's handling of the artist and model subject (which was one so often painted by Picasso) was given a specifically female twist. In their words, "The creative process, which for Picasso remained integrally linked to the male sex drive, is here transported to the less aggressive realm of

sisterhood." While I am not sure that Laurencin's painting was any less motivated by desire, I think there is a sense in which she restores as much balance as she can to the relationship between artist and model.

77. De Zayas's condemnation of Laurencin's work is privately expressed in a letter from him to Alfred Stieglitz dated June 30, 1914, preserved in the Alfred Stieglitz Archive, Beinecke Rare Book and Manuscript Library, Yale University. In the letter he writes: "this clever girl is doing exactly what Davies and his bunch did with 'Cubism' at the Montross. She does not express the present, she has the spirit of the XVIII century represented by the formula of modern art." De Zayas's comments on the show at the Modern Gallery appear in "How, When, and Why Modern Art Came to New York," [Introduction and notes by Francis Naumann], *Arts Magazine* 54:2 (April 1980): 121-22. I would like to thank Ernst Birss for drawing my attention to de Zayas's comments.

78. Roland Barthes, *Mythologies*, selected and translated by Annette Lavers (New York: Hill and Wang, 1978), 144.

Feminist Articulations of the Nation: The "Dirty" Women of Armagh and the Discourse of Mother Ireland

Laura Lyons

In the prison, we used to slag, and say "Mother Ireland, get off our backs." Because it just didn't represent what we believed in. Maybe at one time. But not now. We've been through all that and we're not going back. We're going forward.
—Mairead Farrell, interview in *Mother Ireland*

On August 31, 1994, Gerry Adams, president of the Irish political party Sinn Fein, announced an Irish Republican Army ceasefire. His announcement and the Irish and British governments' renewed commitment to holding meaningful and inclusive talks on resolving the conflict in the north of Ireland suggest that those on the island now have a historical opportunity to reconsider the purpose, necessity, and continued efficacy of the geographical and governmental partition that separates the six counties that make up Northern Ireland from the twenty-six that comprise the Republic of Ireland. In an essay that points to the necessity for gender relations, as well as political borders, to be reimagined in any new Ireland, Una Gillespie, a Sinn Fein city councillor who works at the Belfast Rape Crisis Centre, chronicles the various abuses that women in the north, activist and insurgent, have endured in the last twenty-five years of the struggle: "Republican women have been shot, beaten, abused and imprisoned as a result of their participation in the struggle. . . . To claim that women have only played a supportive role would be totally inaccurate, yet equality both within our republican communities and wider society is still something that we have yet to achieve." [1]

Writing for the first post-ceasefire issue of *Women in Struggle/Mna I Streachailt*, the magazine of Sinn Fein's Women's Department, Gillespie astutely notes a basic homology between gender relations as they develop within the liberation movement and in the larger culture, and thus argues for the importance of gender to any discussion of national liberation:

While it can be said that the Republican movement is one of the most progressive movements in regards to the equal rights of women, it is imperative that it develops sufficiently to challenge the sexist attitudes which constrain our women activists. This struggle for women's liberation must be ongoing with the struggle for national liberation, because the two cannot be separated. If we fail to recognize this, we will only allow reactionary ideas to gain ground and put the women's struggle back years. [2]

As a Sinn Fein activist, Una Gillespie supports placing feminist issues—from gaining reproductive rights to dealing with sexual and domestic violence—on social agendas both within her own party as well as those of other governing bodies. The constraints faced by women activists exemplify and expose those that exist throughout Irish society.

In contrast to Una Gillespie's awareness that feminist issues must be developed both inside and outside of liberation struggles, we might look to a recent exchange between the Irish literary critics Dymphna Callaghan and Seamus Deane, a section of which focuses on gender and armed struggle.

DC: But isn't violence, especially the violence that one associates with, say, the IRA, inherently masculinist? For instance, the struggle for independence seems to require the Irish mother sending the son off to be killed, etc., and this reinforces reactionary notions that then impede any possibility of sexual liberation. This week, homosexuality is supposed to be legalized in the South at long last. Such tardiness seems indicative of the fact that questions of sexuality get addressed only in displaced and belated ways.

SD: I've heard arguments in Provisional IRA circles that the Provisional IRA constitutes an advance on the old IRA not only because many of the activists—a considerable number—are women, but that these women have influence in and (though they could never tell you this) may even be members of the Army Council. This they say is inconceivable in the UVF [Ulster Volunteer Force] or even RUC [Royal Ulster Constabulary]. But I'm not convinced. It isn't clear that if the Provos won tomorrow—whatever winning would mean—the outcome would be sexual and gender equality. [3]

Dymphna Callaghan's comments point out the ways in which certain strands of Irish nationalist discourse have relied historically on gendered representational strategies. In response, Seamus Deane rightly notes that the clandestine status of insurgent movements precludes outsiders from making easy assessments about gender politics within revolutionary groups at a particular moment, and he strategically questions what victory by the IRA would mean for the Irish people as a whole. Nonetheless, their remarks place, at least momentarily, the responsibility for liberatory gender and sexual relations solely on the republican movement. In so doing, they ultimately naturalize the role that both states on the island have played in repressing basic women's rights. In other words, if we ask, following Deane's prognostication, whether, under the status quo, gender and sexual equality would be achieved tomorrow, we would, no doubt, be equally unconvinced.

Gillespie's article and the exchange between Callaghan and Deane demonstrate that the well-known tensions between feminism and nationalism remain a contested area of Irish cultural politics, and these pieces suggest some of the responses, both practical and intellectual, to this problem. In Ireland, as elsewhere, feminism and nationalism are neither monolithic nor entirely unitary discourses.[4] The debates about their relationship have historical precedent in Ireland and elsewhere. Looking at the constraints placed on women following the revolutions in Algeria and Nicaragua, where gender relationships within the insurgent forces had promised to be transformative, we might be skeptical of the claim that "the role a woman plays on the barricades will determine what she has been building (and the role she will play when the fighting has stopped)."[5] The opportunities now available to reconfigure the political terrain in Ireland, in whatever limited ways, make it imperative that we historicize the participation of women in all aspects of this struggle, but particularly in armed resistance, so that the gender politics developed within the republican movement and in "legitimate" government circles might inform the current negotiations for peace. We might understand the complexity of this moment, at least in part, by looking at another event which dramatically forced a reevaluation of the relationship between feminism and nationalism, the "no-wash" protest by women republican prisoners in Armagh Gaol.

In March 1981, after thirteen months in soiled clothing and cells covered with excrement, the women of A wing in Armagh prison ended their no-wash protest for political status within the prisons and courts of Northern Ireland. The women decided to end their protest so as not to detract attention from the men's protest at Long Kesh prison, which had escalated from a no-work program to a blanket and dirt protest to a hunger strike, during which ten men died. If these protests are judged strictly by their stated goals, then they were utter failures. With the ending of the hunger strikes, however, the prisoners won the substance of their demand for political status: the rights to wear their own clothes, to associate freely with other prisoners, to full remission, to organize their own educational programs, and to do work of their own choosing. Margaret Thatcher, however, in her staunch refusal to intervene in the deaths of the ten hunger strikers, withheld any legal recognition of the political nature of the prisoners' action. She refused to retract her declaration "that there is no such thing as political murder, political bombing, or political violence, there is only criminal murder, criminal bombing, and criminal violence."[6]

These protests, however, initiated a public discussion of what actions should or should not be recognized as "political." In particular, the Armagh women's no-wash protest for political status disrupted the discourses of Irish feminism and republicanism, both of which claimed, on different grounds, "to represent women" in their struggle against the state authority. In making such claims, both feminism and republicanism had to come to terms with the already existing system of representation for women. The disruption created by the no-wash protest can be understood in light of Stuart Hall's remarks that "if you are going to try to break, contest or interrupt some of these tendential historical connections, you have to know when you are moving against the grain of historical formations."[7] By moving the question of these women's demand for political status from inside the prison to the outside public sphere, the protest brought the already weakening image of "Mother Ireland" into a state of crisis and raised the possibility of a new connection or articulation of interests between the discourses of feminism and republicanism.

THE DISCOURSE OF MOTHER IRELAND

Edna O'Brien begins *Mother Ireland*, her 1976 autobiographical account of her journey through the real and imagined Ireland of her childhood, by commenting that "Countries are either mothers or fathers, and engender the emotional bristle secretly reserved for either site. Ireland has always been a woman, a womb, a cave, a cow, a Rosaleen, a sow, a bride, a harlot, and, of course, the gaunt Hag of Beare."[8] Similarly, Belinda Loftus observes in her recent study of the images of William III and Mother Ireland that her question about what Mother Ireland meant to two republican women in Belfast was met by a simultaneous assertion of "Everything."[9] According to Loftus, Protestant and Loyalist groups in Northern Ireland occasionally make use of female figures to embody symbolically either their connection to Britain or their own vision of a separatist Ulster. But such female figures differ from that of Catholic or nationalist communities for whom "[Mother Ireland] is not one figure but many."[10] In 1988, the Derry Film and Video Workshop, a feminist collective sponsored by Britain's Channel 4, produced the documentary *Mother Ireland*, which traces the development of the image of Ireland as a woman from the late eighteenth century to the present, focusing particularly on the religious and political meanings of the figure. Although the video includes women of all ages, it is framed by a discussion about how the image of Mother Ireland has affected six women and their different projects: Bernadette Devlin McAliskey, a civil rights activist; Nell McCafferty, a feminist journalist; Margaret MacCurtain (Sister Benvenuta), an Irish historian; Pat Murphy, a filmmaker; Rita O'Hare, editor of *An Phoblacht/Republican News*; and Mairead Farrell, a commanding officer in the Irish Republican Army, who at the time had recently been released from prison and who had participated in the no-wash protest at Armagh. Originally banned in both the Republic of Ireland and the United Kingdom, *Mother Ireland* was eventually shown in the Republic and has become an important document in the on-going project of uncovering the role that women have played in Irish history.[11]

As Margaret MacCurtain explains, the image of the Virgin Mary and the practice of Catholicism underwent a profound transformation following the famine of 1846, when the Catholic clergy first began to enlist the Virgin Mary as a role model for Irish women. As early as the seventeenth century, figurative representations of the Virgin portray her as the active protectress of Ireland. Loftus cites one such iconographic depiction, a "blue flag showing the Virgin carrying the infant Jesus and crushing a serpent's head with her feet. The motto is given as *Solvit Vincula Deus* (God has broken our chains)."[12] In contrast, the mid-nineteenth-century Virgin is "Our Lady of the Sorrows," the suffering mother of the adult Jesus. This change in the image of Mary and the way it came to be promulgated as a model for Irish women occurred at a point in Irish history when there was a need to understand the effects of a "punishing God." Loftus suggests that with the 1854 proclamation of the doctrine of the Immaculate Conception, which denied that the Virgin was subject to human frailty, the clergy found in the Mater Dolorosa a convenient icon of chastity and a proper object for Irish women to reflect upon in their acts of penance. Such an image could counter both the more revolutionary potential of James Clarence Mangan's Dark Rosaleen or the sexual and reproductive associations of older Celtic figures like St. Brigid or Sheela-na-gig.[13] As nationalistic fervor increased from the time of the famine through the first two decades of the twentieth century, this image of the sorrowful Virgin gained both in prominence and political significance. MacCurtain explains that the mothers of Ireland, like Mary, "were losing their sons to a great and noble cause."[14] "Irishmen of the second half of the nineteenth century," Loftus argues, "constantly fused the Virgin and Hibernia. England was seen as a threat to pure, Catholic Ireland, both politically and as a country which led Irish emigrants away from their religion."[15]

The various historical transformations and political uses of "Mother Ireland" exemplify what Stuart Hall calls "articulation." Drawing on the two uses of "to articulate"—"to utter" and "to be connected to another," in the sense of an "articulated lorry truck"—and a theory of articulation that has been developed elsewhere by Ernesto Laclau, Stuart Hall states: "An articulation is thus the form of different, distinct elements that can make a unity of two different elements under certain conditions. It is a linkage that is not necessary, determined, absolute and essential for all time. . . . So the so-called 'unity' of a discourse is really the articulation of different, distinct elements which can be rearticulated in different ways because they have no necessary belongingness."[16] He goes on to explain that the "unity" that matters is "a linkage between that articulated discourse and the social forces with which it can under certain historical conditions, but need not necessarily, be connected."[17] In the various transformations that Mother Ireland undergoes from the time of the famine onward, one notices that while she may be "named" or "articulated" through different means—both Cathleen ni Houlihan and the Shan Van Vocht (Irish for "old woman") were important during the time before the 1916 uprising through the civil war of the 1920s—vestiges of the Virgin, the sorrowful mother, are retained.

Two important pieces of literature from this time illustrate how the

Mother Ireland image could be articulated in different ways. In his play *Cathleen ni Houlihan*, W. B. Yeats used the figure of Cathleen to depict an Irish woman, ugly with age, who seduces a young man on his wedding day. He must fight to restore her four fields, the four provinces of Ireland dating back to the time of the chieftains, as well as her beauty, which only he can see. Cathleen is paradoxically both old and young, seductress and virgin, for as Cathleen herself claims, "If anyone would give me help he must give himself, he must give me all. . . . With all the lovers that brought me their love I never set out the bed for any."[18] Modeled after and first performed by Maud Gonne, Yeats's Cathleen was such an effective figure that many, including Yeats, feared the dramatic character's potential to recruit real men. In the poem "Man and Echo," Yeats asks "Did that play of mine send out/Certain men the English shot?"[19]

In contrast to Yeats, Padraig Pearse, one of the leaders of the 1916 uprising, saw in the position of "mother" a strategic focal point for the nation following the death of nationalist sons. In the poem "The Mother," he appropriates the voice of his mother in prayer in order to parallel her suffering with that of the Virgin Mary: "Lord, thou art hard on mothers:/ We suffer in their coming and their going,/And tho' I grudge them not, I weary, weary/Of the long sorrow—And yet I have my joy:/My sons were faithful, and they fought."[20] For Pearse, the mother's role in the revolutionary process is to mourn the loss of her sons and to celebrate their patriotism, activities that in Ireland are necessarily both public and private. Her loss is shared by the nation. In her mourning clothes, a figure in black, she reminds the nation of what has yet to be accomplished.

A more recent articulation of Mother Ireland hybridizes Yeats's Cathleen with Pearse's mother figure, creating the old woman with the four green fields whose sons and grandsons are recruited to reclaim what has been lost.[21] Tommy Makem's popular Irish folk song of 1969, "Four Green Fields," evokes Ireland's long colonial history; in it the old woman moves through Irish history explaining that she had four green fields which "her fine young sons" "fought and died against strangers" to save. The song continues, moving from the time of the famine and civil war into the age of partition:

> Long time ago, said the fine old woman
> Long time ago, this proud old woman did say.
> There was war and death, plundering and pillage,
> My children starved by mountain, valley and stream,

And their wailing cries, they shook the very heaven,
And my four green fields run red with their blood said she.

What have I now, said the fine old woman,
What have I now, this proud old woman did say.
I have four green fields, one of them's in bondage,
In stranger's hands they tried to take it from me.
But my sons have sons, as brave as were their fathers,
And my four green fields will bloom once again said she.

The image of the mother articulates directly with a nationalist ideology at a historical moment when the problems resulting from partition and the occupation of the six counties in the north exerted a particular social force on the community, a force which needed to be addressed in some way. The song constructs women as noncombatants, who support the struggle by raising sons whose deaths in the name of the nation must be mourned as Makem positions women in the funeral possession rather than in the line of fire. His ballad gained an even more overt nationalistic valence in 1971. During a house-to-house search in her West Belfast neighborhood, Emma Groves refused to take "Four Green Fields" off her record player while soldiers conducted their hunt.[22] She was blinded by a rubber bullet fired at her by security forces through an open window at a range of less than eight yards. For Emma Groves and many other women on both sides of the border, the home—a space traditionally gendered as female and particularly used in the Irish constitution to recontain Irish women—represents not a "safe haven" or depository of family virtues but the site of both repression and politicization.

The use of Mother Ireland images, then, is not without certain effects on those whom it is supposed to represent. In the *Mother Ireland* video, Pat Murphy testifies: "For me, growing up, it meant a very repressive image, the old woman with the harp, and a specifically Irish version of the Virgin Mary"; while Mairead Farrell suggests that young republican women would not identify with this image or see it as representing their political commitments. A previous generation of politically committed women—exemplified by McAliskey, O'Hare, and McCafferty—do see value in representing Ireland as a woman and even a mother, so long as the image of woman "is not one of clinging, [or represents a woman] dependent upon her sons to go fight for her," as Rita O'Hare asserts. For McAliskey, the image acknowledges the place of both women and Ireland in the world: "In its own unconscious way I think that [Mother Ireland] is an acceptance of the oppression of the country and of the oppression of women, so I don't think it's a bad image."

What is at stake in the discussion of the image of Mother Ireland as pure and virginal—and in certain versions politically passive—is the political and figurative representation of Irish women. Nowhere does this issue of representation become more contested in contemporary Irish women's history than the no-wash protest.[23] Some of the social force of an image like Mother Ireland comes from the articulation, the connecting of the political and mimetic senses of representation, which have no "necessary belongingness" but which at certain moments become "complicit." Pat Murphy's and Mairead Farrell's rejection of the Mother Ireland image suggests that while popular social movements, as Hall states, must negotiate the political, cultural, and religious articulations of a given society, the problematics of "buying into, inflecting and developing" that terrain—without reinscribing into new articulations those same conservative or reactionary elements that have prompted the need for new articulations—make this a difficult negotiation at best.

In order to uncover how political and figurative representations are at issue in the no-wash protest, I want to examine why the no-wash protest so effectively undermined the discourse of Mother Ireland, and how that strategy determined representations of the protest directed at audiences outside of the prison. I want to contrast the way that those who participated in the protest inside the prison discuss it with representations of the protest from feminists, who had other, often conflicting agendas.

Part of the difficulty in discussing the no-wash protest is that none of the republican women who were protesting have written full accounts of it. Sinn Fein's publication *Women in a War Zone: Twenty Years of Resistance* is the only source whose discussion and historicizing of the protest are presented in an explicitly republican framework.[24] Excerpts of Mairead Farrell's interviews on the *Mother Ireland* video—sections of which were also used for a PBS Frontline episode, *Death of a Terrorist* in the United States—and in the books *I Am of Ireland: Women of the North Speak Out* and *Only the Rivers Run Free* remain for the present the only works with substantial interviews with republican women about the protest, and thus can hardly be said to constitute instances of self-representation.[25] Margaretta D'Arcy, a feminist and playwright from the Republic of Ireland, wrote *Tell Them Everything*, an account of her three months on the protest in solidarity with the prisoners. Nell McCafferty discusses the protest in her book *The Armagh Women*, but most of her information comes either from prisoners who were not on the protest or from Liz Lagrua, a British feminist who, with D'Arcy, joined the protest for a short time.[26] Of these representations of the no-wash protest, I want to examine Shannon's and D'Arcy's most closely, in part because of a similarity in their textual strategies and because of the ways in which their commitment to different forms of feminism serves to underwrite those textual strategies.

READING THE WRITING ON THE WALLS

In the videotaped interviews, Mairead Farrell insists that the no-wash protest itself was actually brought about by the British government and the prison apparatus as punishment for the riot on February 7, 1980, which was initiated by the search of the prisoners' cells for the black clothing by which they identified themselves as members of the IRA.[27] After the riot, the prisoners were locked up for over twenty-four hours without access to toilets or washing facilities and later only allowed out of the cells for one hour of exercise every day. "We were forced into it," Farrell states, "So we excreted in our cells and smeared it on our walls. There wasn't anything else to do with it. You are in your cell twenty-three hours a day and you have to live with it. Putting it on the wall is the best way."[28] Brendan McFarlane explains that the no-wash and dirt protest in Long Kesh had a similar origin. After receiving repeated beatings by warders going and coming from the showers, the men simply refused to wash.[29] Although the immediate cause for their protest was the riot and the punishment imposed, the women in Armagh had previously volunteered to join the men's strike, a request that the leadership outside, "having enough on the organization's plate trying to cope with the H-Block protest's effect," had vetoed.[30] The dirt strike in Long Kesh had already been on for several years before the no-wash protest in Armagh began. After four years, Farrell suggests, the prisoners had either to escalate the protest or to begin a hunger strike.[31]

By not washing, the women were continuing their official punishment in order to reimpose it upon the prison system itself. Prison is a "shitty place to be" and the women of Armagh made it that way for their jailers as well. Liz Lagrua describes her entry into A wing: "The stench hit me. Urine and rotting food and shit. Two women screws [prison personnel] in masks, blue nylon jumpsuits and white wellington boots, like space age women, brought me in and marched me down this filthy corridor."[32] Tim Pat Coogan, who inspected both Long Kesh and Armagh for his 1980 book *On the Blanket: The H-Block Story*, describes the conditions: "Tissue, slops consisting of tea and urine, some faeces and clots of blood—obviously the detritus of menstruation—lay in the corridor between the two rows of cells. . . . I found the smell of the girls' cells far worse than that at Long Kesh, and several times found myself having to control feelings of nausea."[33]

D'Arcy observes the effect that the no-wash protest had on the female screws: "The more asexual we became with our loose-fitting jeans and streaks of dirt-running down our faces, the more feminine they became, with their elaborate coiffures, their waists nipped in tightly, great whiffs of perfume choking our nostrils every time we left the cells."[34] Just as the state interfered with the bodily functions of the prisoners, so the no-wash protest disrupted the warders' relationships to their own bodies at the most basic level of breathing. Their bodies, too, became subject to a kind of "imprisonment" within the heavy uniforms and masks they must wear. D'Arcy's poetic tribute to her cellmates, "The Armagh Women," reverses the roles of "captor" and "captive":

> But the Armagh women they would never yield.
> They'd never yield to Scott the Governor,
> They'd never yield till they broke him down.
> He and his jailers were all locked in prison
> By the women of Armagh jail.[35]

Given that many of the women in the A wing were introduced to the prison system through internment without trial, the no-wash protest might be considered a kind of ad-hoc writ of habeas corpus on the part of the prisoners. By making it impossible for the prison system *not* to deal with their bodies, the prisoners asserted themselves as bodies in aggressive ways that challenged preconceived notions of femininity as a category discrete or separate from "politics." Here, it might be useful to read the no-wash protest alongside the ending of Mahasweta Devi's short story "Draupadi," in which an Indian Naxalite, after being captured and repeatedly raped, defies her culture's honor codes by refusing to wear clothing. When she is brought to Senanayak, the officer responsible for her capture and torture, she confronts him with her naked and battered body. "Draupadi shakes with an indomitable laughter that Senanayak cannot understand. . . . Draupadi wipes the blood on her palm, and says in a voice that is as terrifying, sky splitting, and sharp as her ululation, What's the use of clothes? You can strip me, but how can you clothe me again? Are you a man?"[36] Challenging Senanayak to "counter her" as his men have, Draupadi transforms her body into a weapon: "Draupadi pushes Senanayak with her two mangled breasts, and for the first time Senanayak is afraid to stand before an unarmed target, terribly afraid."[37] Like Draupadi, the women in Armagh stand before their captors in such a way that their bodies are both targets of repression and weapons of resistance.

Having no other materials at hand, the women use their bodily issues—urine, faeces, and blood—to take control of the prison. The act of putting the body's by-products on the wall, marking the walls with shit, constitutes a form of writing. In fact, the women often used their excrement to write out slogans like "Smash the H-Blocks," or "Status Now." Far from being something to be embarrassed about, bodily issues become a form of ornamentation. Tim Pat Coogan cites a visitor to the prison who claimed, "They have excrement all around their cells. The only thing spared are the holy pictures. You see here and there pictures of the Blessed Virgin on the walls framed in shit. The Loyalist members of the prisoner visitors committee think that's dreadful."[38] The juxtaposition of the Virgin and shit, the sacred and the profane, provides one way of understanding why the women's protest was thought to be so much more horrifying than the men's. Tim Pat Coogan states that the women's cells smelled worse than the men's but never explains why. We might ask if his assertion is not, in fact, based on a common Western cultural assumption that equates women and their sexuality with various odors. Given the emphasis in both Irish Protestant and Catholic culture on the purity of women, the no-wash protest both disrupts and plays with the dichotomies of virgin/whore, purity and cleanliness/danger and dirt.[39] The scene with the prison visitor that Coogan relates suggests that the women reject an idea of femininity associated with purity by deploying an extreme version of the connection between women and filth. Such a reading, however, while explaining something of the cultural backdrop for the protest and its reception, is limited. There is a risk in looking at this protest solely through the screen of Catholicism and of "abstracting" these women's actions from their dirt. The Armagh women's *immediate* struggle was not against a myth; rather they were engaged in a specific historical and political confrontation.

Rather than look only at the pictures of the Virgin for an interpretive key, I want to focus on another part of the wall, the slogans. The writing that we read outside of the prison, most often in mechanically produced print, effaces the body of its author. Writing in prison requires using anything at hand.[40] During both the no-wash protest and the hunger strike, when communication between the leadership inside the prison and that outside was essential, tiny slips of paper were stored in bodily orifices and passed between prisoner and visitor through kisses. The bodies of the prisoners during these protests were like publishing houses, issuing written materials. Writing in prison is an important sign of the body; that is, writing leaves the prison because the prisoner cannot. The slogans (or the visual images and written accounts of them) bring three different kinds of messages together in one gesture. First, the marks of shit on the wall attest to the oppression of the body in prison and "commemorate" a particular moment of excessive abuse in the contest between the prisoners and guards over control of the body. In addition, the women's words insist on what the black clothing would have meant; that is, the slogans become the sign of the women's political affiliation and keep the ideology of the movement before the prison authorities. Finally, by using the prison wall as their writing surface, the prisoners reappropriate the means of containment and point directly at the ways in which the system that has incarcerated them is both morally and literally "full of shit."

What differentiates the no-wash protest in Armagh from the dirt strike in Long Kesh is the addition of another bodily issue, blood. The women's insistence that blood is just another bodily material, like shit or urine, on which their protest can be built—their refusal to grant menstrual blood, the sign of women's potential to reproduce, "special status"—forcefully raises the question of whether or not women can be recognized as political beings both inside and outside of the prison. Menstruation is that bodily function most often invoked to keep women from participating in certain actions that are allowed to men. By remaining in bloodied clothing or by smearing clots of blood on the wall, the Armagh women insisted that what is important about menstruation is not its part in reproduction but its production of materials for protest. What, perhaps, makes the no-wash protest the more nauseating and compelling of the two strikes, to such observers as Coogan, is its complete politicizing of the women's bodies, its refusal to let any part of the body be granted an apolitical status.

Yet, as Mairead Farrell points out in the *Mother Ireland* video, when the protest began the women themselves did not have "the most positive attitude" because they thought of their protest "as being an extension of the men's dirt strike in Long Kesh." Only after they refused to wash or change clothes did the women realize, as Farrell explains, "that we were on the protest for ourselves, that we wanted political status for ourselves as women." In a communiqué from the prison, Farrell, who was recognized by both the republican prisoners and the prison apparatus as the commanding officer of the republican women prisoners, writes: "We are in a war situation. We have been treated in a special way and tried by special courts because of the war, and because of our political activities, we want to be regarded as prisoners of war."[41] This moment is a significant one not just for the women in the prison but for the republican movement as a whole. Farrell explains in the video that "through events we began to understand our oppression as women. We were educating ourselves in there. It was a two-way street you know." It is, perhaps, for this reason that Bernadette Devlin McAliskey states in *Mother Ireland* that she feels "that if you look at the Irish feminist movement today, the best of young Irish feminists are those who have come up through the republican experience, who have come to an understanding of their oppression as women through a growing awareness of all other layers of oppression." During the same video interview, Farrell sketches the attitudes of those outside the movement toward politically active IRA women. She explains that people outside, as well as some in the IRA, felt that participation in the armed struggle was something that would be better left to the men than to the "girls of Armagh," that "women weren't supposed to be politically active, that they ought to be taken care of, looked after and certainly not participating in a no-wash protest."

Such remarks were not without support even within feminist circles. Looking back over the relationship "the national question" has had to Irish feminism, Nell McCafferty asserts in the video that

Irish women have no trouble supporting Winnie Mandela and the ANC, or the guerilla women of the Philippines or the women of Nicaragua, but when it comes to the use of physical force to achieve an objective here at home, they are confused. And I don't expect Irish women, especially feminists in operation the last 17 years, to be any less ambivalent or clearer-minded than the majority of Irish Constitutional Nationalists, as they call themselves, who also can't make up their minds.

In both the video interview and her now-famous editorial, "It Is My Belief that Armagh Is a Feminist Issue," McCafferty points out how divisive the issue of partition was for Irish feminists, so much so that in the 1970s feminists in the south agreed not to discuss it.[42] What guarantees would a thirty-two-county Ireland offer against the continued oppression of women? The no-wash protest further complicated any stand southern feminists might take on the question of the north. How could they support women whom they believed to belong to a patriarchal organization? As McCafferty's article indicates, some feminists struggled with the "self-inflicted" nature of the protest, which led to weight loss, infections of the skin and reproductive organs, and, it was feared, would lead ultimately to sterility or even death. Oddly enough, many of the feminists outside of the prison, who were calling for women to have greater reproductive control on both sides of the border, found it difficult to support women whose political protest might involve the loss of reproductive capabilities. In fact, no known fertility problems have plagued the women who participated in the protest. Many of the Armagh women claim that infection was less frequent than people believe. Others claim that the solidarity of the protest gave them great physical and psychological strength. One might wonder, therefore, if the concern of some feminists outside over the issue of reproduction is not another way of denying or refusing to acknowledge that the immense power of the female body might be located not simply in those body sites that separate them from men, but in the totality of the body with all its productive capabilities.

In her editorial, McCafferty outlines on what basis she feels feminists have an imperative to support the women in Armagh:

> It is my belief that the 32 women there have been denied one of the fundamental rights of women, the right to bodily integrity, and I suggest that an objective examination of the events that gave rise to the dirt strike will support this contention. . . . the women, many of whom suffered bodily injury, were locked in their cells for 24 hours . . . were refused access to toilets or a washing facility during the time.[43]

The rest, she says "is a matter of smelly and filthy history, one chapter of which testifies to a calculated sexual assault upon them—in the early months of the protest, insufficient numbers of sanitary towels were provided and the women were forced to wear bloody, saturated clothing."[44] McCafferty rallies support from the feminist community by appealing to the right to bodily integrity and the specificity of the problems that confront the female body on such a protest and *not* to the right of women to act on their political convictions and to have those actions recognized as "political commitments." It is the issue of "bodily integrity" that has allowed feminists and republican women subsequently to come together over the issue of strip-searching within the prisons. Nonetheless, the issue of bodily integrity might justifiably be seen as a way for feminists to continue to avoid the more difficult question of whether or not they can support the right of all women to act on their political convictions, particularly those beliefs that include armed resistance to the state. As a strategy, appeals based on bodily integrity that overlook the political dimension of the protest indicate a limitation both within certain forms of Irish feminism at the time and the society as a whole. In the case of both the no-wash protest and strip-searching, the women assaulted by the system are attacked not simply because they are women but because they are *republican* women who oppose the state that the prison represents.[45]

In her conclusion to *The Armagh Women*, McCafferty explains that many feminists in both the north and south remain suspicious of and even hostile towards the struggle for national liberation: "It has so far proved easier to feminize republicans, who have much to gain from the inclusion of women in the struggle, than to republicanize feminists, who have much to lose if women's interests are totally subordinated to a resolution of the war."[46] Many republican women would disagree with McCafferty's assessment that women's issues are a secondary part of their struggle. In *Mother Ireland*, republican Rita O'Hare states her conviction: "I still believe in that old saying 'There can be no true women's liberation without national liberation.' How can one section of a society be free if the whole of the society isn't free?" The question, then, that has separated feminists and republican women to varying degrees at different times is one of political representation, as each side claims to represent the interests of women.

Although the no-wash protest did not succeed in forcing the British government to reinstate political status within the prison and court system, one of the unpredictable effects of the protest was an opening up of discussion in both republican and feminist circles about the political status of women in general, and what kind of political agendas could best represent women's interests.

The pressure for the rethink[ing] came from the growing numbers of women, both in the political and military spheres [of the IRA], who were dissatisfied with the oft-repeated statement by other members that there was no sexual discrimination in the movement. . . . Other independent feminist groups, like Women Against Imperialism, had made important criticisms of the movement's lack of analysis and commitment to fighting on women's demands. Their argument gained strength when they embarked on a campaign to highlight the position of women political prisoners in Armagh's Women Gaol. . . . For the first time connections were made between the struggle for national independence and many questions were raised inside the Republican movement as well as outside it. It was an issue that could no longer be ignored. Sinn Fein set up a Department of Women's Affairs aimed at ensuring a unity of struggle which will guarantee women's freedom in a free Ireland.[47]

The debates between and among feminists and republican women over which struggle is more important continue today. Sinn Fein Women's Department works both within the party and with outside organizations on a variety of issues that affect the quality of women's lives, such as child care, greater reproductive freedom, better pay, and benefits for workers. McCafferty stresses that after more than twenty years, feminists have to confront "the national question," which she describes as "a running wound in the body politic of Ireland."[48] The no-wash protest, therefore, succeeded in powerfully disrupting the discourses of feminism and republicanism.

LISTENING TO REPUBLICAN WOMEN: TWO FEMINIST JOURNEYS TO THE NORTH OF IRELAND

In the decade since the no-wash protest, feminism has made important advances in Ireland. In 1990, Mary Robinson became the first woman elected president of the Republic. Late in February 1992, a fourteen-year-old rape victim and her parents were denied exit from the country to obtain an abortion in England, despite the fact that the girl threatened to kill herself if she were forced to continue the pregnancy. Public outcry over the case forced then Taoiseach (Prime Minister) Albert Reynolds to hold a referendum on this controversial issue in November 1992, less than a year after he took office.[49] The referendum involved three issues. Two issues, the right to information on abortion and the right to travel outside of Ireland to obtain an abortion in other countries, both passed by a significant margin. The substantive issue, identified as the "right to life" on the ballot, asked voters to affirm "the right to life of the unborn" except in those cases that presented "a real and substantial risk" to the immediate "life, as distinct from health" of the woman, excluding "a risk of self-destruction."[50] This issue was defeated. Pro-life groups, angered that the government did not give them a chance to vote *no* in all circumstances, saw the substantive issue as the first step towards the legalization of abortion on a broad basis. The pro-choice alliance also asked the electorate to vote against the substantive issue; they argued that the life and health of a pregnant woman cannot be separated. Almost three years later, both abortion information and referrals remain unavailable to Irish women in their country. Similarly, a divorce referendum scheduled to take place this summer has been delayed until the fall.

Although it is unclear what effect these actions will have on women's everyday existence, it is evident that a feminist agenda is one that gradually has found a space, however limited, within "mainstream" politics from which to articulate its position. By contrast, republicans must continue to fight for their rights to take part in formulating public policy. The legacy of governmental censorship of Sinn Fein, only officially ended in January 1994, means that most Irish people are unfamiliar with any of the party's policies—on issues such as women's rights, health care, and economic development—except that of the call for British withdrawal in the north. Because republican women's affiliation with a party in support of armed struggle has limited their potential to represent themselves in public discourse for the past two decades, it is necessary to examine critically feminist representations of republican women.

Both Margaretta D'Arcy in her memoir *Tell Them Everything* and Elizabeth Shannon in her book *I Am of Ireland: Women of the North Speak Out* embark on such a project.[51] The emphasis in their titles on "telling" and "speaking" suggests the degree to which each author envisions her book as a forum for representation. Moreover, early in each of these books, the author foregrounds her position as an outsider relative to the women represented in her book by invoking the role of the traveler.

In a speech about academic freedom in the United States and the Third World delivered at the University of Cape Town in 1991, Edward Said provides two images for the reception of knowledge: *potentates*, who survey everything that comes before them with a presumed detachment that endows them with the authority to make "objective" judgments, and *travelers or migrants*, whose acquisition of knowledge depends upon "a willingness to go into other worlds, use different idioms, understand a variety of disguises, masks, rhetorics."[52] The role of the traveler, as Said defines it, is particularly enabling for investigations of self and other, and, within the context of the academy, helps "to transform what might be conflict, or contest, or assertion into reconciliation, mutuality, recognition, creative interaction."[53] Although neither Shannon nor D'Arcy is attached to the academy in an official capacity, we might ask what kinds of recognitions come from their individual travels. A reading of Shannon's and D'Arcy's trips reveals both their positions as travelers in their narratives. Each writer employs the metaphor of travel in constructing a frame for her account, a frame that both enables the telling and problematizes it.

An "outsider," Elizabeth Shannon enters Northern Ireland for the first time as the wife of the U.S. Ambassador to the Republic of Ireland. She hopes that her book will help to restore those women's voices "which might have had a moderating effect" on the conflict but that "have gradually faded and died away"; thus, she "want[s] to listen to the women in the North in a way that only an outsider can" (4). On her six subsequent trips to the north, Shannon explains, "I visited the homes, farms, offices, shops and schools of many women, of all political shades and social and economic status. These are the stories I heard from them, the women whose soft voices have too long been muted by the drums of violence" (6). In trying to make all those "soft voices" heard, Shannon is careful to announce that she "didn't intend to write another analysis of the political situation in the North, nor is this book meant to be an apology for one side or another" (5). She simultaneously foregrounds and eschews her position as the writing subject. What she writes are other women's stories.

By contrast, Margaretta D'Arcy's prison memoir *Tell Them Everything* is not only about everything she saw and was told in Armagh but also about what it means to have access to particular people and events, as well as what it means to be subject to an imperative to *tell*. The book contains both stories about Armagh and a narrative about D'Arcy's relationship to those stories with regard to her position as an intellectual, a feminist, and a middle-class woman from the Republic. The frames within which Margaretta D'Arcy writes this book become important to the way in which—and *how much* of—what she was told gets represented in her account. Before reaching the first chapter, we pass through a number of points of entry—the cover, the subtitle, the author's note, and the preface—which serve to locate D'Arcy in relation to her text and thus inform our reading.

A worn adage advises against judging a book by its cover, but textual criticism and Marxist critiques of commodity fetishism have demonstrated the ways in which the cover and frontispiece of a text can inform and direct our interpretation. The cover of D'Arcy's book, designed by Michael Mayhew, reveals the complex nature of the writer's position with regard to the material in the book. The title *Tell Them Everything*, in large dark letters, is framed by "the women of Armagh said to me" and "and this I have tried to do" in smaller white lettering. The cover thus locates the production of the book both within the prison—in the imperative to tell—and outside of the prison—in the effort to tell. While most autobiographies and memoirs have a photograph of the author on the cover, D'Arcy's book has on its cover one of the few photographs of a prisoner taken during the protest: Mairead Farrell, standing beside a bed and a wall smeared with feces. What makes this picture even more remarkable is that there is no indication of who took it or how. During the no-wash protest and later the hunger strike, much effort was made to prevent information about those inside the prison, as well as photographs of them, from getting out. This photograph does not merely illustrate D'Arcy's story; rather it acts as contraband evidence of the conditions both in Armagh prison and those under which information about the prison is disseminated.

Like Shannon, Margaretta D'Arcy positions herself, however wryly, as a traveler when, on one of her title pages, she adds the subtitle, "A Sojourn in the Prison of Her Majesty Queen Elizabeth II at Ard Macha (Armagh)." The word "sojourn," which denotes a temporary stay and is associated with travel literature, locates D'Arcy as a temporary and voluntary visitor. By juxtaposing the Queen's formal title with the Irish place name for the prison, she positions her account inside Northern Ireland, where she is subject to British control, and as a part of the political struggle for recognition between the British government and the Irish Republican Army.

That Margaretta D'Arcy is subject to British authority is made more explicit in the author's note, in which D'Arcy offers one of her many qualifications of the title and scope of her memoir:

It is not in fact possible to "tell them everything" because in Britain the intimidating and expensive laws of libel are used by the vested interest of the state as a means of covert censorship. Any truthful book about the oppressive intransigence of the British government's jail policy in the North of Ireland is likely to imperil its publishers and authors. I have regretfully had to accept this. (20)

Here, D'Arcy admits the inadequacy of her account. But she locates the cause of that inadequacy in the British government's legislation on libel which in working to criminalize protest, attempts to extend the walls of the prison to include all of Northern Ireland, as it also attempts to fortify the walls of Armagh and Long Kesh by attempting to insure that information does not pass into or out of the prison. D'Arcy accuses the British government of creating an atmosphere in which to speak the "truth" about oppression is forbidden and where any act of "telling" is heavily circumscribed. In her regret and acceptance of this fact, she acknowledges her responsibility not to endanger either the women inside the prison or those outside, like her publishers and editors at Pluto Press, who participate in the struggle in Northern Ireland by disseminating information on the conflict, particularly on women's participation in it.[54] The constraints placed on D'Arcy's telling are precisely those factors that make it imperative that she does tell, if not "everything" then at least "something," for anything told of the conditions of the women in Armagh "tells on" the oppressive practices of the British government.

In her preface, D'Arcy locates both herself and her book in a number of ways that may at first glance seem contradictory. She begins by stating, "Hundreds of women have been jailed in the fight for Irish freedom" (11). She refers to important women in the history of Irish resistance such as Anne Devlin and Countess Markievicz in order to align them with the one hundred twenty women who have been incarcerated in Armagh since the 1970s "for armed rebellion, or civil disobedience, or merely for being known to hold dissident opinions" and with the many women in the south who have been jailed "for selling *Spare Rib*, resisting evictions or demonstrating outside embassies." Her placing of the Armagh protest and the resistance of "ordinary women" in a larger historical context enables the on-going project of uncovering the roles that women have played and continue to play in the struggle for the liberation of Northern Ireland. The status of women in Ireland as political activists, therefore, concerns not only those political groups to whom they owe allegiance but also feminist projects which hope to expose the varied forms of oppression women encounter. D'Arcy situates her book within the "considerable and acrimonious debate both in Ireland and Britain as to whether the demand for political status by the women in Armagh should be supported as a 'feminist issue' " (11), and she continually frames her discussion of Armagh in relation to international feminism.

Having set up the book in various ways as a "feminist" and "nonindividualistic" account of her three months in Armagh, D'Arcy concludes her preface with two statements that position her somewhat differently. She writes: "This is a non-dramatic and often rather absurd story of one person who found herself in Armagh jail" (13). The phrase "found herself" not only tends to obscure the decidedly active role that she took in getting herself into Armagh prison but also suggests an individual "coming to consciousness."[55] D'Arcy further calls attention to her limited perspective when she states "since so few books have been written about Irish women's experience as political prisoners over the last two centuries I felt it essential to put down my own small experience with all its limitations" (13). Rather than privileging her own experience here, D'Arcy both recognizes the limitations of her own position and further attempts to protect those whose story she tells by making it, for readers outside the prison, *her* story. D'Arcy's "own small experience," then, can be seen to serve as a kind of "cover" under which she attempts to carry out the imperative she claims these women have given her.

Positioning themselves as particular kinds of travelers with particular stories to tell, both Shannon and D'Arcy must negotiate the actual terrain of their journey, a process that involves the movement over both geographical and ideological boundaries. Shannon's first chapter, "Three Towns," provides us with a travelogue of her journeys to the north in a rented Ford Fiesta. On one trip to Derry, Shannon encounters a confusing juxtaposition between physical and political geography. Leaving Limerick in the Republic, she sees no people but "spring fields littered with yellow and white wildflowers.... Neat whitewashed cottages sat sideways on sloping hillsides. New lambs leaped awkwardly over spongy tufts of grass, chasing their mothers' tails. The earth was at peace with itself here" (26). Arriving at the border crossing, Shannon passes through the Irish checkpoint but before traveling the several hundred yards to the British checkpoint, she pulls over to take pictures of "a pretty, travel poster scene" (26). When Shannon turns to go back to her car she finds it gone, slowly rolling down the incline to the British checkpoint. She explains that only five days before Lord Justice and Lady Gibson were killed when driving past an abandoned car planted with a bomb in the no-man's land between checkpoints. Shannon's predicament seems "too horrible to be real. Would they shoot me first, no questions asked, then blow up the car? Or would there be an international incident . . . ? I might be inter-

viewed from my hospital bed if I lived. My family would be humiliated"
(27). Somehow this rather dramatic scene is not witnessed by soldiers at
either checkpoint, and Shannon, on her way to Derry "instantly vow[s] a
litany of good deeds that I would perform with regularity for the rest of
my life. It was like wakening from the worst nightmare" (27).[56]

This scene is illustrative of Shannon's approach to her subject matter.
Her gaze is naturally drawn to the pastoral, highly romanticized, seemingly apolitical, and unpopulated landscape. When her focus shifts to the
car careening down the hill, she must contemplate the possibility that
others will misinterpret her actions, that her work or her carelessness
could put her in the position of being mistaken for a "terrorist," a
particularly humiliating prospect for the wife of an ambassador. But rather
than explore these connections, Shannon promises to perform a set of
good deeds. The rhetoric of Christianity is invoked as both the proper
penance for her mistake and the recompense for having been spared the
agony of "an international incident." Her travel and her work remain
untainted by political implications.

In contrast, it is by proclaiming, indeed insisting upon, her guilt that
Margaretta D'Arcy makes her way into Armagh prison. D'Arcy actually
entered Armagh twice, each time for a different reason. In 1978, D'Arcy
traveled to Belfast at the invitation of the Northern Ireland Arts Council.
She explains that the government had just banned a protest by relatives of
prisoners in the H Block, yet at a poetry reading at a local museum, which
was meant as "a radical protest against censorship and the brutality of
repression on the Falls Road," no mention of the families was made (15-
16). Staging her own counter-demonstration, D'Arcy wrote "H Block" on
the wall of the museum in red marker and was immediately arrested. She
was sent to Armagh, where, after refusing to cooperate with a doctor, she
was put in A Wing, which housed political prisoners. D'Arcy defended
herself by debating "the role of the artist in a time of repression" (17).
Fines were imposed on her and paid by someone else.

Half a year later, D'Arcy returned to Armagh to participate in a
demonstration sponsored by Women against Imperialism, a feminist organization, which picketed for political status of republican prisoners
on International Women's Day, March 8, 1979. D'Arcy writes that the
demonstration was "the first statement to feminists all over the world that
solidarity with the Armagh prisoners and a commitment to oppose British
rule were central issues in the struggle for women's liberation" (19). The

protest ended when four Royal Ulster Constabulary jeeps appeared "out of nowhere," and the protestors were forcibly taken away. Eventually eleven of the women were arrested, including D'Arcy. During the many trial delays and preparations, the women were able to participate in a number of protests, including the next International Women's Day demonstration at Armagh, whose attendance had increased from fifty-three to five hundred people.

Yet factionalization frequently occurred within Women against Imperialism. Among the Armagh Eleven, there was initial resentment that D'Arcy refused to acknowledge the court and wanted to defend herself with "the Human Rights Charter, the Bennett Report and the Pope's speech at Drogheda" (30). The women from outside Northern Ireland, like D'Arcy, were singled out by the court as leaders so that "the world could then be persuaded that we were 'outside agitators' and northern public opinion would lose interest in us" (34). Accounts in the local *Armagh Gazette* claimed that the Armagh Eleven were a group of French feminists. The decision to pay fines further threatened the group's solidarity; some women chose to pay, while others had relatives who paid their fines without telling them.[57] Ultimately only Liz Lagrua, a British woman, and D'Arcy were incarcerated on "behalf of the Armagh Eleven" (37).

The deliberate nature of D'Arcy's efforts to enter Armagh as a prisoner marks her presence in the prison, from the beginning, as different from that of the republican women incarcerated there. During an appointment at the army barracks, she refused to pay the fine and demanded to be arrested. In her discussion of the problems of knowing whom to trust and how far to take her actions once inside Armagh, which indicates her growing awareness of the problems of her position vis-à-vis the other women already inside, she explains: "I had to be very careful not to outdo the militancy of the other prisoners. I did not come from the oppressed minority of the ghettoes. . . . I was there because I objected in principle to the British presence in the six counties, the subjugation of the minority and the treatment of the prisoners" (44). Here, D'Arcy's construction of herself as outsider involves not objectivity but lack of experience. In order to move from B Wing to the remand wing, D'Arcy must refuse to work, see the prison governor, and threaten to pour her urine on the floor. Only when she is ushered into A wing, which housed the prisoners on behalf of whose rights she had demonstrated, does she reach her destination.

Both D'Arcy and Shannon arrive at their "destinations" thanks to carefully planned itineraries formulated on the "outside." Margaretta D'Arcy participates as "an advocate of international socialist feminism, without being a member—or wholehearted supporter—of the IRA" (36). While Shannon makes no attempt to identify her political commitments in so bold a manner, it is clear that despite her claims to objectivity or neutrality an unspoken political analysis pervades her recounting of those "soft voices" of Northern Irish women. To what extent do D'Arcy's and Shannon's commitments constitute itineraries that determine the manner in which they will both encounter republican women and write about that experience?

In Shannon's book, the conflicts between the political commitments of republican or nationalist women in the north and feminists in the south are played out in a particularly dramatic form in a section entitled "Today's Revolutionaries," which features Shannon's interviews with women in Sinn Fein and Mairead Farrell. Shannon comes to these women with the belief that feminism and violence or participation in the armed struggle are irreconcilable. There is something fundamentally "dirty" for Shannon about women whose politics either sanction or directly involve armed struggle. While recounting her interview with Martha McClelland of Derry, "the only American working full time for the Republican cause in Northern Ireland," Shannon remarks that McClelland's apartment in the Bogside "was spotless and cozy. . . . The lackadaisical attitude that most nationalist Irish women have toward housekeeping hadn't yet rubbed off on this adopted daughter of Northern Ireland" (31).[58]

Given her interest in "cleanliness" it is not surprising that Shannon considers the no-wash protest, "the most bizarre political protest I had ever heard of" (124). For example, in her questions to Mairead Farrell about hygienic practices during the protest, Shannon registers her disgust:

"For over a year you didn't wash your hands, your face, your body, or brush your teeth?"
"No."
"What did you do about your periods?"
"I used tampax because I felt that kept me as clean as possible."
"And you didn't get sick?"
"No." (124)

Throughout this section of her book, Shannon pruriently explores the mysteries and secrets of the IRA. For example, she asks Farrell "Just for my own curiosity, how do you plant a bomb?" to which Farrell replies, "I'm not going to tell you any of my secrets" (123). Shannon imagines that the old men whispering, in what is probably the Sinn Fein waiting room, are planning a bombing, murder, or kneecapping. She is surprised to learn that they are only discussing how to fix a refrigerator. In addition, she fantasizes about what secret messages might be in the cigarettes that Sîle, one of the women she interviews, passes to an old woman who comes to the door.

Throughout the interviews with Farrell and other women in the IRA, Shannon insists on having the last word on armed struggle. When Sîle explains how the shooting of a six-year-old boy in Divis Flats by a British soldier served to politicize her, Shannon comments, "How does the death of the child in Divis Flats in any way validate similar kinds of IRA murders, where innocent women and children [have] been killed?" (119). Shannon's question appears to be rhetorical, for her text allows Sîle no response. She employs the same strategy when Father Raymond Murray, the Catholic priest in Armagh Gaol, expresses his admiration for the republican women prisoners' dedication to their cause. Shannon states that it is "sad and pointless for a young woman like Mairead Farrell to be back in the organization, perhaps risking her own life again in an armed struggle when a non-violent, political path is open to her" (125). When Father Murray tells her that she doesn't "understand how they feel, always being second-class citizens in their own country," Shannon retorts: "I understand perfectly. . . . It's something like being a woman in the Catholic Church, a second-class citizen in one's own religion" (125). Shannon's desire to have the last word reveals that she is not so much coming to these women for knowledge to which she does not have access but for confirmation of her political analysis of the conflict, which she only explicitly delineates in the final pages.

For Shannon, the nonviolent, political path open to Mairead Farrell would be paved by women in all thirty-two counties banding together against Northern Irish men's "addiction to revenge, an addiction as insidious as alcohol or drugs" in order to create a more "civilized world" (249). In her view, Ireland's problems stem from psychological dysfunction on a national scale. Shannon discounts the opinions of those Irish women with whom she disagrees in order to uphold her own peculiarly "one-dimensional and non-dynamic feminism."[59] One might add to these adjectives "sanitized" in order to throw into contrast the way in which

Shannon's version of feminism is repelled by the "messy" and "dirty" practices employed by the republican women. Shannon's exasperation that it takes three phone calls to get in touch with "women who are playing leadership roles in the IRA today" perhaps betrays her political naïveté and privileged class position, and these women's rightful wariness in meeting with her.

In the final chapter of her book "In Love and Anger," Shannon writes that "[t]he saddest thing I heard on my travels around the North was women saying, 'Oh, we've played a big part in these Troubles.' Then you find out that their 'big role' was banging garbage lids to signal the arrival of the British army, or making sandwiches and tea for the lads" (248). In commenting on the "growth" that specifically nationalist women have discovered—"that they can run their households and raise their children by themselves if their men are dead or in prison, and many times they discovered that they like it better that way"—Shannon makes an odd statement: "Their 'freedom' is an erosion of the cultural and religious tradition that makes Northern Ireland unique" (249). While Shannon questions how such new familial configurations constitute "freedom," she seems protective of the traditional value system that she feels is eroded by women's new roles. Throughout her book, Shannon paradoxically wants greater equality for and recognition of the hardships endured by certain women but not at the expense of what makes Northern Ireland "unique," its traditions. Such a construction reveals an "exoticization" of Northern Ireland's traditions similar to Shannon's treatment of the pastoral landscape. To be attractive to tourists like Shannon, both the land and its customs must be preserved, remaining pristine and untouched by the country's political troubles. Perhaps what Shannon, as a self-proclaimed feminist, ultimately hopes for the women of Northern Ireland is an arrangement like her own, one with enough economic security to afford them the opportunities for self-actualization that she enjoys within the confines of "traditional" norms of domesticity. To return to Said's metaphors of the traveler and the potentate, Shannon's book reveals that potentates are also capable of travel, but when they travel they take with them their ideological boundaries and superimpose them on the landscape set before their view.

If Shannon sees the women that she interviews, republican or loyalist, as the subjects of her book, Margaretta D'Arcy views the women with whom she is incarcerated on A wing in Armagh as "tour guides." D'Arcy describes her attempts to get to know her fellow prisoners in the three months that she was in Armagh "like passing through maze within maze— each one appearing in front of me just as I had thought I had successfully threaded the last one. I was not only an observer, I was a participant and I had to retain my own individuality as civilian" (68). Getting to know her fellow inmates proved to be a "slow process," as prisoners saw only their own cellmates except during their one hour of exercise in the yard, where they could speak with the other prisoners with the same recreation period. But D'Arcy also comes to realize that the process is slow because of her "own individuality as a civilian," the cultural and class differences between her and the republican prisoners.

On more than one occasion she is brought up against an ideological wall in the maze by her lack of awareness of issues to which the women are sensitive. For example, when she questions one prisoner about how her drinking affects her commitment to political meetings, a complaint is lodged with Mairead Farrell that D'Arcy is "trying to make out like the IRA was nothing but a bunch of alcoholics" (91). After this incident, D'Arcy begins to interrogate her own desire to question her companions, and admits that she "had become the enemy. Every insult that British propaganda had ever brought out was reflected on their faces, and I was British propaganda" (91). When she apologizes, the women explain the importance of solidarity to her. One woman tells her, "We all know each other. . . . But we don't know you. You must understand that we have got to protect ourselves" (91). Another woman forgives her several days later saying: "We can't afford to quarrel in here, or to keep our hurt for a long time; we're all together and get our strength from each other" (92). D'Arcy, unlike Shannon, carefully avoids asking about IRA activity, know- ing that the reply "quite correctly would have been if I wanted to know, I could join; if I just wanted the information I must be a spy" (98). She comes to accept the prisoners' suspicion of her: "What could they make of me? . . . an alleged playwright. . . . I did not come from the North. . . . My world, my standards and values, were incomprehensible to them. What was I doing in here, a middle-aged woman with four sons and a husband; and yet I appeared to be fancy-free" (93).[60] That D'Arcy's companions consider her "fancy-free" may suggest that they recognize the elements of "tourism" that shape D'Arcy's "sojourn" in Armagh. She comes to understand that no information gathered in a place like Armagh is ever "just" information, but is rather an instrument that can be wielded in the service of various conflicting interests. The prisoners distinguish between types, or degrees, of information: they are most reluctant to divulge "insider" information, knowledge that if disseminated on the "outside" might threaten their interests.

In prison, D'Arcy must act as both student and teacher. Giving lectures on feminism at the request of the other prisoners, Margaretta D'Arcy and Liz Lagrua must confront some prisoners' fears that they would not be "intellectual" enough for the visiting feminists, and other prisoners' feelings that feminism is pro-abortion, anti-Catholic, and full of lesbians and men-haters (107). During a series of lectures on the development of the women's movement in relation to other oppressed people—"slaves, the colonial people, the workers, national liberation struggles"—the prisoners reveal their "deep distrust of the Women's Movement, which they felt was implying that the Republican Movement had not recognized their struggle in jail as having an identity of its own, and that it was no more than a support for the men" (107-8). These lectures and debates left a legacy, for although some of the women initially had ambivalent attitudes towards feminism, nonetheless the educational programs organized by and for republican prisoners, women and men, includes feminism.

D'Arcy reports feeling torn apart by the debates: "A lot of what they said was true, for where was the Women's Movement in 1976 when these women were first rounded up, tortured, and thrown into prison?" (107). The women's movement, the prisoners pointed out, had no army or clear organizational hierarchy: "That our battle was the political one of raising consciousness was something from which they could see no direct benefit" (110). Perhaps the most damning evidence against feminism in the prisoners' minds was that D'Arcy and Lagrua received very little tangible support from their women's organization once inside Armagh, and, as D'Arcy remarks, "They were outraged that some of the women arrested with us hadn't bothered to write" (111). D'Arcy concludes: "The more I became isolated from my comrades on the outside, the closer I grew to these women and the more we began to understand our problems together. . . . It is very difficult for those outside to understand this; and to understand how the isolation of the prisoners on the protest reinforces their commitment to the IRA" (112). Here, the knowledge that D'Arcy has gained momentarily destabilizes the boundary between insider and outsider and recalls Said's remarks that "we should regard knowledge as something for which to risk identity, and we should think of academic freedom as an invitation to give up one identity in hope of understanding and perhaps even assuming more than one."[61]

D'Arcy's struggle to determine her position as an intellectual "visiting" the prison involves rethinking her function as an interpreter of the "sights" she took in during her stay. Her intellectual dilemma suggests that we might examine her relationship with the women prisoners in A wing in terms of what Antonio Gramsci calls the "traditional" and the "organic" intellectual. Gramsci's delineation of the functional roles of these two types of intellectuals, and the tensions that can arise between them, is placed in the context of efforts to develop a "global" feminism in Spivak's famous essay "French Feminism in an International Frame." Spivak's comments are of particular relevance to D'Arcy's situation, given the "educational" focus of D'Arcy's and Lagrua's "lectures" to and discussions with the prisoners:

> As soon as one steps out of the classroom, if indeed a "teacher" ever fully can, the dangers rather than the benefits of academic feminism, French or otherwise, become more insistent. Institutional changes against sexism here or in France may mean nothing or, indirectly, further harm for women in the Third World. This discontinuity ought to be recognized and worked at. Otherwise, the focus remains defined by the investigator as subject. . . . However unfeasible and inefficient it may sound, I see no way to avoid insisting that there has to be a simultaneous other focus: not merely who am I? but who is the other woman? How am I naming her? How does she name me? Is this part of the problematic I discuss? Indeed, it is the absence of such unfeasible but crucial questions that makes the "colonized woman" as "subject" see the investigators as sweet and sympathetic creatures from another planet who are free to come and go.[62]

D'Arcy recognizes her own relative freedom "to come and go" late in her account: "I was shortly to be released from Armagh and would not be on the final stages of the expedition on which the travellers would be facing the most dangerous water of the entire journey. For us on the outside, the question should be: how important is the individual life of each Irish republican prisoner?" (117). This question takes its place among the other "unfeasible but crucial questions" that D'Arcy begins to formulate, if not satisfactorily to address, in the course of her sojourn in Armagh. As the appropriateness of the no-wash protest as an example of properly feminist resistance is called into question by feminists "outside" of Armagh, the protest, as D'Arcy comes to view it, calls into question the investments and assumptions of the feminism D'Arcy "found herself" to be representing "inside" Armagh.

We have noted that D'Arcy has not simply "found herself" in Armagh prison but that she took an active part in her arrival at the prison, acting on an itinerary shaped by her commitment to her role as a feminist intellectual. Her "tour" of Armagh prison, then, is a kind of "tour of duty"; D'Arcy sees herself in Armagh "on assignment." What distinguishes D'Arcy from Shannon is her awareness of her own subject position with regard to both the oppressive government of the country she visits and her own intellectual assignment, her intellectual "duty." D'Arcy arrives at her destination through a series of acts of insubordination to the laws of the British dominators; once there, she finds that she is compelled to be, in a sense, "insubordinate" to her own feminist agenda.

Both D'Arcy's and Shannon's texts document the difficulties that different versions of feminism face when confronted with the issue of women and armed resistance. In assessing these accounts and the different versions of feminism that shape them, we might confront the writers, and ourselves, with yet another imperative, the one Spivak offers in the conclusion of her essay "Can the Subaltern Speak?" "Representation has not withered away. . . . The female intellectual as intellectual," Spivak writes, "has a circumscribed task which she must not disown with a flourish."[63] While neither woman disowns the difficult task of representing other women, D'Arcy's text reveals what Shannon chooses to conceal, those factors that circumscribe the act of representation. D'Arcy offers no pretense of objectivity. Acting as what Carolyn Warmbold has called a "narrative courier"—one who brings out information about conditions deemed unrepresentable by the state authorities—she does not erase her position as a middle-class intellectual; rather, she learns from the prisoners how to interrogate that position.[64]

Doing time in Armagh provides D'Arcy with an opportunity not only to expose the grotesque conditions under which the republican prisoners live but also to consider how her own feminist ideals might be complicit in sustaining the structures that confine these women. The questioning to which D'Arcy subjects herself leads to an enabling recognition of the many factors that circumscribe her task, and of the obstacles that she will encounter in bringing "inside" information to the "outside." Such information, as D'Arcy has come to realize and as Shannon's text illustrates, can be wielded to the detriment of the women of Armagh not only by the British government but also by any feminism that fails to interrogate itself thoroughly before making its declarations. *Tell Them Everything* provides an important account of how negotiating the faultlines that emerge from the interaction between women whose feminism is differently articulated by nationalism need not end, as it unfortunately so often does, in impasse.

RECONFIGURING REPRESENTATION

The no-wash protest, insofar as it insisted that women be thought of as political beings who are themselves capable of entering into the "dirty" business of taking political action, including armed resistance, on their own behalf, brought the image of Mother Ireland into a state of crisis. At the end of the *Mother Ireland* video, when the women are asked whether they think Mother Ireland is ultimately a positive image, it is the older generation of women who agree. Bernadette Devlin McAliskey states: "I would still see myself as a child of Mother Ireland . . . I would still hold strongly to it for all her strengths, weakness, contradictions and areas of reaction, and all that she has cost me." Nell McCafferty explains that she would replace Mother Ireland with the ancient fertility goddess, Sheela-na-gig, whose image is on the stonework of ruined places of worship and reminds one of both Ireland's colonial past and the power of the female form. However, it is a new generation of politically committed women—Pat Murphy and Mairead Farrell—who find Mother Ireland not just an inadequate representation of women but a potentially damaging image. Pat Murphy states that she believes that it is a "wrong thing to image a country after a woman" because of the implications for thinking of the country as something that is raped, and that one of the problems of the image of Mother Ireland is that it "always gets connected to these larger figures, like Constance Markievicz, who is seen as a unique figure. . . . This is work that goes on all the time; there are many women to identify with." For her, feminism and republicanism serve the important function of monitoring each other, so that no one side of the struggle is overlooked. Mairead Farrell says, "It wouldn't make me want to go out and fight. In fact, it would have the opposite effect." She jokes that in the prison on the no-wash protest the women would say " 'Mother Ireland, get off our backs.' " The gap between the two generations represented in the *Mother Ireland* video points to a new possibility for articulation as the social formation and historical forces change.

A 1991 Sinn Fein International Women's Day mural attests to the development of a feminist agenda within the republican movement from the 1960s to the present. The mural depicts some of the social forces—from labor issues to social justice campaigns—that have shaped the commitments of republican feminists by focusing on a day in November 1968 when, following an announcement banning all marches within the walls of the Derry by Home Affairs Minister Bill Craig, women in the city's shirt factories abandoned their work to spend the rest of the day marching in and out of Derry's gates. Martha McClelland, who coordinated the mural project, explains: "The mural itself honours the many women who took part in that march and specific women who have played key roles, particularly during the recent years of struggle."[65] In the mural, these anonymous women who "broke the ban" are joined in their protest by Bernadette Devlin McAliskey; Kathy Harkin, who founded Derry Women's Aid; Roisin Keenan Barton, who organized walkouts by women workers during internment; Mairead Farrell and Ethel Lynch, who both died on active service with the IRA; Brigid Bond, who campaigned for housing in the 1960s and 1970s; Suzie Coyle, who defended the rights of republican prisoners; Brigid Shiels, a republican activist who died a few months before the mural was painted; Nell McCafferty, the feminist journalist raised in Derry; and Peggy Deery, whose death in 1989 was related to injuries she received on Bloody Sunday. In addition to these generations of Irish activists, the mural includes three Nicaraguan women in a recognition of Irish solidarity with anti-imperialist struggles throughout the world. Such a visual representation of the varied and collective contributions of Irish women—in the home, in the factory, on the street, and in the prison—McClelland suggests, performs the important intervention of countering an image of republicans as "men of violence."

The present political situation in Ireland raises serious questions about where the marching women depicted in this mural, indeed, all women in Irish society are headed. In the two months leading up to the announcement of the IRA ceasefire in August 1994, a number of organizations sponsored debates and forums on the efficacy of a united Ireland and on the obstacles to creating a lasting peace on the island. Both Time To Go (a broad-based, all Ireland organization dedicated to achieving British withdrawal) and the organizers of the West Belfast Community Festival included in their activities specific forums for discussing the role of women in a new Ireland and in the negotiations for peace. In most accounts of the official peace process, much attention is given to the necessity for a national reconciliation of the "two traditions," Protestant and Catholic. Discussion of how civil liberties based on forms of difference outside of religion and "tradition"—such as gender and sexuality—are to be guaranteed in whatever new social and political configuration may emerge has been largely absent.[66] The struggle of Irish women of today for adequate political representation has its precursor in the struggle of the women of Armagh for the recognition of their political status. The crisis in feminism—both within and outside of the republican movement—brought about by the no-wash protest has important implications for the present. If the uneasy tension between feminism and nationalism experienced within women's organizations and coalitions is to remain politically productive, it is less a question of resolving this tension than of insisting that these debates belong within the formal negotiations on the restructuring of Ireland's political future. The role that women play on the barricades does not always determine their role after the fighting has stopped; perhaps more important in setting a course for Irish women is the place they occupy in negotiating a settlement and reimagining the community that calls itself "the Irish nation." The women represented on the Derry mural and the black captions that frame them pose two crucial questions that all those involved in the current negotiations must also ask: " 'What is Freedom?' and 'Where are women now?' "

NOTES

Several people have provided helpful commentary on this piece: Purnima Bose, Liz Butler Cullingford, Ann Cvetkovich, Cindy Franklin, Barbara Harlow, Katie Kane, Margaret Kelleher, and the readers for *Genders*. In August of 1990 I had the good fortune to meet two women who participated in the no-wash protest and another republican woman who had been incarcerated in Maghaberry Prison. I have not quoted them directly, but their generous answers to my questions helped to shape my analysis, for which I take full responsibility.

1. Una Gillespie, "Twenty-Five Years of Women's Resistance," *Women in Struggle/Mna I Streachailt* (Autumn 1994): 4.

2. Ibid.

3. Dymphna Callaghan, "Interview With Seamus Deane," *Social Text* 38 (Spring 1994): 40.

4. For a discussion of the intersection of feminism and nationalism in other geopolitical sites, see Kumari Jayawardena, *Feminism and Nationalism in the Third World* (London: Zed Books, 1986); and Chandra Talpade Mohanty, Ann Russo,

and Lordes Torres, eds., *Third World Women and the Politics of Feminism* (Bloomington: Indiana University Press, 1991). Barbara Harlow's *Barred: Women, Writing, and Political Detention* (Hanover, N.H.: University Press of New England, 1992) offers the most sustained analyses of writing and theorizing within national liberation movements on this topic.

5. Angela Gilliam, "Women's Equality and National Liberation," in *Third World Women and the Politics of Feminism*, 228.

6. From the video *The H Block Hunger Strike*, written and produced by the republican prisoners in Long Kesh, Northern Ireland, 1991.

7. Stuart Hall, "On Postmodernism and Articulation: An Interview with Stuart Hall," ed. Lawrence Grossberg, *Journal of Communications Inquiry* 10 (Summer 1986): 54.

8. Edna O'Brien, *Mother Ireland* (New York: Harcourt, Brace and Jovanovich, 1976), 11. For a discussion of the imaging of women in Celtic mythology, see Mary Condren, *The Serpent and the Goddess: Women, Religion, and Power* (San Francisco: Harper and Row, 1989).

9. Belinda Loftus, *Mirrors: William III and Mother Ireland* (Dundrum, Co. Down, Northern Ireland: Picture Press, 1991), 44.

10. Ibid.

11. The documentary *Mother Ireland* was written and directed by Ann Crilly and produced by Anne Goldberg, Derry Film and Video Collective, 1988. The interviews with Rita O'Hare and Mairead Farrell prevented the full version of the video from being broadcast. In addition, vintage footage of Maud Gonne speaking about the contributions of the IRA that had never before been seen was also prohibited on the basis that subsequent to the filming of Gonne's speech the IRA was outlawed. Section 31 of the Republic of Ireland's Broadcasting Act of 1960, as amended in 1976, prohibited the broadcast of any interview or part of an interview with a spokesperson for the IRA, Sinn Fein, Republican Sinn Fein, Irish National Liberation Army, or Ulster Defense Association. Although Section 31 was overturned in January 1994, its legacy of censorship effectively curtailed the election of Sinn Fein representatives to city, county, and national government.

12. Loftus, *Mirrors*, 50.

13. Ibid., 58.

14. On August 21, 1879, when crops in Ireland were still failing, fourteen people of the village of Knock in County Sligo claimed to have seen an apparition of the Virgin Mary. See Michael P. Carroll, *The Cult of the Virgin Mary* (Princeton: Princeton University Press, 1986), in which he notes that Knock was particularly hard hit by evictions of tenant farmers that year, which marked the beginning of the Land War. He suggests that the social and economic conditions at the time made the people of Knock susceptible to a Marian apparition. Although the "miracle" of the sighting has never been fully investigated or confirmed by the Vatican, a small tourist industry and an airport flourish there by catering to pilgrims.

15. Loftus, *Mirrors*, 58.

16. Hall, "On Postmodernism," 53.

FEMINIST ARTICULATIONS OF THE NATION 145

17. Ibid. In order to explain what the theory of articulation can account for, Stuart Hall turns specifically to religion as a site of potential articulations. According to Hall, religion exists "historically in a particular formation, anchored very directly in relation to a number of different forces . . . its meaning—political and ideological—comes precisely from its position within a formation. It comes with what else it is articulated to" (54).

18. W. B. Yeats, *Cathleen ni Houlihan*, in *Collected Plays* (New York: Macmillan, 1953), 55. In her book *Gender and History in Yeats's Love Poetry* (Cambridge: Cambridge University Press, 1993), Elizabeth Butler Cullingford points out that Cathleen ni Houlihan was "first used as a figure for Ireland in the late eighteenth century, when the blind poet Hefferan wrote a rousing ballad that promises Irish freedom 'When the Prince is seen with Cathleen ni Houlihan!'" (65). She notes that Yeats wrote an article on Hefferan for the *Dictionary of National Biography* and so would have been familiar with the origins of the figure when he wrote the play.

19. Richard J. Finneran, ed., *The Collected Poems of W. B. Yeats* (New York: Collier Books, 1989), 345.

20. Proinsias MacAonghusa and Liam O'Regain, eds., *The Best of Pearse* (Cork, Ireland: Mercier Press, 1947), 171.

21. For an excellent analysis of representations of Irish women in popular novels about the Troubles, see Bill Rolston, "Whores, Mothers and Villains: Images of Women in Novels about the Northern Ireland Conflict," *Race and Class* 31 (Winter 1989): 41-57.

22. *They Shoot Children* (London: Information on Ireland, 1986), 25. This excellent pamphlet documents the history and use of rubber and plastic bullets by the security forces in Northern Ireland.

23. I have in mind the connection between political and figurative representation that Gayatri Chakravorty Spivak delineates in "Can the Subaltern Speak?" in *Marxism and the Interpretation of Culture*, ed. Lawrence Grossberg and Cary Nelson (Urbana: University of Illinois Press, 1988), 271-313. See especially pp. 276-79.

24. Chrissie McAuley, *Women in a War Zone: Twenty Years of Resistance* (Dublin: Republican News Print, 1989).

25. "Death of a Terrorist," written and produced by William Cran, produced by Stephanie Tepper, *Frontline*, introduction by Judy Woodruff, PBS WGBH, Boston, June 13, 1989. Elizabeth Shannon, *I Am of Ireland: Women of the North Speak Out* (Boston: Little, Brown and Company, 1989). Eileen Fairweather, Roisin McDonough, and Melanie McFaydean, *Only the Rivers Run Free* (London: Pluto Press, 1984).

26. Margaretta D'Arcy, *Tell Them Everything* (London: Pluto Press, 1980). Nell McCafferty, *The Armagh Women* (Dublin: Co-Op Books, 1981).

27. Appetite, a basic bodily drive, was employed by the guards to allow extra time for the search as a special dinner of chicken, chips, and apple pie was served to the women that day. During the dinner, male guards from Long Kesh appeared in the dining hall in riot gear and announced the search. This tactic illustrates one of the many ways that prisoners and guards struggle for control over the body.

28. Shannon, *I Am of Ireland*, 124.
29. From the videotape *The H Block Hunger Strike*.
30. Tim Pat Coogan, *On the Blanket: The H Block Story* (Dublin: Ward River Press, 1980), 118.
31. Shannon, *I Am of Ireland*, 124.
32. McCafferty, *Armagh Women*, 11.
33. Coogan, *On the Blanket*, 215-16.
34. D'Arcy, *Tell Them Everything*, 64.
35. Margaretta D'Arcy, "The Armagh Women," in *Ten on Ten: Memories of the 1981 Hunger Strike* (Dublin: Republican Publications, 1991), 54.
36. Mahasweta Devi, "Draupadi," trans. Gayatri Chakravorty Spivak, in *In Other Worlds: Essays in Cultural Politics*, ed. Gayatri Chakravorty Spivak (New York: Routledge, 1988), 196.
37. Ibid.
38. Coogan, *On the Blanket*, 118.
39. For a detailed account of the history and bases of such dichotomies, see Mary Douglas, *Purity and Danger: An Analysis of the Concepts of Pollution and Taboo* (London: ARK Paperbacks, 1984); and Julia Kristeva, *The Powers of Horror: An Essay in Abjection*, trans. Leon S. Roudiez (New York: Columbia University Press, 1982). For a less anthropological and more historically grounded analysis of dirt and filth within the Irish context, see Cullingford's excellent discussion of the emphasis on excrement in the public debate over Irish sexual identity and censorship current during the 1920s in her chapter on Yeats's "Crazy Jane" poems in *Gender and History*, 227-41.
40. In *Detained: A Writer's Prison Diary* (London: Heinemann Educational Books, 1981), Ngũgĩ wa Thiong'o explains that because the toilet paper in prison is often meant as yet another punishment, it makes an excellent writing surface: "Toilet paper: when in the sixties I first read in Kwame Nkrumah's autobiography, *Ghana*, how he used to hoard toilet paper in his cell at James Fort Prison to write on, I thought it was romantic and a little unreal despite the photographic evidence produced in the book. Writing on toilet paper? Now, I know, paper, just about any paper, is about the most precious article for a political prisoner, more so for one like me, who was in detention because of his writing" (6). For an analysis of Irish republican prisoners' relationship to writing, see Allen Feldman, *Formations of Violence: The Narrative of the Body and Political Terror in Northern Ireland* (Chicago: University of Chicago Press, 1991).
41. McAuley, *Women in a War Zone*, 30-31. One of the ironies of the revocation of political status is that although the British authorities refused to recognize, in an official manner, these prisoners' political affiliations, the prison authorities relied on the way in which the republican prisoners organized themselves in prison (i.e., following the structure of the IRA, as a company with a commanding officer who represented the company in administrative dealings and negotiations with the prison governor) to help run the prison more efficiently.
42. Nell McCafferty, "It Is My Belief that Armagh Is a Feminist Issue," in *The Best of Nell* (Dublin: Attic Press, 1984), 133-35. For a discussion of the historical

development of feminism and its relationship to nationalism, see Carol Coulter, *The Hidden Tradition: Women, Feminism, and Nationalism in Ireland* (Cork, Ireland: Cork University Press, 1993).

43. McCafferty, "It Is My Belief," 133.

44. Ibid.

45. For a more complete discussion of this issue, see Laura Lyons, "At the End of the Day: An Interview with Mairead Keane, National Head of Sinn Fein Women's Department," *boundary 2* 19 (Winter 1992): 260-86. The hunger striker Bobby Sands insists upon the political focus of the prison protests: "But the issue at stake is not 'humanitarian,' nor about better or improved living conditions. It is purely political and only a political solution will solve it." *The Diary of Bobby Sands* (1981; reprint, Dublin: Republican Publications, 1990), 34.

46. McCafferty, *Armagh Women*, 90.

47. Fairweather, McDonough, and McFaydean, *Only the Rivers Run Free*, 262-63.

48. From the videotape *Mother Ireland*. The nationalist question and issues involving republican women still have the potential to split women's coalitions. Two pamphlets from Attic Press's LIP series demonstrate how the Armagh protest acts as a marker around which different feminisms get defined. Edna Longley's excoriation of feminists who supported the republican prisoners in Armagh indicates how vitriolic the debate can become: "While admiring the bonding that tough circumstances beget, and perceiving these circumstances as tragic, I do not accept that either the supportiveness of the ghetto or the essential survival-strategy in Armagh Gaol affords a model for Irish women in general. It remains true that the vast majority of republican women come from republican families— recruited by and for a patriarchal unit. The Irish women's movement, instead of walking away or vaguely empathising, might examine the role of nationalist conditioning in all this: the ideological forces which played a part in sending Mairead Farrell to be shot." "From Cathleen to Anorexia" in *A Dozen Lips* (Dublin: Attic Press, 1994), 182. In the same series, Geraldine Meaney offers this critique: "Edna Longley's denial that it is possible to be both feminist and republican is not only an historical absurdity, it runs the risk of making Irish feminism no more than a middle class movement directed towards equal participation by privileged women in the status quo. Indeed, a feminism which refuses to engage with the hard realities of Ireland can be no more than that. . . . Instead of lecturing republican women on their political and moral failings as women we might pause to listen. Perhaps they could teach us to address those women for whom Mother Ireland is still a powerful enchantment. Perhaps they know better than the academics, writers and pamphleteers how to expose and destroy that enchantment." "Sex and the Nation: Women in Irish Culture and Politics" in *A Dozen Lips*, 195-96. A special issue of *Feminist Review* 50 (Summer 1995) revisits the problematics surrounding Irish feminism and nationalism. My thanks to Karen Steele for providing me with copies of these sources.

49. The referendum was part of the November 25, 1992, general election, called when the coalition government formed by Reynolds disintegrated in late

October. A new coalition of Fianna Fail and Labour was finally formed in early January 1993. Following a scandal over a government appointment late in 1994, Fianna Fail fell from government, and the Labour Party formed a governing partnership with Fine Gael and the Democratic Left. The current Taoiseach is John Bruton of Fine Gael.

50. Quoted from the leaflet *Alliance for Choice*, distributed in Dublin in November 1992.

51. References to these texts will be given parenthetically in this section of the essay. See Ellen MacDonald, *Shoot the Women First* (London: Fourth Estate Press, 1991), for an examination of "guerilla women" in Ireland, Korea, occupied Palestine, Germany, and the Basque region of Spain.

52. Edward Said, "Potentate or Traveler: Academic Freedom in U.S. and Third World Academies," *The Irish Reporter* 2 (Fall 1991): 13.

53. Ibid., 14.

54. As a playwright, D'Arcy would be particularly sensitive to the ways in which the British are capable of censoring materials. In 1971, when she and John Arden chose James Connolly, an Irish socialist and a leader in the 1916 uprising, as the subject of a radio-play commission, the British Broadcasting Company revoked the commission stating that the subject would "inflame passions in Northern Ireland." Liz Curtis, *Ireland: The Propaganda War: The British Media and the "Battle for Hearts and Minds"* (London: Pluto Press, 1984), 212.

55. Harlow, *Barred*, 65.

56. In late May 1992, a Northern Ireland Tourist Board report suggested that "the curiosity factor" with regard to the Troubles should not be overlooked as a drawing card for tourists. Shannon's incident at the checkpoint suggests why that recommendation was widely denounced as irresponsible at the time. The promotion of tourism in a post-ceasefire Northern Ireland was part of the agenda at a conference on the development of trade with Ireland held in Washington, D.C., May 25, 1995, and sponsored by the Clinton administration and the two governments in Ireland.

57. The costs were not always only monetary; D'Arcy reports that the in-laws of the first woman to be jailed used the situation in order to return her children to her ex-husband.

58. In a discussion at the panel "Women and Insurgency" at the Gender and Colonialism conference in Galway, Ireland (May 1992), McClelland expressed her frustration at having discussed with Shannon the political problems facing the six counties for three hours, only to have Shannon focus more closely on her housekeeping abilities. Anne Crilly, director of *Mother Ireland*, suggested in the same discussion that because Derry women are conscious of how a lack of cleanliness might be used to dismiss their political commitments, they are particularly "house proud."

59. Cheryl Herr, "The Erotics of Irishness," *Critical Inquiry* 17 (Autumn 1990): 25.

60. When I asked two women who had been on the protest what they thought of D'Arcy's book, they explained that it accurately described conditions in the

prison, even though they felt that D'Arcy's individualism did not allow her to adequately represent their collective experience. They also generously noted that D'Arcy must have learned a great deal from being in prison on the protest.

61. Said, "Potentate or Traveler," 14.

62. Gayatri Chakravorty Spivak, "French Feminism in an International Frame," *Yale French Studies* 62 (1981): 50.

63. Spivak, "Can the Subaltern Speak?" 308.

64. Carolyn Warmbold, "Women of the Mosquito Press: Louise Bryant, Agnes Smedley, and Margaret Randall as Narrative Guerrillas," Ph.D. diss., University of Texas at Austin, 1990, 6.

65. Martha McClelland, "Celebrating International Women's Day," *The Irish Reporter* 2 (1992): 23.

66. For a critique of the current peace process, see Bernadette Devlin McAliskey's "Wrong Road to Peace," *Red Pepper* (January 1996): 24-25. My thanks to Barbara Harlow for bringing this article to my attention.

FIVE

Reproduction and Malthusian Economics: Fat, Fertility, and Family Planning in George Eliot's *Adam Bede*

Eileen Cleere

Most critics have tended to read the sexual, social, and moral teleology of George Eliot's *Adam Bede* against the perpetual juxtaposition of Hetty Sorrel and Dinah Morris, the principal female protagonists. As exemplified by the foundational work of Sandra Gilbert and Susan Gubar, the ideological program of *Adam Bede* is saliently "dedicated to dramatizing the discrepancy between the antithetical faces of Eve," by providing "subversive evidence that the fallen murderess is inalterably linked to the angelic Madonna."[1] Moreover, any uncomfortable similarities between Hetty and Dinah are summarily neutralized when the murderess is banished and the Madonna becomes the cynosure of a newly emerging nuclear family, a family framed, significantly, by the historical backdrop of *Adam Bede*—the dawn of industrial capitalism. In this way, Eliot's manipulation of female sameness and difference is not limited to seemingly transhistorical categories of "fallenness" and "purity": if Dinah's "purity" becomes a signifier of a particularly middle-class brand of domesticity, the idiom of female difference in *Adam Bede* is fundamentally economic.

It is also the case that differences between and among women in *Adam Bede* are not always played out by the overdetermined pairing of Hetty and Dinah. Within the boundaries of the working-class Poyser family, for example, female difference is an inevitable result of the economic shape of the household, a shape casually exposed by the Poysers' utilitarian motives for adopting their orphaned niece Hetty, and their sanguine views about her potential marriage to Adam Bede:

> Though she and her husband might have viewed the subject differently if Hetty had been a daughter of their own, it was clear that they would have welcomed the match with Adam for a penniless niece. For what could Hetty have been but a servant elsewhere, if her uncle had not taken her in and brought her up as a domestic help to her aunt, whose health since the birth of Totty had not been equal to more positive labour than the superintendence of servants and children?[2]

With this unidealized outline of the social heterogeneity of the Poyser household, the narrator reveals the affective space of the family to be organized around an unarticulated principle of difference between nieces and daughters—a facet of Poyser family life that is easily obscured by the more evident comparisons fostered between Hetty and Dinah. The Poysers' consciousness that Hetty could only have been a "servant elsewhere" lends her position within the family a distinct liminality: as a "penniless niece," Hetty's family title is also her economic title, and if she is not exactly a servant at Hall Farm, the Poysers' home, she is still a "domestic help to her Aunt" rather than one of the children.

In order to read the family romance of *Adam Bede* against the grain of more dominant "nuclear" narratives of development, this chapter takes advantage of recent trends in both historical research and literary criticism. In the wake of Foucault, historical work on the evolution of modern kinship has been increasingly willing to assign the ideology of the "traditional" family to the reign of Freud rather than to Victoria.[3] By enforcing a monolithic site of power in the "law" of the father, the hegemony of what has been generically labeled "patriarchy" works to obscure an entire network of familial power relations which operate in and around the seemingly autocratic nuclear core. Similarly, Eve Kosofsky Sedgwick's recent summons to "Forget the Name of the Father" as well as the deeply laid psychoanalytic consciousness that the phrase immediately and necessarily invokes, has suggested that it might be something more than a matter of semantics to address the differences between daughters and nieces, fathers and uncles, as crucial to our understanding of the social development of the family.[4] From a contemporary perspective, it is important to question any narrative that privileges a nuclear family at the expense of other family types. From a sociocultural angle, moreover, it becomes possible to view the extended family as a site of material changes in nineteenth-century discourses of individualism, productivity, and value.

In *Adam Bede*, the depiction of the extended family under industrial
capitalism is intensified both by the historical period it spans—the transition between the eighteenth and the nineteenth century—and by the way
this narrative of extended family development is mapped out against a
working-class crisis of economic individualism that ostensibly forced a
fledgling middle class into existence. By focusing here on the figure of the
niece, and specifically on the way that this figure is located at the fringes
of the traditional affective family, I argue that Hetty Sorrel's illegitimate
and invisible pregnancy becomes an emblem of both economic and familial crisis in *Adam Bede:* an emblem that registers thematically and metaphorically as a failure of ownership. The text's preoccupation with female
"fat" provides the linchpin between economic concerns and familial
tropes, as the bloated, distended, fat female body perpetually insists upon
comparisons between nieces and daughters, economic production and
female sexual appetite, conspicuous consumption and maternity. The
rhetoric of fat is also central to the final sections of my essay, as I suggest
that a distinctly Malthusian understanding of population, production,
and labor interpolates *Adam Bede*, filtering the text's economic discourse
through a mathematical (and misogynous) understanding of sex and marriage, and repeated images of fertility that are finally, inevitably barren.[5]

FAMILY ECONOMIES

Of course, in privileging what may be called an avuncular model over a
paternal paradigm, and in telling a story of nieces rather than a story of
daughters, Eliot's novel disrupts an idiom that Catherine Gallagher has
identified as nearly ubiquitous to novels of industrial development: the
rhetorical program of social paternalism; and the "tropes of reconciliation" between parent and child that provide the closing tableaux for
novels ranging from Elizabeth Cleghorn Gaskell's *Mary Barton* to Benja-
min Disraeli's *Sybil.*[6] Arthur Helps's *The Claims of Labour* was probably
the most influential doctrine of paternalist philosophy written in the
1840s, and its thesis that "the parental relation will be found the best
model on which to form the duties of the employer to the employed"
found a receptive audience among social philanthropists, novelists, and a
segment of society that J. S. Mill snidely identified as "the more favored
classes."[7] In Mill's opinion, the affective metaphor of paternity obscured
the fact that any relationship between employer and employed cannot

exist without "a countervailing element, absolute power, or something approaching to it, in those who are bound to afford this support, over those entitled to receive it."[8] Furthermore, Mill pointed out that it would be ultimately impossible for modern industrial society to disguise its economic objectives and fend off a revolution of the class system with the antiquated "claims of labour": "The age that produces railroads ... is not an age in which a man can feel loyal and dutiful to another because he has been born on his estate."[9]

In *Adam Bede*, class rivalry between owners and workers is neatly rescripted as sexual rivalry between Arthur Donnithorne and Adam, with Hetty Sorrel serving as the index and icon of both brands of exploitation. Rather than reifying the social paternalist project with a hyperaffective tableau of "reconciliation," Eliot brings Arthur and Adam to blows over Hetty in order to diminish the class difference that informs their connection: Adam's patience and subservience only give way because he has decided that "in this thing we're man and man" (354) rather than owner and worker. While Margaret Homans has pointed out that Adam's egalitarian epiphany privileges "shared gender" over "class difference," it is crucial to recognize that gender sameness is only allowed to transcend class rivalry when both Arthur and Adam share a desire for Hetty Sorrel.[10] If the alienation of capital is an intangible, vague concept for Adam and the other precapitalist inhabitants of Hayslope, the alienation of women is the condition under which economic power is visible and recognizable: the site at which the paternalist metaphor begins to erode. Deliberately confusing the linearity of the paternal bond through such devices as the "coming-of-age" party for the young Squire and Arthur's memories of learning carpentry—the Bede family trade—from working-class Adam, Eliot drives home the fact that paternalism is an inadequate recipe for making sense of social and economic inequities.

Furthermore, by perpetually denying an affective parent-child relationship thematic centrality in *Adam Bede*, and by rescripting the normatively affective space of the family as an economic network regulated by the principles of production and consumption, Eliot problematizes the paternalist notion that bonds of sympathy and understanding should "naturally" transcend both the economic rivalry between classes and the material conditions of family life. As we will see, tensions between production and consumption, supply and demand, will infect even the expected sanctity of the mother-child bond, in that Hetty's act of infanticide is pointedly described as an assertion of economic autonomy: a choice to nourish her own body at the expense of her child's. Likewise, Adam's perpetual struggle to make up for the loss of income caused by his father's slack work habits and alcoholism makes it impossible for him achieve economic independence or even marry until Thias Bede accidentally drowns on his way home from the pub.

Although Adam's problems with his father are conveniently swept away in the early pages of the novel, it is repeatedly made clear that even the most affective sites of family interaction in *Adam Bede* are rhetorically marked by more material claims of paternity. For example, Adam's adult dealings with his father are painfully contrasted with his happier memories of a vibrant, productive man and by the way his childhood identity was entirely constituted by being known as "Thias Bede's lad" (92). Given the fact that other families in the Hayslope community are attracted to similar modes of identification, and that two female cousins who share the name of Bess are distinguished from each other by the names of their respective fathers (either "Chad's Bess" or "Timothy's Bess"), it is quite evident that this language of ownership translates the law of the father into a linguistic dominion, one that confers identity as it simultaneously circumscribes individuality. These patronymic chains even extend to Timothy's grandson, who goes by the "notorious" name of "Timothy's Bess's Ben" (65). Such paternal "narcissism," as explained by Luce Irigaray, is the benchmark of patriarchal authority: "Commodities [that] share in the cult of the father, . . . never stop striving to resemble, to copy, the one who is his representative."[11]

Yet it is also the case that the idiom of ownership in the working-class community of *Adam Bede* is perpetually deflected from the commercial sphere where possession is impossible to discursive signs of paternity. Even the more gentile domestic interiors of *Adam Bede*, spaces that are far removed from working-class occupations and concerns, assert the claims of paternity through a discourse of commodification and possession. The "handsome, generous-blooded clergyman, the Rev. Adolphous Irwine" (111) is introduced under the unfortunate status of perpetual bachelor: a man who would have lived a very different sort of life if he had not the heavy financial responsibility of a widowed mother and two spinster sisters, and "would have had tall sons and blooming daughters—such possessions, in short, as men commonly think will repay them for all the labour they take under the sun" (111). With sons and daughters figured as units of value that reward both paternal "labour" and the failure to possess within the commercial sphere, the previously addressed distinction between daughters and nieces will begin to take shape over the discourse of commodification.

Avuncular patronage is radically different from paternal possession in *Adam Bede*, and measures female value by the principles of utility rather than the compensatory pride of ownership, or to use Irigaray's term, "accumulation." This double standard resembles what Irigaray has recognized as a "schism" in the women-as-commodities system that is the bedrock of capitalist patriarchy, a system that determines wealth on the basis of accumulation rather than use-value: "Women-as-commodities are thus subject to a schism that divides them into the categories of usefulness and exchange value; into matter-body and an envelope that is precious but impenetrable, ungraspable, and not susceptible to appropriation by women themselves; into private use and social use."[12] While "private use" implies both the hidden domestic labor of women and their ability to reproduce and social use denotes exchange value, Irigaray attributes both brands of female utility to the symbolic system represented by the name of the father.[13] The smooth operation of this social order depends upon women's transition from usefulness to exchange, a "passage that never takes place simply" in Irigaray's opinion.[14]

In the case of *Adam Bede*, the circulation of women is threatened by the fact that nieces are not authorized by the name of the father—not appropriated by the idiom of paternal possession—and cannot be seamlessly accumulated for circulation within the social order. While it is evident that the set of cousins who share the same name are meant to mirror a more central pair of female cousins (the modest maternity of one "Bess" significantly contrasted with the easy virtue, gaudy dress and large earrings of the other), it is also clear that the name of the father is the immediate factor separating Dinah and Hetty from their counterparts. While we know very little about Dinah's parentage, we do learn that Hetty's father, "that good-for-naught" Sorrel, married Hetty's mother against the wishes of her family, the Poyser clan, and soon brought his own household to financial ruin (383). Hetty's paternal heritage is a history of economic distress, of failed accumulation, and her body itself is tainted by the fact that she has "Sorrel's blood in her veins" (383). Given that Hetty's body circulates the faulty authority of the father, it seems inevitable that it should eventually become—as it does—both an icon of paternal failures and an index of paternalistic exploitations. Uncle Poyser's attempt to use his niece and accumulate her, too—to retain the utility of Hetty's private labor while placing her within the social economy of exchange—will fail because Hetty's "labor" is, in fact, like his own: always already possessed by the Donnithornes.

Just as Hetty's paternal heritage is economic failure, her maternal heritage is a form of bodily crisis associated with *reproductive* failure. Old Mr. Poyser complains that Hetty's mother married "a feller wi' on'y two head o' stock when there should ha' been ten on's farm," and died "o' th' inflammation afore she war thirty" (383). As I will be taking up the issue of Malthusian economics later in the chapter, it is important to note here that the undoing of the Sorrels is blamed not only on a failure to economize but on a disregard of arithmetic: a failure to recognize the material difference between two and ten. Yet as the subject will soon turn toward the place of reproduction within a labor theory of value, I want to point out that the effects of the Sorrels' economic crisis descend to Hetty paternally through a diseased circulatory system, and maternally through "inflammation." The mysterious "inflammation" which killed Hetty's mother is the same illness that now inhibits Mrs. Poyser's ability to labor (120), and although the precise nature of the disease is vague, Mr. Poyser localizes his wife's discomfort by referring to the habitual "pain in thy side" (192). In this way, "inflammation" is coded as a trauma to the reproductive capacity of the female body: a malignant swelling that displaces other, procreative outgrowths. This illness not only links Mrs. Poyser's nonproductive body with her deceased sister-in-law's, it identifies "inflammation" as part of Hetty's maternal heritage. Hetty's circulation may be tainted by her father's bad blood but as old Mr. Poyser ominously notes, she also "takes arter her mother" (383).

FARMING ECONOMIES

The way that Hetty's problematic body becomes a resonant metaphor for the circulatory difficulties endemic to the Poysers' tenure on the bountiful Hall Farm can be clarified by an interrogation of the socioeconomic status of tenant farmers in the late eighteenth and early nineteenth century. F. M. L. Thompson's analysis of landownership and economic growth in eighteenth-century England, for example, identifies most turn-of-the-century tenant farmers as "middling consumers—exactly on a par in income terms with the lesser clergy and dissenting ministers, slightly more affluent than innkeepers, slightly less well off than naval and military officers, or shopkeepers."[15] This carefully qualified economic scale allows Thompson to suggest that "without committing ourselves to the view that the farmers did form one-third of the middle class, we may still hold that very many farmers were indeed in that social and economic category."[16] As tentative as Thompson's definition of "middle class" may seem, it does seem to reflect certain aspects of *Adam Bede*'s preindustrial world. While the class system in Hayslope is flexible enough to dispense with any "rigid demarcation of rank between the farmer and the respectable artisan" (142), Mr. Poyser's "latent sense of capital and of weight in parish affairs" (142) is associated with a newly developing but still dormant middle-class identity; a feeling of self-importance conferred by economic accumulation that effectively separates penniless nieces from portioned daughters within the boundaries of his own family.

Yet while the socioeconomic position of farmers such as Mr. Poyser may be loosely termed middle-class, it is important to recognize that "there was no statutory control of the relations between tenant and landlord" until the Agricultural Holdings Act was passed in 1875.[17] Throughout the eighteenth and for most of the nineteenth century, therefore, relations between landowner and tenant were governed by a vague set of customary laws that presumed landlords would be motivated by a paternalistic sense of social duty in all dealings with their tenantry. According to J. V. Beckett, "by 1750, a rough division already existed whereby the owner undertook to provide fixed capital, and the tenant the working capital . . . the landlord's capital consisted of the land, the farm buildings, fences, hedges, gates, access roads, drainage works and river and sea defences, all of which required an annual outlay on the maintenance."[18]

An 1880 pamphlet directed "To the Tenant Farmers of Great Britain" thus describes the "ideal" landlord/tenant relationship as depending entirely upon the landlord's good will:

The ideal of the English system of large proprietors and of tenants hiring the land they farm instead of owning it, is where the landlord, being a capitalist, is able to relieve the tenant of all expenditure of a permanent character, and to leave him the full employment of his capital in his trade of farming, in stocking and cultivating the land . . . if these functions are performed by the landlord; if he has the capital and does what is recognized as a duty, nothing can be better from an economic point of view than the... relationship of Landlord, Tenant, and Labourer.[19]

Understandably, by the time Eliot published *Adam Bede* in 1859, the question of "tenant right" had a long and contentious history, and the difference between an improving and unimproving landowner was tantamount to a farmer's economic prosperity. Despite some middle-class pretensions, tenant farmers had little ready capital at any given time to enact their own improvements, and as nineteenth-century agriculturist James Caird explained, "unlike that of the landowners, much of it is in daily use, circulating among tradesmen and labourers."[20] As we know from Mrs. Poyser, Squire Donnithorne is no improver, and his tenant's requests for repairs and innovations have been perpetually ignored: "my husband's been asking and asking till he's tired, and to think o' what he's done for the farm, and he's never had a penny allowed him, be the times bad or good" (126). Not only has the Squire denied the Poysers their customary tenant rights, he has forced Mr. Poyser to put his relatively scarce capital into the enrichment of land that he does not actually own, without any legal right to compensation for the long-term improvements he may effect.

Tenant's compensation was at the crux of nineteenth-century agricultural controversy, especially in cases where short-term leases were insisted upon by landlords. In his 1850-51 analysis of English farming systems, Caird observed that since "the investment of a tenant's capital in land seldom contemplates an immediate return ... an improving tenant has no legal security for the capital he invests in the cultivation of another's land."[21] Similarly, in 1848 tenant-farmer Charles Higby Lattimore claimed he had been evicted from his farm because he voted against his landlord's interests in a local election and consequently appealed to the law for compensation for the "unexhausted" improvements he had effected at the coincidentally named Bride Hall Farm. Lattimore writes:

With extreme reluctance, but animated by the conviction of public duty to my brother farmers, I was compelled to test the law in order to ascertain (what I had ever doubted) whether there is any *legal recognition* of the floating capital of a tenant-farmer sunk in the soil, or expended upon the premises of another person ... the result proved to be that an agreement—good in law, if applied to commercial or trading matters—was not available to a tenant-farmer against a landlord ... no such phrase legally exists as *tenant-farmer's capital.*[22]

Under Caird's and Lattimore's analysis of "Tenant Right," the ambiguous "latency" of Martin Poyser's capital takes on a very tangible nineteenth-century commercial significance. Without any legally recognized capital, Mr. Poyser isn't really a capitalist, and his apparent wealth in property is as illusory as his blooming abundance of nieces. Although the Poysers have cultivated the Hall Farm for generations, it seems that they renew their lease with Squire Donnithorne every three years (393): a period of time too short for a tenant to reap the benefits of long-term improvements, especially in light of the perpetual threat that the Squire will choose to terminate their occupancy.[23] Moreover, as Mrs. Poyser will declare when Squire Donnithorne actually does menace them with imminent eviction,

I should like to see if there's another tenant besides Poyser as 'ud put up wi' never having a bit o' repairs done till a place tumbles down—and not then, on'y wi' begging and praying and having to pay half—and being strung up wi' the rent as it's much if he gets enough out of the land to pay, for all he's put his own money into the ground beforehand. (394)

If the Poysers' capital is figuratively latent because it is unrecognized by law, it is also literally latent because it is always either buried in the soil or perpetually circulating in the form of seed money, stock, and laborer's wages.

Interestingly, Mrs. Poyser's understanding of farming is actually more canny than her husband's and reveals the false prosperity and hand-to-mouth nature of tenantry: "As fur farming, it's putting money into your pocket wi' your right hand and fetching it out wi' your left. As fur as I can see, it's raising victuals for other folks, and just getting a mouthful for yourself and your children as you go along" (125). While Lattimore's plea for legal compensation aligned him with his "brother" tenant farmers over his paternalist landlord, Mrs. Poyser's economic perspective on tenantry is articulated in the familial idiom of parents and children. Tenant farming, in Mrs. Poyser's representation, is a process by which parents are forced to privilege the economic imperative to feed other people over the affective responsibility of nourishing their own family. Many agricultural writers throughout the nineteenth century similarly viewed the controversy over tenant right as a social conflict between the "real" family and the meta-phoric family: a choice between a paternalist's duty to his workers and a father's responsibility to his children. I. S. Leadam, for example, insisted that the English custom of primogeniture prevented any landowner from being as financially supportive of his tenantry as he might have been under different circumstances: "The landlords of this country cannot provide the needful capital because they are not the real owners, they enjoy a life-interest on the estate which with or without their will, goes upon their death to their eldest sons. The less capital, therefore, that they expend upon the land the more they have for their younger children, who are also provided for by charges out of the estate.[24]

Likewise, Caird insists that the customary rights accorded to tenants will not protect a farmer from the fact that an eldest "son does not always inherit the virtues of his father."[25] A breakdown in the affective connection between a landowning father and son, in other words, could produce subsequent breakdowns in the affective philosophy of social paternalism. On the tenant side of the family spectrum, moreover, a farmer who failed to stand up for tenant right was a bad father, who allowed the economic future of his own children be sacrificed for the prosperity of his landlord's heirs. Lattimore, for example, hopes that the moral of own his story will direct tenant farmers to consider

the insecure position in which they must leave their children under the present law—a circumstance of peculiar interest to every good man at the close of his life. I can never forget that my father assured me upon his deathbed, in 1834, the last time I ever conversed with him, that the only earthly anxiety he felt at that time was his regret for my exposure to the possible consequences of my occupation of this farm, under the thralls of the owner and his agents.[26]

According to mid-century agriculturists, the economic tensions between the "real" family and the social family finally could not be elided by the affective rhetoric of paternalism: in a world mediated by supply and demand rather than by custom or tradition, "the relation is and must become one of business, and not merely of mutual confidence."[27]

Mrs. Poyser is certainly able to detect the incompatible economic claims of the literal family and the social family, and she recognizes that tenantry puts too much Poyser labor into circulation outside of the family, feeding bodies other than Poyser bodies, and nourishing children other than Poyser children. Unfortunately, however, she cannot notice her niece's body as the weakest link in the family cycle of labor and nourishment, the site at which Poyser "victuals" are most egregiously appropriated to nourish non-Poyser bodies. The question of who is producing and who is consuming is central to an economic understanding of the working-class household, as Wally Seccombe's recently published *A Millennium of Family Change* makes clear. By viewing maternity as a form of economic production (as the *literal* reproduction of labor power), Sec-

REPRODUCTION AND MALTHUSIAN ECONOMICS

combe is able to envision the household not as an affective space but as a tenuously balanced network of producers and consumers: adults capable of productive labor, and members such as children and aged people unable to contribute to their own subsistence.[28] Seccombe explains:

> The lifespan pattern of productive capacity is roughly in symmetry with the maturation of procreative capacity as well. The middle generation commands both elements of labour-power, while children and the aged are incapable of sustaining either of the two basic conditions of life. It is therefore necessary for every class of adult producers to generate continuously a "subsistence surplus" (in addition to any surplus which may be extracted from non-productive classes) in order to reproduce itself from one generation to the next.[29]

In this Malthusian understanding of the history of family development, the "middle generation" of productive adults is the linchpin of economic stability in the working-class household and must be periodically stabilized either through the limitation of births or the inclusion of extra adult members to bridge the gap between familial consumption and production. For Seccombe, this horizontal expansion of the working-class family is indicative of new and powerful ideologies of work, production, and especially, of reproduction.[30]

In the context of *Adam Bede*, of course, it is this last term that is the most provocative, as Hetty Sorrel's illegitimate pregnancy is arguably the focus of the novel. Yet even before Hetty's seduction, the production of children as a form of economic production is suggested by the figure of Mrs. Poyser, whose last experience of childbirth, as we remember from the opening quotation, has rendered her permanently unfit for "more positive labour." Registering in both the idiom of domestic work and childbirth, Mrs. Poyser's inability to "labour" must be compensated by the addition of what Seccombe terms "middle-generation" family members: productive bodies to make up for the "subsistence goods" Mrs. Poyser is now unable to supply, as well as for the absence of future sons and daughters. This ratio of consumers to producers in the Poyser family is repeatedly thematized by the parodies of labor enacted by Mr. Poyser's elderly father: for example, his "job" of holding the farmyard gate open for his family as they set off for church, "pleased to do his bit of work; for, like all old men whose life has been spent in labour, he liked to feel that he was still useful" (233).

At the other end of the generational spectrum are the mischievous and sometimes destructive antics of the Poysers' young children, especially three year-old Totty. In her more quiet moments, Totty parodies the domestic labor of the busy household by "arduously clutching the handle of a miniature iron with her tiny fat fist" (120) and demanding that her harried mother participate in the farce by warming the toy in the fire. Yet, Totty's playful mimicry soon erodes the positive effects of her mother's labor, as she takes advantage of "her momentary leisure, to put her fingers into a bowl of starch, and drag it down, so as to empty the contents with tolerable completeness on to the ironing sheet" (120). In light of Totty's unhelpful participation in the rites of domestic work, it is clear that adult nieces are actually more *economical* family additions than daughters. Dinah and Hetty, with their contributions of real work, are necessary components of productivity at Hall Farm; this is especially true of Hetty, who resides with the Poysers on a full-time basis and is solely responsible for the making of butter in Mrs. Poyser's large and well-respected dairy. Nevertheless, the Poysers' narcissistic investment in their own daughter "blurs the seriousness of utility," making labor less valuable than exchange, and nieces less valuable than daughters.[31] Under a capitalist regime, in other words, "wealth amounts to a subordination of the use of things to their accumulation" (174). Uneconomical accumulation, furthermore, is like "inflammation" and will register directly upon Hetty's body.

BODILY ECONOMIES

Although I earlier introduced the problem of economic autonomy as an important factor in the social organization of the family, it is also clear that the economic awkwardness of tenantry within *Adam Bede*—a text that negotiates identity through the trope of possession—is first encountered as a bodily awkwardness. In the opening paragraphs of the second chapter, the reader is confronted with the oddly bifurcated body of Mr. Casson, caretaker of the Donnithorne Arms Inn:

On a front view it appeared to consist principally of two spheres, bearing about the same relation to each other as the earth and the moon: that is to say, the lower sphere might be said, at a rough guess, to be about thirteen times larger than the upper, which naturally performed the function of a mere satellite and tributary. But here the resemblance ceased, for Mr. Casson's head was not at all a melancholy-looking satellite, nor was it a "spotty globe," as Milton has irreverently called the moon; on the contrary, no head and face could look more sleek and healthy, and its expression . . . was one of jolly contentment, only tempered by that sense of personal dignity which usually made itself felt in his attitude and bearing. This sense of dignity could hardly be considered excessive in a man who had been butler to the family for fifteen years, and who, in his present high position, was necessarily very much in contact with his inferiors. (59)

Mr. Casson is the reader's first perspective on the Hayslope commercial community and on the socioeconomic conditions which divide farmers from artisans and pub owners from the gentry. If Mr. Casson's past occupation as "butler to the family," the Donnithorne family, has given him an air of social superiority, his present occupation as innkeeper to the family now separates him from his customers, places him in a liminal economic position linked to Mr. Poyser's through the idiom of tenantry. As a tenant, Mr. Casson can participate in the enterprise of capitalism, leasing the Donnithorne Arms and the "pretty take" of land attached to it (58). His capital itself, however, is like Mr. Poyser's "latent" capital: unable to circulate within the larger economy because it is always already possessed by the Donnithornes. The two engorged "spheres" that constitute the innkeeper's physical person are part of the thematic representation of this economic latency, as they suggest an innate failure of the whole to possess its disparate parts. Furthermore, as Eve Kosofsky Sedgwick has recognized in her work on *Our Mutual Friend*, this kind of bodily disruption is a metaphor for economic crisis: "the illusion of economic individualism."[32]

Sedgwick's argument implies that the generic bodily icon of struggling bourgeois independence is male, and posits bodily metaphors of digestion and anality as signifiers of the failure to "possess." However, Mr. Casson's disembodied head and swollen gut merely introduce an economy of the body into *Adam Bede* that will eventually be grafted upon its representation of Hetty Sorrel, a reinscription that ultimately suggests that the female body enacts a similar crisis of ownership when it is unable to register the signs of its own pregnancy. The novel's two famous mirror scenes provide a telling map of Hetty's body, both before and after she is pregnant, as her disfigured and disfiguring bedroom mirror is "fixed in an upright position, so that she could get only one good view of her neck and arms" (194). Likewise, the small, hanging mirror she removes from Dinah's room "would show her nothing beneath her little chin, and that beautiful bit of neck where the roundness of her cheek melted into another roundness shadowed by dark delicate curls" (294). Just as neither

of Hetty's mirrors will reflect her lower body, neither the Poyser family
nor the Hayslope community are able to see Hetty in relation to her
corporeality; like the broken mirror, they are "fixed in an upright position" and refuse to reconcile the much-admired "roundness" of Hetty's
head, neck, and arms with the other, more disturbing "roundness" of her
emerging middle.

Hetty's invisible pregnancy has been widely commented upon by scholars of the Victorian novel: for example, Helena Michie suggests that
Hetty's "fleshy" body is unreadable because it belies physiognomy, and
finally is unassimilable with her kittenish looks and flower-like delicacy.[33]
However, it is also the case that Hetty's distended middle belies the
economic autonomy of her class status, as her very "fleshiness" is a mark
of the economic exploitation that infects the Poyser family's commercial
position within the Hayslope community, and especially in relation to the
Donnithornes. Other critics have allowed Hetty's extreme egoism and
vanity to deflect from the strangeness of the mirror scenes in *Adam Bede*:
John Kucich, in fact, describes Hetty as psychically "driven to imagine
herself as she wants others to see her."[34] Hetty's lack of bodily integrity,
however, is not a simple inscription of her vanity but rather a portrait of
an already vague sense of subjectivity unravelling under the mutually
reinforcing ideologies of class and gender that began to shape social
identity in the late eighteenth century. As noted by Leonore Davidoff,

the same forces which produced a world view dividing the society between masculine and feminine, working class and middle (upper) class, urban and rural, also
separated physicality, e.g., bodily functions in general and sexuality in particular,
from the public gaze. This is an example of the privatization we have come to
associate with the development of industrial capitalism and was part of a changing
view of men's and women's positions in the cosmos and of their relation to
Nature.[35]

Although Davidoff's argument has been criticized for suggesting that
precapitalist notions of the body were uninformed by any distinction
between public and private, it is important to register the way that the
social body was organicized, naturalized by an image of the literal body:
"The adult middle class (or aristocratic) man, representing the governing
or ruling group, was seen as the Head. . . . The Hands were unthinking,
unfeeling "doers" without characteristics of sex, age, or other identity. . . .
Middle-class women represented the emotions, the Heart, or sometimes
the Soul, seat of morality and tenderness."[36] The unmentionable regions

of the body were, of course, rounded out by the social outcasts: prostitutes, criminals, and other brands of poor who were finally as unnarratable or invisible as those body functions normatively concealed from the "public gaze."

With this social mapping of the body in mind, Hetty's bisected form becomes an assortment of gendered, class-inflected parts organized around the principles of private and public. If her buttermaking links her literal hands with the "doers" of the social body, and her beautiful head and neck function as false barometers of her "Soul," her unrepresentable lower body, with its mysteriously developing roundness, marks her as a social criminal by betraying her sexual capacities. Read along the axis of gender, Hetty's body literalizes the popular Victorian myth of women's lack of conscious sexual desire or bodily curiosity and serves as a corporeal emblem of the stereotypical female failure to integrate the various uses of the body into an organic whole. If the potential for male exploitation of women's schooled ignorance is not made abundantly clear by Hetty's seduction, it brutally reverberates at the end of the novel when Tommy Poyser is seen "amusing himself" with his sister's legless doll, "turning Dolly's skirt over her bald head, and exhibiting her truncated body to the general scorn" (522). Read along class lines, however, Hetty's failure to integrate her body links her with Mr. Casson's tenantry, and translates her bodily failure into a problem of ownership: a failure to possess the fruits of labor. Similarly, because Hetty is seduced by Arthur Donnithorne, her sexual exploitation is rewritten as an economic exploitation: just as the baby that no one is willing to "see" is Arthur's illegitimate child, the unacknowledged Donnithorne heir, the bountiful farm on which the Poysers' labor is owned and controlled by Arthur's grandfather the Squire.

Although the problems with metaphorizing political economy have been widely discussed, reading Hetty's bodily metamorphoses in terms of commercial oscillation is imperative in light of a specifically Victorian tendency to use the female body as an economic icon. Susan Walsh dubs this gender-specific representation of financial crisis "climacteric economy," explaining that "Women's bodies, as advertisements, medical handbooks, and health manuals made clear, were the human bodies most agitated by cyclical 'crises.' "[37] Although Walsh's argument primarily focuses on the way that an image of the elderly female body was used textually and pictorially "as a potent analogue for economic as well as reproductive 'bankruptcy,' " she insists that medical discourse surrounding the health and well-being of the female body at any stage of development provided a plethora of metaphors for representing economic instability.[38] "In nineteenth-century parlance . . . the 'obstruction,' 'constriction,' or 'depression' of an 'ill-regulated circulation' in women meant more than digestive or circulatory arrest: these terms were code words for stopped menses, whether the result of delayed menarche, pregnancy, menopause, or a general overine-uterine 'derangement.' "[39] Walsh uses a series of *Punch* cartoons featuring the Old Lady of Threadneedle Street in order to drive home this point: they uniformly depict an ancient woman with a ballooning bottom-half as a comic metaphor for the Bank of England. If these bifurcated female images remind us immediately of Mr. Casson and his engorged lower sphere, they should remind us eventually of Hetty, and of the way Hetty's own "stopped menses" provide a resonant metaphor for the "ill-regulated circulation" of her uncle's tenant-capital.[40]

FERTILITY, FATNESS, AND THE FAMILY:
MALTHUSIAN PERSPECTIVES

At first glance, Hall Farm seems to be a place of infinite productivity and fertile richness; in fact, many critics have pointed out the edenic nature of this garden where Adam will find first the wrong, and finally the right Eve.[41] Yet, closer inspection of the metaphors of plenty and fecundity reveal the seeds of degeneration and decay: not only was the Hall Farm once the Hall, the place where the local gentry lived, but "one might fancy the house in the early stages of a chancery suit, and that the fruit from the grand double row of walnut trees on the right hand of the enclosure would fall and rot among the grass" (115). Although Hall Farm is filled to capacity with milch cows and hens, and Mrs. Poyser's dairy makes the finest butter and cheese in Hayslope, the once "well-tended kitchen-garden of a manor house" is now littered with "unpruned fruit trees, and kitchen vegetables growing together in careless, half-neglected abundance," flowers that are "large and disorderly for want of trimming," and "a huge apple tree making a barren circle under its low-spreading boughs" (263-64). This ominous "barren circle" seems to plant potential scarcity at the root of economic plenty, despite the narrator's disarming, disingenuous dismissal: "what signified a barren patch or two? The garden was so large" (264).

Thomas Robert Malthus's *First Essay on Population* was published in 1798, a year before Hetty Sorrel's crisis in family planning is played out against the historical backdrop of *Adam Bede*. Written in the wake of the French Revolution, at a time when the issue of society's "perfectibility" was a central economic and philosophical concern, Malthus's essay dispels the more utopian scenarios of social improvement put forth by such theorists as Condorcet and William Godwin by insisting that certain laws of necessity inevitably regulate the progress of mankind.[42] The most famous of Malthus's "laws" is the one that reflects the codes of production and consumption in *Adam Bede* and explains the inevitable decay that is shrouded within the deceptive richness and ripeness of Hall Farm:

Population, when unchecked, increases in a geometrical ratio. Subsistence increases only in an arithmetical ratio. A slight acquaintance with the numbers will shew the immensity of the first power in comparison with the second.

By that law of nature which makes food necessary to the life of man, the effects of these two unequal powers must be kept equal. This implies a strong and constantly operating check on population from the difficulty of subsistence. This difficulty must fall some where; and must necessarily by severely felt by a large portion of mankind.

Through the animal and vegetable kingdoms, nature has scattered the seeds of life abroad with the most profuse and liberal hand. She has been comparatively sparing in the room, and the nourishment necessary to rear them. The germs of existence contained in this spot of earth, with ample food, and ample room to expand in, would fill millions of worlds in the course of a few thousand years. Necessity, that imperious all-pervading law of nature, restrains them within the prescribed bounds. The race of plants, and the race of animals shrink under this great restrictive law. And the race of man cannot, by any efforts of reason, escape from it. Among plants and animals its effects are waste of seed, sickness and premature death. Among mankind, misery and vice.[43]

In Malthusian rhetoric, therefore, the barrenness implicit in fertility is an economic and mathematical given, as an economy of plenty, a period of uninterrupted production and uncircumscribed reproduction, will eventually give way to an economy of scarcity: a time when the production of food cannot keep up with the increase in population.[44] By associating fertility with social distress instead of prosperity, Malthus's brand of political economy, according to Catherine Gallagher, "occluded the possibility of using the healthy body to signify the healthy society."[45] Instead, the healthy reproductive body loses, "in the very power of its fecundity, the integrity of its boundaries, and hence comes to be a sign of its opposite.

The blooming body is only a body about to divide into two feebler bodies that are always on the verge of becoming starving bodies. Hence, no state of health can be socially reassuring."[46]

Within the context of *Adam Bede*, the blooming body that becomes a Malthusian precursor of social decay is of course Hetty Sorrel: the health of her body measures not economic prosperity but the potential enfeeble-ment of uncontrolled reproduction. But Eliot's economic metaphors also allow us to interpret the *family* body as an index of commercial distress, and to read the hyperbolic prosperity of the Poysers as the harbinger of future atrophy. If the flexibility and amorphousness of the Poyser family, its seemingly benevolent ability to incorporate two orphaned nieces, reg-isters at one time as a sign of affective health, its lack of integrity as a unit will eventually become "a sign of its opposite." While paying lip service to the affective ideologies of the paternal family, the avuncular family mistakes fat for fertility, fertility for prosperity, and economic expediency for family sentiment. Obsessed with one side of the Malthusian drama—the production and consumption of food—the Poysers finally cannot keep up with the mathematical teleology of the population principle.

Food is increasing at such a rate at Hall Farm that it becomes more and more difficult for the Poyser family to monitor its various sites of productivity, and Malthus's image of the "profuse and liberal hand" of nature resurfaces in the way that the corn itself is "ripe enough to be blown out of the husk and scattered as untimely seed" (337). Moreover, the corn is not the only bearer of "untimely seed" in Hayslope, and the empty circle concealed by the apple tree's profusion of leaves, blossoms and fruit is not the only source of potential barrenness within the fecun-dity and verdure of Hall Farm. The narrator reminds us of what exagger-ated sites of fertility so often conceal, "an image of great agony—the agony of the cross" (409):

If there came a traveller to this world who knew nothing of the story of man's life upon it, this image of agony would seem to him strangely out of place in the midst of this joyous nature. He would not know that hidden behind the apple blossoms, or among the golden corn, or under the shrouding boughs of the wood, there might be a human heart beating heavily with anguish: perhaps a young blooming girl, not knowing where to turn for refuge from swift-advancing shame ... such things are sometimes hidden among the sunny fields and behind the blossoming orchards; and the sound of the gurgling brook, if you came close to one spot behind a small bush, would be mingled for your ear with a despairing human sob. (409-10)

This image of illegitimate reproduction at the mainsprings of economic plenty links the blooming Hetty with the rapid overgrowth at Hall Farm and with the Malthusian laws that circumscribe both brands of production. From the overripe cornfields, to the "half-neglected" kitchen garden, to their niece's unregulated sexuality, the Poyser family, for all its adherence to the principles of domestic economy, is finally unable to police its own fertility, to control the productivity of its various parts.

On the one hand, it seems uncharacteristic for Mrs. Poyser to be negligent about the state of overripeness on the farm and in her dairy: if she is aware of the exact moment that the currants in the garden need to be picked, she is also perpetually poised to nip her servants' burgeoning sexuality in the bud. All expressions of desire on the part of her housemaid, for example, are immediately translated into sexual desire, as Molly's seemingly innocent request to sit down to her spinning "according to Mrs. Poyser, shrouded a secret indulgence of unbecoming wishes which she now dragged forth and held up to Molly's view with cutting eloquence":

> Spinning, indeed! It isn't spinning as you'd be at, I'll be bound, and let you have your own way. I never knew your equal for gallowsness. To think of a gell o' your age wanting to go and sit with half-a-dozen men! . . . That's the way with you—that's the road you'd all like to go, headlong to ruin. You're never easy till you've got some sweetheart as is as big a fool as yourself; and you'll be finely off when you're married, I daresay, and have got a three-legged stool to sit on, and never a blanket to cover you, and a bit o' oatcake for your dinner, as three children are a-snatching at. (118-19)

Yet while Mrs. Poyser vigilantly polices her servants' bodies and their sexuality, she fails to discern that her niece also participates in the sexual economy of Hall Farm and shares the capacity for "labour" with the housemaid. What is more, Arthur Donnithorne does not constitute a sexual threat that Mrs. Poyser can recognize. To the Poysers, their future landlord signifies the potential for economic improvement rather than exploitation, and while they fiercely guard their farmyard from the "loiterers" and transient laborers who may lead their young female servants astray, Arthur, in the role of benevolent paternalist, is allowed to enter at will.

Ironically, the tenants of Hayslope are not the only people convinced of Arthur Donnithorne's potential largesse as a landlord. Arthur views himself as the antithesis of his grandfather, a potential improver of property who busily studies agricultural writers in preparation for his succession to the estate. In conversation with Reverend Irwine, Arthur eagerly describes his future plans:

I've been reading your friend Arthur Young's books lately, and there's nothing I should like better than to carry out some of his ideas in putting the farmers on a better management of their land; and, as he says, making what was a wild country, all of the same dark hue, bright and variegated with corn and cattle. My grandfather will never let me have any power while he lives; but there's nothing I should like better to do than to undertake the Stonyshire side of the estate—it's in a dismal condition—and set improvements on foot, and gallop about from one place to another and overlook them. I should like to know all the labourers, and see them touching their hats to me with a look of good will. (214-15)

The Reverend approves of Arthur's enthusiasm, but tries to temper it with a warning: although "increasing the quantity of food" is a noble endeavor, "You must make it quite clear to your mind which you are most bent upon, old boy—popularity or usefulness—else you may happen to miss both" (215). Irwine's advice penetrates to the heart of what will be Arthur's premature failure as an improver. By confusing affection for Hetty with economic interest in the Poysers, Arthur brings fertility to the wrong side of the estate, and instead of increasing the quantity of food, only ends up increasing the population. For all his benevolent impulses, the young heir proves to be as appropriative of tenant capital as his grandfather the Squire.

In fact, Arthur's initial contact with Hetty is actually enabled by Mrs. Poyser, as her pride in her dairy leads her to believe that Arthur is "really interested in her milkpans" (126), rather than in her beautiful buttermaker. Hetty's liminality—of body, of class, and of family—allows her to evade the perimeters of her aunt's normally rigid supervision; furthermore, in the context of the dairy, Hetty is merely another implement of labor to her aunt, a set of "hands" that makes the butter, and her actions can only seduce Arthur's regard for economic efficiency. Yet it is the sensuality of Hetty's "attitudes and movements" that are of primary interest to Arthur while he watches her work, and her "hands" register in an entirely different nexus of meaning: the "tossing movements that give a charming curve to the arm, and a sideward inclination of the round, white neck . . . little patting and rolling movements with the palm of the hand, and nice adaptations and finishings which cannot at all be effected without a great play of the pouting mouth and the dark eyes" (129).

While Mrs. Poyser quickly transforms the domestic productivity of her housemaid into a tale of potential *re*productivity, her niece's labors remain in the economic realm, and at the end of Hetty's performance she is merely pleased by the material fact that Hetty "is particularly clever at making the butter" (129).

Even Arthur's solicitation of Hetty to partner him in two dances at his upcoming birthday feast is carried out with Mrs. Poyser's unthinking approbation: "Indeed sir, you're very kind to take notice of her. And I'm sure, whenever you're pleased to dance with her, she'll be proud and thankful, if she stood still the rest o' the evening" (129). Mrs. Poyser is finally unable to see the workplace as the scene of her niece's initial seduction because it is a cross-class seduction: an exchange that has only economic significance at Hall Farm. Although Mrs. Poyser's natural sagacity is renowned throughout Hayslope, and Mr. Poyser is "secretly proud of his wife's manner of putting two and two together" (235), it is a shame that Bartle Massey, the Hayslope schoolteacher, has never taken the time to teach the couple his brand of Malthusian mathematics. Following Malthus's assertion that sexual passion "may always be considered in algebraic language, as a given quantity," Bartle calculates that the principles of "simple addition" clearly indicate that if you "add one fool to another . . . in six years time six fools more—they're all of the same denomination, big and little's nothing to do with the sum" (291).[47] Bartle even comments upon the issue of human perfectibility that inspires Malthus's first *Essay*, as he blames Adam's mistaken faith in Hetty's fidelity and innocence on his lack of mathematical knowledge: "If he hadn't had such hard work to do, poor fellow, he might have gone on to the higher branches, and then this might never have happened—might never have happened" (463). Like Malthus, Bartle realizes that the daily realities of work keep the lower classes from the "higher branches" of intellectual development and prevent them from understanding—what the Reverend Irwine also knows—that human affections can interfere with economic prosperity. This crucial lesson is the one with which the Poysers and others in their economic situation are grappling; it is the inaugural factor of middle-class identity and the reason Malthus rests all hopes for human improvement on the rise and empowerment of the middle classes through the "established administration of property" (Malthus, 286).

Like Arthur Donnithorne, the Poysers have confused "the established administration of property" with family sentiment and have allowed rhetorical assessments of what "a good father" Uncle Poyser has been to elide the fact that Hetty's place in the family registers economically rather than affectively. The mistaken impulses of paternalism have been inadvertently replicated by the Poysers, and despite the sentimental idiom that allows the Poysers to understand themselves as a family, the economic and affective claims of their own children perpetually obscure what is due to their metaphoric daughter. Uncle Poyser's proprietorship of Hetty is finally like his tenant-farming: a secondary form of appropriation that has nothing to do with ownership. Although he expects to channel Hetty's fertility into a mutually empowering marriage with the innovative, up-wardly mobile Adam Bede, Uncle Poyser's interest in his niece will prove to be as latent as his "stuck in the soil" capital: cultivated by the Poysers but devoured by the Donnithornes.

Furthermore, when Hetty's economic productivity becomes reproduc-tivity, it signals that another of Bartle Massey's ominous predictions has come true, that sooner or later, a woman's food "all runs either to fat or to brats" (285). Bartle's misogynous words return us finally to the problem of fatness, a problem that has been previously addressed both under the delicate euphemism of "fleshiness" and under the sign of Mr. Casson's distended frame. Although Hetty's brand of fleshiness, her uneconomical form of productivity, is unnoticed by her family, other kinds of fat are hysterically and repetitiously recognized and celebrated by the Poysers.[48] As much as Hetty's uneconomical fatness belies the Poysers' financial independence, Totty Poyser's "fat" body is a sign of the idealized economy of plenty at Hall Farm. The difference between daughters and nieces in *Adam Bede* finally materializes over the discourse of fat, marking the bodily excess of daughters as an illusory sign of accumulation, a displaced embodiment of wealth. Conversely, the fleshiness of Hetty's body is an ignored site of exploitation, and the true measure of Poyser economic status. From the time we first glimpse four-year-old Totty "in retreat towards the dairy, with a sort of waddling run, and an amount of fat on the nape of her neck, which made her look like the metamorphosis of a white sucking pig" (120), it is clear that Totty functions within *Adam Bede* as a hyperbolic image of Hetty, her fat body standing in for the unarticu-lated "metamorphosis" of her cousin.

Even Hetty's first rendezvous with Arthur in the Fir-tree Grove is italicized by the way that she returns home to find, despite the lateness of the hour, that her aunt is still awake "trying to soothe Totty to sleep"

(189). As Hetty enters the room, Totty "raised herself up, and showed a pair of flushed cheeks, which looked even fatter than ever now that they were defined by the edge of her linen night-cap" (189). Although Mrs. Poyser initially begins to scold her niece for her tardiness, she soon digresses into a description of her daughter's unusual "fever for what I know . . . and nobody to give her the physic but your uncle, and fine work there's been, and half of it spilt on her nightgown" (190). Paradoxically, Totty's restlessness and "fever" both supply the otherwise absent symptoms of Hetty's late-night tryst with Arthur, and finally draw Mrs. Poyser's attention completely away from her wayward niece, as a new bout of crying from her daughter erupts just as Mrs. Poyser complains that Hetty would like her clock to be "set by gentlefolks time" (190), rather than the time at Hall Farm. Yet another stain (this one, significantly, on Totty's nightgown) literalizes Hetty's sexual stain, fixing Totty's "fat" body as a hyperbolic emblem of concealed sexuality: an exaggerated narrative record of Hetty's bodily transgressiveness.

Returning now to Malthusian logic, "fatness" takes on even greater significance, as the habit of turning rich agricultural land over to the "fatting" of high-grade cattle is one of Malthus's pet peeves: "A fatted beast may in some respects be considered, in the language of the French economists, as an unproductive labourer; he has added nothing to the value of the produce consumed."[49] As Catherine Gallagher points out, this fatted beast is an "immediate threat to society's well being . . . a distension, an overgrowth of its own circulatory system."[50] Similarly, Totty Poyser is the very embodiment of nonproductive value, a healthy sign of economic plenty that is simultaneously a swollen marker of unregulated consumption. We frequently catch glimpses of Totty in the garden of Hall Farm, undoing the picking, gathering, and unearthing of harvest-work by stuffing everything she takes from tree or soil directly into her mouth. Adam Bede is looking for Hetty in the garden one evening when he instead encounters Totty,

Yes—with a bonnet down her back, and her fat face dreadfully smeared with red juice, turned up towards the cherry-tree, while she held her little round hole of a mouth and red-stained pinafore to receive the promised downfall. I am sorry to say, more than half the cherries that fell were hard and yellow instead of juicy and red; but Totty spent no time in useless regrets, and she was already sucking the third juiciest when Adam said, "There now, Totty, you've got your cherries. Run into the house with 'em to mother." (264)

Totty's red-stained face will soon be reflected by the "deep red" blush that spreads over Hetty's face when Adam finally finds her—an appropriately metaphorical "stain" because Adam has interrupted her fantasies about Arthur Donnithorne. What is more, the dangerous sexual imagery of this passage is matched by an equally problematic economic message, and the two lines of signification collide in the slippery "hole" of Totty's open mouth. If the sexual signs are self-explanatory, the economic signs should perhaps be qualified by a term that Malthus recognizes as a "vulgar" but accurate expression: "hand to mouth" subsistence.[51] Malthus's complaint that the labouring classes are prevented from planning for the future by the "hand to mouth" manner in which they must live echoes both Bartle Massey's feeling that Adam's daily labors keep him from important economic knowledge, and Martin Poyser's sense that his capital is latent, unable to circulate properly within the larger social economy. In this way, Totty's fat body and stained mouth not only stand in for Hetty's concealed sexual identity but for the "fatted beast" in her father's failed circulation of capital, the fleshy middle that is grossly out of proportion with the rest of the economic body.[52]

What is more, Arthur Donnithorne's admiration for Totty, or as he calls her, that "funny little fatty" (130), is represented in a manner that clearly exposes the economic effects of his seduction of Hetty. While on one of his infamous visits to the dairy, he pleases Mrs. Poyser enormously by his benevolent attentions to the child:

"Totty's a capital name. Why she looks like a Totty. Has she got a pocket on?" said the Captain, feeling in his own waistcoat pockets.
Totty immediately with great gravity lifted up her frock, and showed a tiny pink pocket at present in a state of collapse.
"It dot notin' in it," she said, as she looked down at it very earnestly.
"No! What a pity! Such a pretty pocket. Well, I think I've got some things of mine that will make a pretty jingle in it. Yes; I declare I've got five round silver things, and hear what a pretty noise they make in Totty's pink pocket." (131)

If the exchange of money for the lifting of a frock resembles prostitution in this scenario, the metaphor will retain the same valence when a pregnant and abandoned Hetty is finally forced by economic necessity to convert the expensive jewelry Arthur has given her into cash and run away from Hayslope. Capitalism, or as it is glossed by Malthusian language, "the established administration of property," will become Hetty's last hope for survival, as we painfully watch her apply "her small arithmetic and knowledge of prices to calculate how many meals and how many rides were contained" (418) in her small stock of funds. Realizing, perhaps too late, that "There's nothin you can't turn into a sum, for there's nothin but what's got a number in it" (282), Hetty's fears take on a distinctly economic bent:

> Now, in her faintness of heart at the length and difficulty of her journey, she was most of all afraid of spending her money, and becoming so destitute that she would have to ask for people's charity; for Hetty had the pride not only of a proud nature but of a proud class—the class that pays the most poor-rates, and most shudders at the idea of profiting by a poor-rate. (418)

Hetty's intuitive economic sense becomes an instinct for self-preservation that even prevents her from committing suicide: "It was no use to think of drowning herself—she could not do it, at least while she had money left to buy food, and strength to journey on" (434). Not only food, but the bodily strength derived from nourishment is a commodity that can be given numerical value, or "turn[ed] into a sum." Although her mother died under the dual oppressions of "inflammation" and Mr. Sorrel's economic incapacities, Hetty's emerging fatness brings out the latent economic characteristics of her "proud class" as she confronts the principles of "simple addition" that shape middle-class identity.[53]

While Hetty's education in the ways and means of capital is no doubt abrupt, her earlier insights into the economic realities of her pregnancy are primarily marked by her vague desires to move away from Hall Farm before her secret is revealed. Before she finally settles on a marriage to Adam as the only feasible way of altering her living conditions, she first asks the Poysers for permission to enter domestic service in the capacity of a lady's maid. Mr. Poyser is quick to assert the sufficiency, and more importantly, the autonomy of economic production at Hall Farm as the primary reason Hetty's request is ridiculous, appealing to his aged father for corroboration: "my family's ate their own bread and cheese as fur back as anybody knows, hanna they father?" (383). Similarly relying on the principles of supply and demand, Mrs. Poyser's scornful response throws us once again into the vernacular of "fatness," this time with an interesting twist:

> I'll never gi' my consent to her going for a lady's-maid, while she's got good friends to take care on her till she's married to somebody better nor one o' them valets, as is neither a common man nor a gentleman, an' *must live on the fat o' the*

land, an's like enough to stick his hands under his coat tails and expect his wife to work for him. (384, emphasis mine)

In this invocation, "fat" is not the illusory emblem of capital, an emblem that is—within fledgling middle-class culture—symbolic, metaphorical and finally, unproductive; rather, "fat" is *capital itself,* a general synecdoche for the rich upper classes and an immediate sign of the Donnithornes.

It is in this context that Squire Donnithorne's late-breaking desire to negotiate a business deal with the Poysers resonates within the larger nexus of *Adam Bede,* and particularly Hetty's story. Delicately indicating that the Poysers' perpetual dread of eviction may become reality if their compliance is not received, the Squire proposes that they turn over a sizeable portion of their corn land to the potential tenant of Chase Farm in return for an increase in their dairy land—an exchange that will nominally give the Poysers the privilege of supplying the manor house with "milk, cream and butter at the market prices" (391).[54] Mrs. Poyser penetrates the Squire's objectives as easily as she discerned her house-maid's, however, and she refuses his offer in an explosive moment of class consciousness: "I'll not consent to take more dairy work into my hands, either for love or money; and there's nayther love nor money here, as I can see, on'y other folks love o' theirselves, and the money as is to go into other folks's pockets. I know there's them as is born't own the land, and them as is born to sweat on't" (392). Confronted with this exemplary tableau of business-as-usual at Hall Farm, the local mechanisms of economic exploitation become apparent to the Poysers, and their pretense of autonomy crumbles under the actualities of tenantry. The plentiful "bread and cheese" that the Poysers have eaten for generations is simply another manifestation of Donnithorne *fat:* like the domestic servants that Mrs. Poyser criticizes, the Poysers are neither "common" nor "gentle," and the unpossessed richness of Hall Farm places them in a similar socioeconomic position to those who must "live on the fat o' the land."

This exchange with Squire Donnithorne represents a major economic triumph to the Poysers, as they manage to circumvent eviction while forcing the Squire to abandon his scheme of monopolizing dairy produc-tion at Hall Farm. Apparently, the prospective tenant of Chase Farm refused to negotiate a lease without the promised corn land, and "it was known throughout the two parishes that the Squire's plan had been frustrated because the Poysers had refused to be 'put upon' " (396). Yet if Mrs. Poyser believes that she has also circumvented Bartle Massey's econometric on female nourishment and has literally prevented her dairy goods from running to Donnithorne fat, she will eventually realize that it is too late: her food has already run to fat in the form of the emerging fleshiness on her niece's body and in the illegitimate Donnithorne child that has been indirectly nourished by Poyser labor. Ironically, it will be Hetty's own belated understanding of the operations of capital that finally, permanently, prevents Poyser goods from running to fat, as her act of infanticide, her refusal to nourish another body at the expense of her own, is an assertion of individualism that replicates Mrs. Poyser's refusal to give her milk to the Donnithornes instead of retaining it for her own family.[55] While this seemingly smooth equation of infanticide with economic individualism is politically unpalatable, it is impossible not to identify the redundancy of the two incidents, especially when we are confronted with the gruesome fact that Hetty is arrested at the site of the baby's grave with "a big piece of bread in her lap" (481), literally putting her own need for nourishment before her child's. It is also telling that the baby's death is coterminous with the death of his unknowing grandfather, Squire Donnithorne, as if Hetty's refusal to nurse her child and Mrs. Poyser's refusal to provide milk products for the Manor House have, at either end of the generational spectrum, the same effects.

ECONOMIES OF REPLACEMENT: THE REDISTRIBUTION OF FAT AND MIDDLE-CLASS EMPOWERMENT

With this pair of Donnithorne deaths, fat begins to redistribute itself throughout the body of the novel, and the economics of replacement take over the management of both the family plot and the marriage plot. If at one point in the text Arthur Donnithorne's birthday feast for his tenants and laborers underscored the feudal organization of Hayslope, by the end of *Adam Bede*, the Poysers' boisterous Harvest supper has disrupted and rewritten the brand of class-consciousness that informed Arthur's party. Martin Poyser enjoys the role of the "young master" (562) during these latter festivities, but unlike Arthur, Mr. Poyser sits at the head of one large table "helping his servants to the fragrant roast beef, and pleased when their empty plates came in again" (560). With this celebration of economic plenty replacing the paternalistic significance of the local gentry's "coming-of-age," middle-class power emerges in the guise of collectivism to foster more harmonious relations between the "head" of the social body and its "hands." Yet if the philosophy of social paternalism has been overthrown by the end of *Adam Bede*, another ideological program has taken its place: as Margaret Homans notes, Mr. Poyser's feast is only for men.[56] By literally segregating the women from the "fat," the Victorian doctrine of separate spheres begins to shape the social economy of *Adam Bede* in time to neutralize the sexual dangers inherent in representations of capitalist excess.

Although the socioeconomic privileges attached to ownership and autonomy are finally awarded to the Poysers, they still must be disciplined for mistaking economic expediency for affection in their early confusion about the differences among nieces, daughters, and servants. When the Poysers attempt to replace one niece with the other—to make Dinah compensate the loss of Hetty's labor at Hall Farm—and fail, it is apparent that some brands of accumulation are unwelcome in the new social order. Despite her aunt's wheedling, Dinah realizes that the position of the perennial niece in the Poyser household is a service-oriented rather than family-oriented role:

"An' now I can trust you wi' the butter, an' have had all the trouble o' teaching you, an' there's all the sewing to be done, an' I must have a strange gell out of Treddles'on to do it—an' all because you must go back to that bare heap o' stones as the very crows fly over an' won't stop at."

"Dear aunt Rachel," said Dinah, looking up in Mrs. Poyser's face, "it's your kindness makes you say I'm useful to you. You don't really want me now; for Nancy and Molly are clever at work, and you're in good health now, by the blessing of God." (518-19)

By quietly pointing out that Nancy and Molly, the servants, are what Mrs. Poyser "really wants" instead of a niece, Dinah refuses to be absorbed into Hall Farm's economic grid and reduced to a redundant pair of hands in the Poyser family dairy. After all, once the dangerous collusions of fat and femininity are eliminated from *Adam Bede*, buttermaking is the last occupation that the newly domesticated Dinah can undertake. This kind of productivity, as Hetty has made abundantly clear, is both uneconomical and antithetical to middle-class empowerment.[57]

Although Dinah refuses to replace her cousin at Hall Farm, Hetty's enforced emigration allows Dinah to marry Adam, her thin body gaining in "fullness" and health (581) as she adapts herself to new conventions of domesticity and maternity. The metaphors of dilation and distention proliferate as this exchange is explored, describing Adam's love for Dinah as "the outgrowth of that fuller life which had come to him from his acquaintance with deep sorrow" (574). Within *Adam Bede*'s vernacular of fatness, Dinah is an "outgrowth," a product of Hetty's "fullness" that will clean up after sexual misconduct, renaturalize maternity and restore the integrity of the social body through a rapid deployment of domestic ideology. Accordingly, within the seven year gap between the end of the novel proper and its epilogue, just as Dinah's thin, "starved" body has begun to bloom and reproduce, Adam has come into some capital and owns the timber-yard where he used to work. As new "outgrowths" replace more deviant forms of fatness, it becomes increasingly clear that successful "possession" and the rise of the middle class are simultaneous socioeconomic events. In good Malthusian form, *Adam Bede*'s economic philosophy is cyclical: Hetty gives way to Dinah, barrenness gives way to plenty, and the accumulated wealth of the upper classes begins to circulate and finally settle around the "middle" regions of the social body.

NOTES

1. Sandra Gilbert and Susan Gubar, *The Madwoman in the Attic: The Woman Writer and the Nineteenth-Century Literary Imagination* (New Haven: Yale University Press, 1979), 496. See also Nina Auerbach's *Woman and the Demon: The Life of a Victorian Myth* (Cambridge: Harvard University Press, 1982), 175; and Helena Michie's *Sororophobia: Differences among Women in Literature and Culture* (New York: Oxford University Press, 1992). For those unfamiliar with *Adam Bede*, the plot primarily revolves around the seduction of a farmer's niece (Hetty Sorrel) by the local Squire's grandson (Arthur Donnithorne), her secret pregnancy, and subsequent act of infanticide. The titular Adam is Hetty's wronged fiance, a struggling artisan who is finally able, by the end of the novel, both to establish himself as a business-owner and to transfer his affections from the undeserving Hetty to her virtuous cousin, Dinah Morris.

2. George Eliot, *Adam Bede* (New York: Penguin, 1985), 143. All further references to this edition will be made within the text.

3. For example, David Cressy, "Foucault, Stone, Shakespeare, and Social History," *English Literary Renaissance* 21.2 (1991): 121-33; James Casey, *The History of the Family* (New York: Basil Blackwell, 1989); Jeffrey Weeks, *Sex, Politics, and Society: The Regulation of Sexuality since 1800* (New York: Longman, 1981); Beatrice Gottlieb, *The Family in the Western World from the Black Death to the Industrial Age* (New York: Oxford University Press, 1993).

4. Eve Kosofsky Sedgwick, *Tendencies* (Durham, N.C.: Duke University Press, 1993), 58. Sedgwick's simultaneous advice to "Think about your Uncles and

Aunts" (59), is also relevant to my argument here. I agree with Sedgwick's assertion that a "relegitimation of the avunculate" would "appeal backward to precapitalist models of kinship organization, or the supposed early-capitalist extended family, in order to project into the future a vision of 'family' elastic enough to do justice to the depth and sometimes durability of nonmarital and/or nonprocreative bonds, same-sex bonds, nondyadic bonds, bonds not defined by genitality, 'step'-bonds, adult sibling bonds, nonbiological bonds across generations, etc." (71). This expansive assessment of the use-value of avuncular reading has the potential to dislocate or at the very least disrupt the nuclear family paradigm wherever it has been naturalized.

5. By "Malthusian" I refer to economic theories put forth by Thomas Malthus's "principles of population" rather than to any debates surrounding contraception or abortion that Malthus's work has spawned. In this chapter I have chosen to use Malthus's first *Essay on the Principle of Population* (1798) as a theoretical touchstone rather than any of the revised editions primarily because *Adam Bede*, although first published in 1859, attempts to account for economic and social changes occurring at the turn of the century—more specifically, between 1799 and 1807. Rather than asserting that Malthus is the definitive subtext of Eliot's novel, I am suggesting that the partial operations of Malthusian economic discourse can be traced within *Adam Bede* in a manner that assumes, in the words of Catherine Gallagher, "no fixed hierarchy of cause and effect." See "Marxism and the New Historicism," in *The New Historicism*, ed. H. Aram Veeser (New York: Routledge, 1989), 37.

6. Catherine Gallagher, *The Industrial Reformation of English Fiction: Social Discourse and Narrative Form, 1832-1867* (Chicago: University of Chicago Press, 1985).

7. Arthur Helps, *The Claims of Labour: An Essay on the Duties of the Employees to the Employed* (London: William Pickering, 1845); J. S. Mill, "The Claims of Labour," *Edinburgh Review* LXXXI (April 1845): 498-525. The review was unsigned, but it has been identified as Mill's by subsequent bibliographies.

8. Mill, "The Claims of Labour," 507.

9. Ibid., 513.

10. Margaret Homans, "Dinah's Blush, Maggie's Arm: Class, Gender, and Sexuality in George Eliot's Early Novels," *Victorian Studies* 36 (Winter 1993): 161.

11. Luce Irigaray, *This Sex which Is Not One*, trans. Catherine Porter (Ithaca: Cornell University Press, 1985), 178.

12. Ibid., 176.

13. Ibid., 173.

14. Ibid., 185.

15. F. M. L. Thompson, "Landownership and Economic Growth in England in the Eighteenth Century," in *Agrarian Change and Economic Development: The Historical Problems*, ed. E. L. Jones and S. J. Woolf (London: Methuen, 1969), 41-60.

16. Ibid., 59.

17. Christabel S. Orwin and Edith W. Whetham, *History of British Agriculture* (Devon: David and Charles, 1971), 153.

18. J. V. Beckett, "Landownership and Estate Management," in *The Agrarian History of England and Wales*, vol. VI, ed. G. E. Mingay (Cambridge: Cambridge University Press, 1989), 597-98.

19. S. S. Lefevre, quoted in I. S. Leadam, *To the Tenant Farmers of Great Britain: Farmer's Grievances and How to Remedy Them at the Next Election* (London: National Press Agency, 1880), 5.

20. James Caird, *The Landed Interest and the Supply of Food* (New York: M. Kelley, 1967), 60.

21. James Caird, *English Agriculture in 1850-1851* (London: Longman, 1852), 12-13.

22. Charles Higby Lattimore, "A Plea for Tenant Right" (London: Ridgway, 1848), 12-13.

23. As Caird notes, "the great proportion of English farms are held on yearly tenure which may be terminated at any time by a six months notice." *English Agriculture*, 503.

24. I. S. Leadam, *To the Tenant-Farmers of Great Britain*, 5.

25. Caird, *English Agriculture*, 505.

26. Lattimore, "A Plea for Tenant Right," 17.

27. Caird, *The Landed Interest*, 149.

28. Wally Seccombe, *A Millennium of Family Change: Feudalism to Capitalism in Northwestern Europe* (New York: Verso, 1992), 21. Although Seccombe is specifically interested in working-class families, it is important to recognize that the Poyser household is working-class to the extent that every able adult member of the household labors on the farm or in the dairy. I am arguing here that the very "latency" of tenant-farmer's capital kept farmers who rented their land (like Mr. Poyser) on the socioeconomic cusp of middle-class existence until much later in the nineteenth century, when tenant's right was finally codified.

29. Ibid., 21.

30. Leonore Davidoff and Catherine Hall's *Family Fortunes: Men and Women of the English Middle-Class, 1780-1850* (Chicago: University of Chicago Press, 1987) also argues that a more flexible notion of family is needed to understand the economic vicissitudes of middle-class life.

31. Irigaray, *This Sex which Is Not One*, 177.

32. Eve Kosofsky Sedgwick, *Between Men: English Literature and Male Homosocial Desire* (New York: Columbia University Press, 1985), 170.

33. Helena Michie, *The Flesh Made Word: Female Figures and Women's Bodies* (New York: Oxford University Press, 1987), 27.

34. John Kucich, *Repression in Victorian Fiction: Charlotte Bronte, George Eliot, and Charles Dickens* (Berkeley: University of California Press, 1987), 193.

35. Leonore Davidoff, "Class and Gender in Victorian England," in *Sex and Class in Women's History*, ed. Judith L. Newton, Mary P. Ryan, and Judith R. Walkowitz (London: Routledge and Kegan Paul, 1983), 18.

36. Ibid., 19.

37. Susan Walsh, "Bodies of Capital: *Great Expectations* and the Climacteric Economy," *Victorian Studies* 37 (Fall 1993): 73-98.

38. Ibid., 76.

39. Ibid., 76.

40. Interestingly, the first sign of Squire Donnithorne's contemplated exploitation of Hall Farm occurs at the birthday feast for Arthur, when he appears to be uncharacteristically concerned about Mrs. Poyser's health and proceeds to give her medical advice: "he gave his most elaborate civility to Mrs. Poyser to-night, inquiring particularly about her health, recommending her to strengthen herself with cold water as he did, and avoid all drugs. Mrs. Poyser curtsied and thanked him with great self-command, but when he had passed on, she whispered to her husband, 'I'll lay my life he's brewin' some nasty turn against us. Old Harry doesna wag his tail for nothin'" (328).

41. For example, see Nancy L. Paxton's chapter on *Adam Bede* in *George Eliot and Herbert Spenser: Feminism, Evolutionism, and the Reconstruction of Gender* (Princeton: Princeton University Press, 1991), 43-68.

42. Malthus's late eighteenth-century economic views are obviously more apocalyptic than Arthur Helps's mid-Victorian paternalist theory; on the other hand, Mill identifies Malthus's "Essay on Population" as the origin of the social paternalist movement because it represents the first time "the economic condition of the working classes had been regarded as susceptible of permanent improvement" (Mill, "The Claims of Labour," 500).

43. Thomas Robert Malthus, *First Essay on Population: 1798*, reprinted for the Royal Economic Society (London: Macmillan, 1926), 14-15.

44. Ibid., 14.

45. Catherine Gallagher, "The Body versus the Social Body in the Works of Thomas Malthus and Henry Mayhew," *Representations* 14 (Spring 1986): 85.

46. Ibid., 85.

47. Malthus, *First Essay on Population*, 128.

48. Although Mrs. Poyser is unable to recognize the fact that Hetty is pregnant, it is important that she *does* recognize a change in her niece that she unknowingly characterizes in the economic idiom previously associated with Arthur Donnithorne: "Mrs. Poyser thought she noticed a surprising *improvement* in Hetty... she thought much less about her dress, and went after the work quite eagerly, without any telling. And it was wonderful how she never wanted to go out now—indeed, could hardly be persuaded to go ... it must be, after all, that she had set her heart on Adam at last" (398, emphasis added).

49. Malthus, *First Essay on Population*, 318.

50. Gallagher, "The Body versus the Social Body," 97.

51. Malthus, *First Essay on Population*, 86.

52. If we know where to look for the fat at Hall Farm, it is also the case that we know where to find the lean—on the body of yet another niece, Dinah Morris. The "naked hills" (121) and scant natural resources of Snowfield are repeatedly contrasted with Hayslope's rich valleys and fertile farms: as Dinah warns Seth Bede when he offers to return home with her, "It's a bleak and barren country there, not like this land of Goshen you've been used to" (80). Just as Totty's fatness is a sign of the idealized economy of plenty at Hall farm, a plenty that

Hetty's unrecognized "fatness" ultimately belies, Dinah's thin "starved" body is a constant marker of Snowfield's struggling industrial work-force: a brand of labor against which the Poysers' (via perpetual contrast) measure their own economic identity. Added to the Poysers' abiding fear that "she'll never marry anybody if he isn't a Methodist and a cripple" (555), Dinah's starved body takes on the signs of reproductive barrenness: an infertility that initially locates Dinah instead of Hetty as the weak link in the Poysers' economics of fat.

53. It is also the case that Malthus deplores the "Parish laws of England" because they undermine British individualism (67).

54. Squire Donnithorne's offer is little more than extortion, of course: Eliot informs us that summer flooding in the Midlands has rapidly driven up the price of bread and the Hayslope farmers currently have a unique opportunity to make the most of their cornlands (337). Furthermore, according to Adam Smith's 1776 *Wealth of Nations*, dairyland was generally believed to be less valuable than corn land in the eighteenth century: "the dairy is not reckoned a more profitable employment of land than the raising of corn, or the fattening of cattle" (New York: Random House, 1937), 227.

55. Malthus refers to infanticide as an economic rather than criminal resource—a "check to population" directly resulting from insufficient food.

56. Homans, "Dinah's Blush, Maggie's Arm," 165.

57. Buttermaking was literally as well as figuratively uneconomical at the turn of the century. According to B. A. Holderness, in most circumstances profits from butter and cheese "were never ample and barely recompensed the dairyman for his trouble." B. A. Holderness, "Prices, Productivity, and Output," in *The Agrarian History of England and Wales*, vol. VI, ed. G. F. Mingay (Cambridge: Cambridge University Press, 1989), 183.

Effaced into Flesh: Black Women's Subjectivity

Jennifer DeVere Brody

When do we start to see images of the black female body . . . made as acts of auto-expression, the discrete stage that must immediately precede or occur simultaneously with acts of auto-critique? When does the present begin?
——Lorraine O'Grady, "Olympia's Maid"

Artist Lorraine O'Grady's questions pose an important problem for black feminist theory: how can black female flesh be represented as other than an other's other given that the coherence and specificity of black female subjects is effaced by the logic that cannot produce her positionality except paradoxically?[1] Reading black female bodies in literary discourse is difficult because, to use Kimberle Crenshaw's term, the "intersectionality" of the black female subject positions her at the crossroads of competing discourses of race and gender.[2] This "intersectionality" is problematic because "such a formulation erases the specificity of black women's experiences, constituting her [only] as the point of intersection between black men's and white women's experience."[3] By being represented in or as the nexus of a schematic that denies her existence, the symbolic black female subject is forced to occupy the false and often oppositional position between race and gender. Too many feminist accounts read this black female subject as an "oxymoronic singularity."[4] Such readings do not take seriously black feminist theory's central tenet that race and gender are mutually constitutive, not mutually exclusive.[5]

This essay asks if and how it is possible to develop a reading strategy that does not replicate the effacement of black women's subjectivities. It calls for black feminist criticism that argues for the specificity and diversity of African American women's experiences in the United States by working against the categories available which are unable to account for black female subjects' complex but not necessarily incoherent differences. If black feminist theory requires that one read race and gender together in order not to efface black women as "coherent" subjects, perhaps the black female's present presence will begin when black feminist theory is employed as a weapon/tool for thinking about the ways in which race and gender work in literary culture. The following discussion of Ann Petry's prize-winning short story "Like a Winding Sheet" (1946) dramatizes the difficulties incurred by denying the dynamic differences of black female subjects.[6]

"Like a Winding Sheet" delineates the impossible position of black female flesh in American cultural discourse. An apt subtitle for this tale might be: "All the Women Are White, All the Men Are Black, and Some of Us Are Brave"—the title of the well-known anthology of feminist writing by women of color.[7] This phrase summarizes the central characters in "Like a Winding Sheet," who are two racist white women; a black man, Johnson; and his not-fully-fleshed-out "brave" black wife, Mae. The story demonstrates that the shifting positionality of Mae's body—whose very name suggests her (im)possibility and instability—can only constitute her as a contingent, incoherent subject.

In Petry's piece, various binaries are dissolved and/or reconfigured in and between a black man and a black woman. The black woman's body straddles the multiple identities—is fixed as flesh rather than as a coherent, stable body. Petry's parable of race/gender relations in the United States exquisitely distills the difference between socially constructed (white) woman and the black female who, as Hortense Spillers explains, is figured as *flesh* in a violent American landscape.[8] Here, the black woman's body proves to be only a fictionally and temporarily stable ground. If in "same-race" encounters the difference that gender makes seems to be highlighted, this essay, by calling for reading black women as coherent subjects—demonstrates that even in such same race encounters, the black woman's specificity must not be erased. In short, Petry's story vividly illustrates the danger of relying on a binary opposition between race and gender.

So too, it illustrates the limitations of critics who would argue that visibility and voice are the crucial assets required for a viable black female social subject. It does so because in the story, Mae's visibility and voice are revealed to be liabilities rather than assets for this black female subject whose presence is (mis)read as being purely paradoxical: "This paradox, that only the black female stands *in the flesh*. . . . This problematizing of gender places her . . . out of the traditional symbolics of female gender, and it is our task to make a place for this different social subject. In doing so, we are less interested in joining the ranks of gendered femaleness than gaining the insurgent ground as female social subject."[9] In order to combat the tendency to represent black female social subjects as "split," silent, and therefore disempowered subjects, theorists must work to eliminate the various categories and discourses that continue to inscribe black women as incommensurate and oxymoronic rather than "merely" complex entities.[10]

I analyze the erasure and/or impossibility of the black female subject with the simultaneous construction of her as "ungendered flesh." This simultaneous facing and effacement of the black woman is a key integer in the calculus that formulates American race and gender in this story. The gendered performances represented in Petry's story form the genesis of my argument that "black woman" is an incommensurate construction in much official U. S. discourse that continues to associate "race" with blacks and "gender" with women.[11] Too often, then, the conjunction "race and gender" works to occlude women of color because race can only signify "blackness" and "gender" stands in for (white) women. It is from this perspective that one can read Petry's story as a paradigmatic parable of race and gender relations in U. S. culture.

"Like a Winding Sheet" poignantly describes a day in the life of a working-class black couple in the 1940s at the same time that it portrays and plays with the triangulated constructions of race and gender. The story focuses a fateful Friday the 13th in the 1940s when Mr. Johnson, a black man, is ravaged by the racism he encounters at his factory job and in a New York restaurant. The time period is significant because World War II "marked an important break with the historic allocation of work by race and sex."[12] For the first time in history, "blacks" and "women" entered manufacturing jobs in record numbers—especially in the North where the story takes place.

The story begins and ends in the Johnsons' apartment, which is the only space where Mrs. Johnson appears. Indeed, her body frames the text in both senses of the word. The story is representative, perhaps even stereotypical, in that, baldly stated, it is the tale of a (black) man beaten by a (capitalist) system who then beats his (black) wife. What keeps Petry's piece from being cliched (besides the fact that such abuse continues to occur) is Petry's deft employment of structural repetitions and her overt attention to the conflicting constructions of gender across the fault lines of racial injustice.

In American discourses, the invisible forces of racism, classism, and sexism often materialize in the flesh of working-class black females. The imbricated identity of this black female subject serves as the locus for other competing identities on the national landscape. Thus, Mae's body simultaneously disintegrates into and materializes as the *flesh* that binds and repels signs of (white/black, male/female) power. Despite the analogies made between Mae, the black wife, and the other (also working-class) white women in the text (for example, all wear red lipstick), the story concludes with the black woman becoming "soft flesh" (22) that is pummelled repeatedly by her race-plagued husband, who "could never bring himself to hit a 'woman' "—even a racist white woman. The problem of "what it is to be a woman" is an important issue in Petry's text.

Initially, the opening exchanges between Johnson and his wife in their bedroom are sanguine, but they quickly degenerate when Mae's dialogue directs the reader's attention to Johnson's pain-ridden body. Unlike her body, which is an absent presence throughout the story, his body is fetishized and palpable by Mae's discourse as well as the narrator's. This reversal of the conventions of narrative description works to "feminize" his body at the same time that it erases Mae's body and makes her immaterial. She is the touched and unseen—a present absence. We know she has a body because she has a voice, and she puts on overalls, but it is Johnson's body, weary from work, that "stands out" and is made tangible by Mae and the author.

Throughout the tale, seen almost exclusively through Johnson's eyes, the reader never really sees Mae. She is heard in the bathroom in the opening paragraph. The narrator does not describe her physical characteristics; rather, Johnson's conversation with Mae is recorded in the dialogue. The only sense of Mae's body comes from a momentary description of her overalls. Unlike Janie Crawford's overalled body in Zora Neale Hurston's *Their Eyes Were Watching God* (1937) that registers and evokes an exalted and debased body whose femaleness is both encased in and bursting forth from this typically ungendered, class-marked clothing, Mae's overalls cover all of her body: they are the androgynous uniform of "a worker."[13] Mae's overalls mask her individuality.

Mae's greatest power here is her voice. Moreover, her words work as a weapon against her husband in a manner analogous to the scene in *Their Eyes Were Watching God* when Janie cuts/kills/castrates her second husband Joe "Ah God" Starks with her words. Mae sees her husband and proclaims that he looks as if he is wrapped in "a shroud" (199). She tells him, "You look like a huckleberry—in a winding sheet—" (Ibid.). She highlights Johnson's body as he awakens in twisted bedsheets. Even before the sheet is identified as being explicitly "white," readers familiar with American iconography assume that it is white. Indeed, it must be for the simile to work. Mae's statement echoes the vernacular phrase "like a fly in butter-milk" and functions as a metaphor for the individual black being who too often is belittled and engulfed by an oppressive white system.[14] The title recalls "the big white backdrop that people of color have charged against for ages making a mark here and there."[15] This metaphoric configuration of the national body constructs colored minorities as belated blemishes on the white amorphous face of America. Mae's reading of Johnson as a being enmeshed *in* the constraining fabric of American culture opposes this latter configuration of the color that stains a foundational, already-woven entity. Petry exposes the fallacy of a purely white America by pointing out the similarities and therefore the differences between the characters in her classic American tale.

At this point in the story, Johnson and his wife are still capable of compassionate communication. They discuss whether or not it is wise to venture out on Friday the 13th and it is Johnson who soothes his wife's superstitions by endorsing rational capitalism that claims wages as the most salvational fruits of work. He quips "Friday is payday—always a good day" (201). The fact that his statements convince Mae demonstrates the extent to which she too is trapped in the values of this system. The necessities of surviving in the urban jungle cancel the value of Mae's traditional folklore. Thus, Johnson succeeds in convincing Mae that it is safe to leave the house.

Pleased with his ability to allay Mae's fears—although it has made him late for work again—the narrator confides that "He couldn't bring him-self to talk to her roughly or threaten to strike her like a lot of men might have done. He wasn't made that way" (200). We learn, however, by the end of the story that he was made to be that way when he lashes out at Mae, hitting her repeatedly. He comes to believe that he is a victim of "the system"—of hypocritical American values. Ironically, Mae's sense of doom and danger *is* realized in the story; but not as she had imagined it. Rather than being abused by the world outside her home, Mae is obliterated in her own bedroom—in the most private and intimate spaces of her life. This serves as a metaphor for the pervasive, insidious (and for too many individuals invisible) force of racism. The reach of racist discourse can be seen even in Mae's jesting with her husband.

Mae's racially inflected commentary objectifies her husband. She stresses the fact that Johnson knows himself only in contrast to the white of the sheet—as merely a "silhouette against the white spread of the sheets [that outline his body]" (199). Mae's objectification of him as well as the fact that she ushers in his metaphorical death through her naming of the "shroud" interrupts the previously lighthearted mood of the story. Her voice strikes a discordant note and causes Johnson to protest against her statements. He retorts, "That's no way to talk, early in the day like this" (199). Although Johnson is just waking up, it is not "early in the day"; rather, it is four o'clock in the afternoon. Since Johnson works the late shift at the plant, he is required to sleep in the day. What is described as the "off-time" of his waking marks his class positionality. He leads an "unnatural" life in that he has been forced by the circumstance of the war to work "odd" hours.

Like many other workers, including Mae, he leads a highly regulated and restricted life that is centered on earning wages. In Petry's naturalistic narrative, bodies respond to external conditions. The workers' bodies, as Elaine Scarry has asserted, often take on the characteristics of their work. Johnson epitomizes those "disinherited from time and reified in space; [these disenfranchised black bodies in America] are presented with death. For to remove people from the voice, from signification, from time, to immure them in obscurity and obdurate materiality is to figure and enforce their death—but a death by no means natural. On the contrary, this death is the upshot of perpetual murder."[16] The workers in the tale are subjected to the rigidity of this capitalistic system. At work, Johnson is subsumed by his animalism. As Hurston claims of the workers in *Their Eyes Were Watching God*, "Mules and other brutes [occupy the workers'] skin" (10). Speech is nearly "impossible" in the plant where the whir of the machinery mutes all. The men and women themselves are reduced to machines—their mouths move but no sounds are audible from a distance.

Johnson, as well as the other workers in the plant, is perpetually late. His lateness serves as the impetus for his white female boss's racist remarks.[17] His boss, named Mrs. Scott, chastises Johnson for his chronic tardiness. She complains, "The niggers is the worse . . . I'm sick of you niggers" (202). Johnson softly replies, "You got the right to be mad. You got the right to curse me four ways to Sunday but I ain't letting nobody call me nigger." This calm verbal defiance contrasts with his hard body language as if to underscore again the mind/body split that continues to be refigured in the story. The narrator explains that "His fists . . . doubled [and] . . . a vein on his forehead stood out, swollen thick" (202). The forelady slowly backs away and mumbles "it slipped out, I didn't mean nothing by it." It is only in the slip, the moments of rupture, that the violence of systemic racism reveals itself.

It should not surprise the reader, then, that Johnson's first confrontation with the boss comes in the form of a glance—in the privileged realm of the mind's eye. This glance signals the psychosexual aspects of Johnson's encounter with his white female boss. "He pushed his cart toward the foreman. He never could remember to refer to her as the forelady even in his mind" (201). She is not called a forewoman (the term used to describe the white female factory boss in Audre Lorde's *Zami*); but a fore*lady* whose race is inscribed in her gender.[18] Johnson thought that "It was funny to have a white woman [which should signify a lady] for a boss in a plant like this one." He describes her eyes as being "half-shut until they were slits." He "couldn't resist stealing a glance at her out of the corner of his eyes. He saw the edge of the light-colored slacks she wore and the tip end of a big tan shoe." The partial, obscured, and furtive glance is revealing. It suggests Johnson's conflicting desires toward his female boss. He cannot remember yet cannot forget to call her "forelady." So, too, as such signifiers as slacks and big shoes suggest, her gendered status is altered by her performance of the boss's role. She becomes masculinized, while he is feminized.

It is important to remember that the wartime economy has placed both Johnson and the forelady in a power relation which is both systematically absolute and culturally tenuous. The white man's absence opens a space in which both characters struggle to assert the power promised by her race and his gender. This is to say that, the wartime economy may have offered black men the "promise" of employment only to reinscribe their disempowerment by placing white women in this space. That Petry has chosen to have white women implicated in the racism of America is important. This strategy refigures the paranoid image of black men and white women fostered by the paradigmatic film *Birth of a Nation* and strengthens the alliance between white and black at the same time that it foregrounds gender. In other words, in hegemonic representations of black men and white women, the latter often is figured as victim, the former as violator; however, in Petry's piece the black man becomes, momentarily, the victim of a white woman's racism.

The female foreman's official role of authority requires that Johnson be subservient to her; however, it is his recognition of her gender that keeps him at bay. Johnson vainly tries to control his body, virtually to no avail since his fists remain clenched and ready to strike. Johnson "turned away from the sight of the red lipstick on her mouth that made him remember that the foreman was a woman. And he couldn't bring himself to hit a woman" (203). The female foreman's presence in the factory, particularly since she occupies a position of power, calls Johnson's own gender into question. He is positioned as a "black boy" and thus his manhood is rendered not definitive but rather always in the process of being defined by others. Like Shadrack in Morrison's *Sula*, Johnson loses control of his hands, they become monstrous instruments.[19]

And he thought he should have hit her anyway, smacked her hard in the face, felt the soft flesh of her face give under the hardness of his hands. He tried to make his hands relax by offering them a description of what it would have been like to strike her because he had the queer feeling that his hands were not exactly part of him any more—they had developed a separate life of their own over which he had no control. So he dwelt on the pleasure his hands would have felt—both of them cracking at her ... if he had done that, his hands would have felt good now—relaxed, rested. (203-4)

This sexualized description of tension and the release that would have "satisfied" him is reminiscent of Bigger Thomas in Richard Wright's *Native Son* (1940) as well as the unnamed narrator in Ralph Ellison's *Invisible Man* (1952) who wants to "caress [the blonde] and destroy her, love her and murder her."[20]

As Abdul JanMohammed has asserted, "in the economy of racialized sexuality, white women represent exchange value between white men and black men, whereas black women represent only use value for both. If

Mary [who is white] constitutes a metaphor of desire on the racial border, then Bessie [who is black] functions as a metonymy of that metaphor."[21] Of course, in Petry's story the white man is the missing integer. Thus, there is a tension between her whiteness (as power) and her femaleness that can in part be resolved by Johnson's disguised rape fantasy. The forelady here is simultaneously a victim of sexism and a perpetrator of racism. Johnson diffuses his competing desires in this dense passage in which he imagines the pleasure of release from his painful position. "The only trouble was, he couldn't bring himself to hit a woman. A woman couldn't hit back the same way a man did. But it would have been deeply satisfying to have cracked her narrow lips wide open with just one blow, beautifully timed and with all his weight at the back of it" (204). This rape fantasy reveals Johnson's desire to have a fair fight and to fight the fair.

Johnson holds on to a chivalrous code "one should not hit a woman," that, though cast in the unconditional, disregards conditions of context. This code is "outmoded" for Johnson, who faces a female foreman. As James Thurber, another important 1940s American writer, remarks, "Word has somehow got around that the split infinitive is always wrong. That is of a piece with the outworn notion that it is always wrong to strike a lady."[22] Johnson's control of his own anger preserves the power structure. In other words, by refusing to hit his female foreman he refuses to break the archaic maxim (to split the imperative)—"one must never hit a woman."

What Johnson sees and hears and marks as "woman" are the "signs" of womanliness. He stumbles over the female foreman as a problematic figure that disrupts the "cult of true womanhood" ideal of white women in America—but he still manages to see her as a "woman" even if only furtively and with frustration. He catalogues her "womanly" features such as her "angry red mouth" (vagina dentata?) and, in the second instance, a waitress's "feminine" gestures. Ultimately, Mae's mimicking of these white women's words and gestures provokes her husband to strike her. Whereas earlier in the story, Johnson manages to restrain himself from actually hitting the white women, the penalty for which might have been death by castration and lynching—he is unable to control these impulses with Mae.

The second incident in the story confirms and concretizes Johnson's conflict with (racist) white women. After his painful, alienating work at the plant, he confronts the long commute home to Harlem. Emerging from the crowded underground subway, he stops outside a restaurant window. Though artificial, the place and its fetishized objects are repeatedly described as "alive." He catalogues "the steam from the coffee urn, with its lively dancing blue flame, the imitation marble counter" (205), finding this artificial life of stimulants, bells, time-clocks, and automatons somehow seductive. He focuses "on the men's hands holding the thick white cups of coffee. He did not pay attention to the white girl who was serving the coffee at the urn" (206). He becomes the coffee surrounded by thick white world. The very detailed description of the coffee cup with its "bubbles bursting on the brim" is almost Keatsian. Such a sensuous description of the coffee serves to sharpen the waitress's snub and may also suggest her action as a kind of sexual snub.

When Johnson's turn to get coffee comes, the white waitress tells him: "No more coffee for a while. . . . He wanted to hit her so hard that the scarlet lipstick on her mouth would smear and spread over her nose, her chin, out towards her cheeks, so hard that she would never toss her head again and refuse a cup of coffee to a man because he was black" (207). His desire to strike out has increased after having been exacerbated by the forelady. In this scene, he seems to want to hit the waitress *because* she is a woman who will not serve him, rather than in spite of this fact. Again, the minute differences in power are revealed in Petry's careful prose. "He forced himself to lower [his hands], to unclench them and make them dangle loose . . . he couldn't hit her. He couldn't even now bring himself to hit a woman, not even this one, who had refused him a cup of coffee" (207). He continues to assign, ascribe, and invest gender with specific characteristics requiring prohibitions. As the world sees him perpetually bleeding back into a black stereotype, a "nigger," so the white women materialize before his eyes as "women not to be hit." Even in his rage, Johnson records his antagonists as gendered bodies that he recognizes as women as he is distinguished from and recognized as being different from the other "men" in the line.

Although the white women in the story are Johnson's actual targets, his wrath warps the face of Mae, whom he transforms and marks as black female flesh in the face of his sexualized racism and racialized sexism. This is to say that Mae, as her name suggests, functions as an ambivalent substance whose black femaleness is and is not secured. The danger with such a figuration is that it ultimately denies black women's subjectivity since they cannot be read on their own terms. Black women do not emerge as "coherent" (which is not the same thing as essential) subjects in this equation.

Here, Johnson's violence against his wife is reminiscent of Teacake's violence toward Janie. Hitting the female flesh, "relieved that awful fear inside him. Being able to whip her reassured him in possession . . . he just slapped her around a bit to show her who was boss" (Hurston, 85). The blows meted out by these male characters are meant to ensure their own limited power. Johnson's deformation of his wife's body is similar to Eldridge Cleaver's grotesque quest to defile white women in which he "refined [his raping] technique . . . by practicing on black girls in the ghetto—in the black ghetto where dark and vicious deeds appear not as aberrations or deviations from the norm, but as part of the sufficiency of the Evil of a day."[23]

When Mae unwittingly "lifts the hair from the back of her neck," *exactly* as the white waitress had done, she replicates the white women's gestural femininity and reminds her husband of the racism he had encountered. In this scene where Johnson reads Mae's gestures, the reader learns nothing of the racism she may have encountered in her day; rather, Mae's story is relegated to the background which allows Johnson to be the central racial subject. His reading transforms Mae by relying upon the unethical aesthetics of Jim Crow whose goal it was "to produce in the mundane gestures of everyday life a pervasive theater of comparison."[24] Mae becomes an accessible target when she tenderly teases her husband and jokingly calls him "nigger." Johnson's unstated rationale for hitting Mae requires that he misread this utterance as if it were the same as the white woman's "nigger." This misreading unfairly casts Mae's playful "nigger" as "the same" as his white boss's denigrating usage.[25]

Johnson's rage at Mae's otherwise innocuous comment is recorded as follows: "The funny tingling started in his fingertips . . . and sent his fist shooting straight for her face . . . there was the smacking sound of soft flesh . . . she screamed . . . he had hit her in the mouth—so hard that the dark red lipstick had blurred and spread over her full lips, reaching up . . . and . . . down . . . and out toward her cheeks" (210).[26] In this description, Johnson has effaced Mae and replaced her face with her genitals. The open and bleeding orifices framed by lips and cheeks are one in this rhetorical gesture. At this moment, he understands her only through a dangerous analogy. This "violence of sameness—exerts a different kind of violence, a violence that occurs to a group whose difference is effaced."[27] In the evanescent spatio-temporal moment between facing and effacement—reading the relation between sameness and difference—the problem of representing black female subjectivity appears. In this situation,

[the non-white woman's] place is outside what can be conceived of as woman. She is the chaos that must be excised, and it is her excision that stabilizes the West's construct of the female body, for the "femininity" of the white female body is insured by assigning the non-white to a chaos safely removed from sight.

Thus, only the white body remains as the object of a voyeuristic, fetishizing male gaze. The non-white body has been made opaque by a blank stare . . . [or in Mae's case, a frank fist]. (O'Grady, 14)

In short, the imbrication of race and gender is inextricable. Moreover, it is the power of Johnson's fist that identifies this unbreakable juncture.

Johnson's clenched fist, the fist of the black man, is both weapon and tool. Elaine Scarry delineates the difference between a weapon and a tool by maintaining that one can distinguish between these instruments according to the surfaces on which they fall.[28] She gives the example of the clenched fist and claims that the fist "may be either a weapon or a tool" (173). Unfortunately, Scarry does unpack the meaning of these differences. Johnson in a way is only weapon or tool—limited, restricted, and operated at the behest of an unseen general system. He is generic, as his name implies, and without individuality or humanity. If we accept this reading, then we see that Scarry does not make space for those whose primary value is *only* as weapons or tools—often black bodies in America. To continue, the weapon/tool dichotomy is dependent upon the difference between sentient and nonsentient surfaces. "The hand that pounds a human face is a weapon and the hand that pounds the dough for bread . . . is a tool" (Ibid.). And what of the hand that pounds black female flesh?

In light of the problematic placement and particularity of black female flesh, this question disrupts Scarry's reading of the supposedly fixed binary of sentient and nonsentient surfaces that distinguishes between tools and weapons. What Johnson thinks is a weapon against a racist system is simultaneously a tool operated by the system to keep such power in place. Black men and women, among others, have been positioned in hegemonic structures as only tools and weapons and that is the violence of this system. To label something a weapon when it is aimed at an unsanctioned target and a tool when it hits a sanctioned target is to assume one knows the "identities" of "surfaces" in advance when surely the tool/weapon would construct the meaning of the surfaces. The substitution of the black woman for the white woman effects the material transformation and substantiation. The black woman stands in for the (im)material white woman and problematically illustrates the (in)difference of wounding and creating. Mae is a floating signifier who is pounded into symptomatic meaning by Johnson's blows. She is reduced to the role of (un)marked flesh between two incommensurate structures in the American law.

At the moment that Johnson tests his own destructive power against the soft flesh of Mae, he also discovers his own limitations. Jean-Paul Sartre's formulation of the fascinating power of viscous material and its relationship to structures of identity-formation might also help to summarize the meaning of the eruptive ending of Petry's story. Sartre's reading of the slimy (which he tellingly labels feminine and exemplifies as honey) concurs with my reading of Mae's body as it is inscribed at the climax of this story. Sartre writes:

> The slimy substance, like pitch, is an aberrant fluid. The slimy reveals itself as essentially ambiguous because its fluidity exists in slow motion. There is a sticky thickness in its liquidity. It presents itself as a phenomena in the process of becoming . . . for the soft is only an annihilation which is stopped halfway; soft is what furnishes us with the best image of our own destructive [and constructive] power and its limitations.[29]

The compressible complexity of Mae's black female body—her position as the "doubly so" in a process of becoming is created and destroyed by Johnson's blows. She is stopped halfway. Precisely at the moment that Johnson strikes Mae, he marks her as a woman *and* as black female flesh. She is a "fixed instability" (Sartre, 778). She is the double marker that he in one blow creates and destroys. The concluding action of the story must be read as a double gesture—in (at least) two ways. For, with the final blow, Johnson does ultimately hit a woman, but with the crucial difference that he hits a black woman who is also his wife. This last detail is important because he has a specific claim of ownership and power over her that is missing in his relationships with the white women. Johnson's idea of difference adheres to what Monique Wittig describes as "difference as a concept . . . [used] to mask at every level the conflicts of interest, including ideological ones."[30]

Sartre's trope of viscosity provides us with a means to "explain" the difficulty of figuring black female flesh. Feminist critics who take up

Sartre's reading, such as Mary Douglas, do not think about "race" or see that such theories of flesh may also be used to designate aspects of black women's subjectivity. From a eurocentric perspective that seeks to make (white) woman *the* body of Western metaphysics, one misses the fact that so-called Third World figures have also been forced to fill the devalued half of the Cartesian split. By reading viscosity as a trope that produces black female subjectivity, we can begin to question the singular foundations and efficacy of certain theories.[31] It is just such a different culturally inscribed reading that might begin to undo the overly specific valences that Douglas and Sartre, among others, associate with viscosity.

Although she does not specifically name black women as potential subjects, Elizabeth Grosz's contention that "Identity itself is the solidification or coagulation of . . . potentially volatile and unstable differences,"[32] is also applicable to my argument. According to this reading, Grosz's so-called momentary solidification is a goal for black female subjectivity—especially where black women are seen only as volatile and unstable. Black female flesh seems always to be broken down, unable to be read even in specific situations as performing coherence and difference simultaneously. This construction runs counter to the previous ones we have seen that insist on reading black female flesh from outside as that which must be feared because it *"has no boundaries of its own* [italics mine] This is not a property of the viscous itself; in keeping with Douglas's claims about dirt [which she defines as matter out of place], what is disturbing about the viscous . . . is its refusal to conform to the laws governing the clean and the proper, the solid and self-identical" (Grosz, 195). The difficulty of reading black female subjectivity, which in certain frames is understood as being "diffuse in itself" or without clear boundaries, is not a property of black female flesh per se; rather, this flesh must be recognized by cultural rules that tend to prohibit her representation as an actual agent of her own subjectivity. Again, despite the fact that none of these feminist critics references black women in particular, their formulations of flesh can be used to denote black women.

The black woman as she is produced at the end of Petry's story resembles Luce Irigaray's generalized "awoman" who "mixes with bodies of a like state, sometimes it dilutes itself in them in an almost homogeneous manner, which makes the distinction between the one and the other problematical; and furthermore that it is already diffuse 'in itself' . . . disconcerts any attempt at static identification."[33] Why is the black woman read as being always already "diffuse in itself" when all postmodern subjects are in theory "not one thing" but rather defined differently and able to exert power differentially in certain contained contexts? If there is no absolute sovereignty, then black women do/can have agency and subjectivity—just none recognized by the law. In juridical discourse she must always be only other's (as in black man or white woman) other and therefore she cannot be "other to herself." Again, this reading occludes the differences among black women themselves vis-a-vis ideology, sexuality, class, and/or color not to mention individual personality. Thus, the black female subject continues to be reproduced as an interstitial ideal.

In her article "Interstices: A Small Drama of Words," black feminist theorist Hortense Spillers criticizes artist Judy Chicago's 1970s installation piece "The Dinner Party" for (mis)representing black women. Chicago's art work, completed over several years by a collective of artisans, commemorates more than one hundred women who have been "swallowed up and eaten by history."[34] The piece pays tribute to selected individual feminist "heroes" by depicting each of them with a unique "vaginal" image painted on a plate.

The only black female represented with a plate of her own among the dinner guests at Chicago's party is Sojourner Truth of "Ain't I a Woman" fame. As in many feminist works, Sojourner Truth is cast as the most privileged black woman at the gathering. She appears as feminism's "metonymic black woman."[35] Truth's representation gestures toward my central problematic because it points precisely to the difficult gendering of black female flesh. Unlike Lorna Simpson's "counter-realist" phototexts in which the artist's "choice not to show faces—articulate[s] the limits of the dominant representations of black women, which have shown everything only to de-face black women as subjects," Judy Chicago's replacement of Truth's face is also a displacement of her genitals and a double denial of the black woman's subjectivity.[36] "This denial or effacement works because ... as the female figures around [Truth] are imagined through ingenious variations on the vagina, *she* is inscribed by three faces. As Alice Walker comments, 'There is of course a case to be made for being personified by a face, rather than by a vagina, but that is not what this show is about.'"[37] Walker's point is important given the historical valorization of black women's vaginal capabilities, especially in the slave economy.

What, then, are we to make of Chicago's marking of Truth? Does the representation disrupt the historical representation of black women's "genetic/genital" difference or does it subtly replicate this history through distortion? Does it suggest that black women have been or are "desexed" in a specific form of racial violence as black men were and are castrated in lynching? Spillers argues that in Chicago's piece, Truth is "a face whose orifices are still searching for a proper role in relationship to the female body" ("Interstices," 78). She continues:

> The structure of the unreality that the black woman must confront originates in the historical moment when language ceases to speak, the historical moment at which hierarchies of power, (even ones to which *some* women belong) simply run out of terms because the empowered meets in the black female the veritable nemesis of degree and difference. Having encountered what they understand as chaos, the empowered need not name further, since chaos is sufficient naming within itself. ("Interstices," 77)

This commentary clearly presents the problem of reading black women as "chaos." So too, this description of how black women can become the "nemesis of degree and difference" is, as we have seen, the central subject of Petry's short story. Moreover, Spillers's use of the term "flesh" coincides with other definitions of this trope. For example, "Flesh is the term Merleau-Ponty uses to designate being, not as plenitude, self-identity, or substance but as divergence or non-coincidence—being's most elemental level" (Grosz, 100). This understanding of flesh allows us to see how black women, without a "unified" subjectivity, continue to be cast as figures in the-process-of-becoming—as being(s) still searching for a proper discursive relationship to a politicized social body. Thus, even in the various feminist critiques of the Enlightenment subject that seek to "break-down" the coherent subject—black women desire what they "cannot not want" (to quote Gayatri Spivak)—namely a "coherent" subjectivity.

The most commonly repeated story about Sojourner Truth's body involves the baring of her breasts. In the various accounts of this action, her breasts become *a* if not *the* privileged signifier of her womanliness. The mere fact that Truth was exposed in this manner served to mark her not solely as "woman" but more accurately as a "black" woman. That she became a spectacle, like the famous Venus Hottentot—precisely marked her as different from the company of women who were never in this sociohistorical moment asked to bare their bodies. This display did not reveal Sojourner Truth's "private" parts (let alone the "truth" of her identity); rather, the display allowed her to perform her particular and peculiar position as a black female possessing flesh but not owning a proper (*propre*) body. The exposure underscored her position as a particular order of flesh that was gendered because "raced" differently.

Most of these feminist accounts of Truth's story efface the historical specificity and context of her claims. For example, Donna Haraway's argument concludes by claiming Truth as the ground to Trinh T. Minh-ha's theory of the "inappropriate/d other" and then places Gloris Anzaldua's "lesbian mestiza" borderlands in the middle of this unholy trinity. Haraway claims that "Truth's speech [at a feminist meeting in Akron, Ohio, 1851] was out of place, dubious doubly; she was female and black; no, that's wrong—she was a black female, a black woman, not a coherent substance with two or more attributes, but an oxymoronic singularity who stood for an entire excluded and dangerously promising humanity" (Haraway, 92). It is interesting that Haraway documents rather than edits out her own struggle to grant black women their own specifically situated identities. For while black women, as Haraway understands, are raced and gendered, they cannot function metonymically for the imbrication of race and gender. In short, they cannot continually be reproduced as the ultimate postmodern subjects.

Haraway's desire to "face [Truth's] specificity" (95) still erases Truth in certain ways. She comes to "meaning" only as a token subject whose exceptionality makes her the ground for a new ideal which she cannot on her own terms represent. Again, the only way that the black woman can be seen to be the ideal postmodern subject is if she comes to stand as the only figure who "has" or "does" race and gender together. This is a problem because, as my reading of this story has shown, *all* subjects are raced and gendered albeit in different ways. In other words, the black woman must not be seen as the "the Border-State"[38] *par excellence*; rather, critics must follow black feminist theory's focal shift to examine "how the borders [of difference and identity] are cut and by whom."[39]

If the black woman has become a representative of "cultural unrepresentability ... within prevailing philosophical ontology ... in which all elements are subordinated to the privilege of the self-identical, the one, the unified" (Grosz, 195), then is her representability dependent upon the possibility of her own unification? Perhaps it is important to recall that the (im)possibility of her appearance is not a quality of the black woman herself, but rather depends upon the systemic possibility of producing her as a subject in dominant discourses. The abrupt ending of Petry's story stops short of creating the space for the entrance of this conditional subject but it allows us to see that merely being heard or seen will not help us to "solve" the problem of our (un)representability. What needs to be theorized more carefully then is the discursive conditions which allow complex subjects to appear as singular social agents. This desire must be denied or rather endlessly deferred because it is an (im)possibility in the present.[40]

NOTES

I would like to thank Elizabeth Alexander, Evelynn M. Hammonds, Ann Kibbey, Katherine Kinney, Carole-Anne Tyler, Ashraf Rushdy, and the anonymous members of the *Genders* editorial board for their helpful comments on this essay.

1. Lorraine O'Grady, "Olympia's Maid: Reclaiming Black Female Subjectivity," *Afterimage* (Summer 1992): 15. Subsequent references to this essay will be noted in the text.

This chapter is dedicated to the memory of Lieutenant Lisa Bryant, a recent Princeton University graduate who was shot to death by a black male Sergeant at Fort Bragg, N.C., on July 10, 1993. I want to remember Lt. Bryant because I want her name and the violence done to her to serve as a marker for the everyday violence/erasure of black female subjects. Neither the *New York Times* nor the *Trentonian* (the New Jersey paper that reported her murder) mention Bryant's race, only her gender. When race is a factor in media descriptions, such black male/female battles are reported by the media as either evidence of black male brutality (as in the tragic case of Mike Tyson) or as evidence of gender trouble in postmodern (white) America (Thomas-Hill). Here, I allude to the fact that white feminists have made Anita Hill their emblem of sexual harassment—paying little attention to her racial specificity. As Kimberle Crenshaw has argued, Clarence Thomas's invocation of lynching erased Anita Hill's black female subjectivity as it simultaneously secured his own blackness. It was Clarence Thomas who deployed effectively the discourse of racialized sexuality epitomized by lynching. While I by no means condone or am an apologist for these contemporary crises, they do seem to be emblematic (but certainly not representative) of a particular scripted subject position in modern America.

2. Kimberle Crenshaw, "Whose Story Is It, Anyway? Feminist and Antiracist Appropriations of Anita Hill," in *Race-ing Justice, En-Gendering Power: Essays on Anita Hill, Clarence Thomas, and the Construction of Social Reality*, ed. Toni Morrison (New York: Pantheon Books, 1992), 402-36.

3. Valerie Smith elaborates on points made by Barbara Smith and Elizabeth Spelman. See Smith's "Black Feminist Theory and the Representation of the

Other," in *Changing Our Own Words*, ed. Cheryl Wall (New Brunswick, N.J.: Rutgers University Press, 1987), 47.

4. Donna Haraway, "Ecce Homo, Ain't (Ar'n't) I a Woman, and Inappropriate/d Others: The Human in a Post-Human Landscape," in *Feminists Theorize the Political*, ed. Judith Butler and Joan Scott (New York: Routledge, 1992), 92. Subsequent references to this piece will be noted in the text. I will discuss this problem more fully in the last section of this chapter.

5. See Valerie Smith, "Split Affinities: The Case of Interracial Rape" in *Conflicts in Feminism*, ed. Marianne Hirsch and Evelyn Fox Keller (New York: Routledge, 1990).

6. Ann Petry, "Like a Winding Sheet," in *Miss Muriel and Other Stories*, ed. Deborah McDowell (Boston: Beacon Press, 1989). All subsequent references to this edition will be noted in the text. The story was included in *Best American Short Stories of 1946*.

7. Gloria Hull, Patricia Bell Scott, and Barbara Smith, eds., *All the Women Are White, All the Men Are Black, and Some of Us Are Brave* (Old Westbury, Conn.: The Feminist Press, 1982). Here, I reference a larger black feminist project that designates the "race of gender" as a phrase that underscores the fundamental imbrication of race and gender. For more on black female subjectivity, see Phillip Brian Harper, *Framing the Margins: The Social Logic of Postmodern Culture* (New York: Oxford University Press, 1994), 90-115.

8. Hortense Spillers, "Mama's Baby, Papa's Maybe: An American Grammar Book," *Diacritics* 17.2 (Summer 1987): 67-82.

9. Hortense Spillers, "Interstices: A Small Drama of Words," in *Pleasure and Danger: Exploring Female Sexuality*, ed. Carol Vance (Boston: Routledge and Kegan Paul, 1984), 80. Subsequent references to this edition will be noted in the text.

10. The dilemma of black female flesh is related to other feminist theorizations of "woman's" body. One useful example is provided by Jeanie Forte's reading of feminist performance artists. She asks, in a similar vein to this inquiry, "How might it be possible for a feminist performer to express 'female' pleasure, especially in terms of the female body, without resorting to essentialist categories? [She] believe[s] that . . . a partial answer resides in a concept of erotic agency . . . that women artists, manipulating imagery in order to inscribe themselves in discourse as erotic agents [who as Eileen O'Neill notes, feel their very fleshiness] might then transgress the limits of representation, and construct a different viewing space where both the spectator and the performer become differentiated subjects" (257). This idea resonates with Lorraine O'Grady's plea that serves as the epigraph for this essay. See Jeanie Forte, "Focus on the Body: Pain, Praxis, and Pleasure in Feminist Performance," in *Critical Theory and Performance*, ed. Janelle Reinelt and Joseph Roach (Ann Arbor: University of Michigan Press, 1992), 248-62.

11. For example, at present, anti-discrimination law does not recognize the "compounded" category "black woman"; rather, one must bring suit either as a black person or as a woman.

12. See Karen Tucker Anderson, "Last Hired, First Fired: Black Women

Workers in World War II," *Journal of American History* 69 (June 1982): 82-97, and Ruth Milkman, *Gender at Work: The Sexual Division of Labor during World War II* (Urbana: University of Illinois Press, 1987).

13. See the first chapter of *Their Eyes Were Watching God*, where Janie returns to the incredulous stares of her former community. The residents exclaim, "What she doin' coming back in dem overhall's? Can't she find no dress to put on? . . . The men noticed her firm buttocks like she had grape fruits in her hip pockets; . . . then her pugnacious breasts trying to bore holes in her shirt. They, the men, were saving with the mind what they lost with the eye. The women took the faded shirt and muddy overalls and laid them away for remembrance. It was a weapon against her strength." Zora Neale Hurston, *Their Eyes Were Watching God* (Urbana: University of Illinois Press, 1991), 11. Subsequent references to this edition will be noted in the text.

14. In American iconography, the white sheet functions as a symbol of the white power movement as the raised black fist serves as the symbol for black power/liberation. Petry's piece juxtaposes these "power symbols" so that their structural resemblance and dependence is unmasked.

15. Kathy Doby, "Long Day's Journey into White," *The Village Voice*, April 28, 1992, 29.

16. Lindon Barrett, *In the Dark: Issues of Value, Evaluation, and Authority in Twentieth Century Critical Discourse*, Ph.D. diss., University of Pennsylvania, 1991, 86.

17. Some vernacular inscriptions of time that might be relevant here are *PC* as in "precapitalist" time and/or the racially inscribed *CP* (colored people's) time.

18. Audre Lorde, *Zami: A New Spelling of My Name* (Watertown, Mass.. Persephone Press, 1982). Here, it may also be useful to note that, according to my mother who grew up in the segregated South of the 1930s and 1940s, public bathrooms were marked for "White *Ladies*" and "Colored *Women*."

19. Toni Morrison, *Sula* (New York: Alfred A. Knopf Publisher, 1994), 9.

20. Ralph Ellison, *Invisible Man* (New York: Vintage Press, 1952), 19.

21. Abdul JanMohammed, "Sexuality on/of the Racial Border: Foucault, Wright, and the Articulation of Racialized Sexuality," in *Discourses of Sexuality: From Aristotle to AIDS*, ed. Domna Stanton (Ann Arbor: University of Michigan Press, 1992), 111.

22. James Thurber, quoted in *The Writer's Quotation Book*, ed. James Charlton (New York: Bantam Books, 1986), 27.

23. Eldridge Cleaver, quoted in *Cavalcade: Negro Writing from 1760-the Present*, ed. Arthur Davis and Saunders Redding (Boston: Houghton Mifflin, 1971), 850.

24. Amy Robinson, *To Pass/In Drag: Strategies of Entrance into the Visible*, Ph.D. diss., University of Pennsylvania, 1992, 8.

25. As Naomi Schor explains, "If othering involves attributing to the objectified other a difference that serves to legitimate her oppression, saming denies the objectified other the right to her difference." See her excellent article, "The Essentialism which Is Not One: Coming to Grips with Irigaray," in *differences* (Summer 1989): 38-58.

26. A different violent ending occurs in Petry's novel *The Street* (Boston: Houghton Mifflin, 1946). The novel also ends with a terrifying scene of intraracial violence. The climactic slow-motion catalogue of blows the main female character, Lutie Johnson, throws at the end of *The Street* are "finally, . . . at the white world which had thrust black people into a walled enclosure from which there was no escape" (*The Street*, 442). Lutie's sentiments echo those of Johnson when she says of her employer/exploiter: "She wanted to hit out at him, to reduce him to a speechless mass of flesh, to destroy him completely" (*The Street*, 433). Lutie's murder transforms what was once Boots Smith, the black band leader, into a "thing." The crucial difference between the texts is in degree and gender—it takes much more overt and prolonged oppression for Lutie to strike Boots Smith, whereas Johnson strikes his wife after only two incidents. Each of Petry's "Johnson" characters acts differently according to his or her gender. Thus, Lutie defends herself from rape, whereas Johnson's violence works as the equivalent of rape. Our knowledge of Johnson's life is limited by the fact that he materializes in a very short story whereas Lutie's life is detailed in more than 300 pages.

27. Elizabeth Grosz, *Volatile Bodies: Toward a Corporeal Feminism* (Bloomington: Indiana University Press, 1994), 208.

28. Elaine Scarry, *The Body in Pain: The Making and Unmaking of the World* (Oxford: Oxford University Press, 1985), 173.

29. Jean-Paul Sartre, *Being and Nothingness: A Phenomenological Essay on Ontology*, trans. Hazel Barnes (New York: Washington Square Press, 1956), 775. Subsequent references to this edition will be noted in the text.

30. Monique Wittig, "The Straight Mind," in *Out There: Marginalization and Contemporary Culture*, ed. Russell Ferguson et. al. (New York: The New Museum of Contemporary Art, 1992), 55.

31. Here, one would have to be careful not to overread Kristeva's gloss that sees the viscous as abject. See Julia Kristeva, *Powers of Horror: An Essay on Abjection*, trans. Leon Roudiez (New York: Columbia University Press, 1982).

32. Grosz, 110. Subsequent references to this edition will be noted in the text.

33. Luce Irigaray, *The Sex Which Is Not One* trans. Catherine Porter (Ithaca: Cornell University Press, 1985), 111.

34. Judy Chicago, *The Dinner Party: A Symbol of Our Heritage* (Garden City, N.Y.: Anchor Books, 1979), 8. For new feminist readings of this work see *Sexual Politics: Judy Chicago's "The Dinner Party" in Feminist Art History*, ed. Amelia Jones (Berkeley: University of California Press, 1996).

35. In an interesting article, Deborah McDowell notes the ways in which feminist critics have deployed Sojourner Truth. Specifically, McDowell cites Denise Riley and Jane Gallop for, in the former case, rewriting Truth's "ain't I a woman," as "ain't I a floating signifier" in the opening of her justly acclaimed *Am I That Name? Feminism and the Category of Women in History* and, in the latter case, for claiming that "the feelings [she] used to have about French men such as Lacan, [she] now has about African-American women like McDowell." McDowell's excellent discussion of this problem does not discuss the work of Judy Chicago or Donna Haraway; however, her reading of Truth's use in and value for feminist

theory concurs with my reading. See Deborah McDowell, "Transferences: Black Feminist Discourse: The Practice of Theory," in *Feminism Beside Itself*, ed. Diane Elam and Robyn Wiegman (New York: Routledge, 1995), 93-118.

36. Saidiya V. Hartman, "Excisions of the Flesh," in *Lorna Simpson: For the Sake of the Viewer*, ed. Saidiya V. Hartman and Beryl Wright (New York: Universe Publishing, 1992), 61.

37. Hortense Spillers, "Interstices," 77. It should be noted that Ethel Smyth, a lesbian composer, is represented by a piano in Chicago's piece.

38. This is purportedly the term Frederick Douglass used to refer to his first wife, who was black. See Henry Louis Gates, Jr., "A Dangerous Literacy: The Legacy of Frederick Douglass," *New York Times Book Review*, May 28, 1995, 16.

39. Hortense Spillers, "Introduction," *Comparative American Identities: Race, Sex, and Nationality in the Modern Text* (New York: Routledge, 1992), 5.

40. Here, I refer to Judith Butler's mandate "not to celebrate each . . . new possibility *qua* possibility, but to redescribe those possibilities that already exist, but which exist within cultural domains designated as culturally . . . impossible." Butler, *Gender Trouble: Feminism and the Subversion of Identity* (New York: Routledge, 1990), 148-49.

SEVEN

Feminism and the Problem of Epistemic Displacement: Reconstructing Indigenous Theories

Poonam Pillai

You who understand the dehumanization of forced removal-relocation-reeduca-tion-redefinition, the humiliation of having to falsify your own reality, your voice—you know. And often cannot say it. You try and keep on trying to unsay it, for if you don't, they will not fail to fill in the blanks on your behalf, and you will be said.   —Trinh T. Minh-ha, *Woman, Native, Other*

In her essay "Under Western Eyes: Feminist Scholarship and Colonial Discourses," Chandra Talpade Mohanty suggests two simultaneous projects that are key to "third world feminist" inquiry, namely, "the internal critique of hegemonic 'Western' feminisms, and the formulation of autonomous, geographically, historically, and culturally grounded feminist concerns and strategies."[1] This chapter is primarily concerned with the latter enterprise. One issue that is central to articulating women's struggles within particular social, cultural, and economic formations is the formulation and use of "theories" that draw upon "third" and "fourth" world epistemological traditions, though not exclusively, in order to critique existing socioeconomic relations and bring about transformative change within society. Although analytic and explanatory frameworks embedded within these traditions are actively used by women and men in struggling with and resisting dominant structures of social and political authority, they are virtually invisible within mainstream feminist scholarship.

My purpose here is to bring one such framework already emergent within rural and peasant women's environmental struggles in India into visibility, and to suggest ways in which we can articulate "indigenous theories."[2]

The term *theory*, as many critics have pointed out, is not a monolithic construct.[3] Rather, it is a site of contestation and cultural struggle. The debate is oriented around a wide range of issues including: "What is theory?" "What is the project of theory?" "Who is the subject of theory?" "What is the relation between theory and politics?" "In what ways do theories construct issues of identity and difference?" "How do theories articulate questions of race, ethnicity, class, gender, sexuality, nature, and so forth?" "How do theories travel from one place to another?" "What role do they play within the current dynamics of nationalism and transnationalism?" and so on. For the purposes of this essay, I draw upon Teresa Ebert's notion of theory to refer to "materialist explanatory critiques" which provide a fundamental critique of existing socioeconomic institutions and practices and participate in transformative change within society.[4] Though the issue of the hegemony of Western theoretical production that I problematize in this chapter, is not addressed by Ebert, her definition of theory is compelling in that it understands theories not just as affirming, describing, and enlisting cultural differences, but in terms of explaining exploitative relations of power at the level of both discursive and material practices. Within such a perspective, different categories of sociality such as race, gender, and nation are critiqued not only at the level of signifying practices but "within a system of exploitation and the social struggle it engenders."[5] Theory according to Ebert "is a double operation: it is both the frame of intelligibility through which we organize and make sense of reality, and the critical inquiry into and contestation over these modes of meaning making."[6] It is a political practice in the sense that it provides a historical understanding of how "meanings are materially formed and social reality is constructed in relation to various strategies of power."[7]

One instance where the epistemologies of rural poor third world women have been used to critique and contest existing socioeconomic conditions is found in the work of Indian writer, activist, feminist, and ecologist Vandana Shiva, especially in her text *Staying Alive.*[8] Here, her argument is that the systematic marginalization and displacement of rural Indian women and men is linked fundamentally to the displacement and devaluation of indigenous knowledges brought about through the imposition of the profit oriented development paradigm. What is significant from my perspective is that while negotiating with the work of various "third world" as well as metropolitan writers to critique the development paradigm, Shiva articulates an alternative to this paradigm from the epistemologies of rural women and peasants, and integrates them into an oppositional framework that informs political action. Although the issue of "theory" is not directly addressed in her work, it is in this effort that I locate in her text the outlines of an "indigenous theory."

Specifically, this involves an interactional strategy for theorizing feminist politics that engages rather than dismisses the significance of marginalized non-Western epistemologies, without casting them as ahistorical. The notion of nature as *prakriti*,[9] as mobilized by the Chipko activists, struggling for survival in northern India, is rearticulated by Shiva within a feminist framework where the project is not simply to transform gender based social relations but to challenge ecological destruction and the structural and institutional exploitation of poor third world women within the dynamics of global capital. For Shiva, *prakriti* becomes the organizing principle for a feminism without "gender" which provides an alternative way of conceptualizing the relation between people and nature. It assumes difference to be a survival issue where the survival of the other is taken to be central to one's own survival. It provides a critique of modern development paradigms by providing alternative ways of conceptualizing "growth," "productivity," and "development." Shiva's formulation, as I discuss later, is quite problematic. However, despite the limitations of her critique, the central advance she makes is to reconstruct the "indigenous" as a subject of theory. It is important to point out here that my interest in this essay is more on the process through which Shiva negotiates with the worldviews of the Chipko activists and less on establishing the "authenticity" of their views, which would require a separate study. It is for this reason that I limit my analysis to her work in this chapter.

What is at issue here is not simply the concern that there should be greater partnership between academics and activists. Indeed, as many "first" and "third world" feminists have argued, this is necessary in order to connect academic theories to lived realities and to bring about fundamental socioeconomic changes within society. Nancy Hartsock,[10] for instance, argues that theories can provide a broader perspective to political activism by foregrounding how specific issues affect women in similar and dissimilar ways, while a sustained engagement with activism outside the university can allow academic feminists to remain connected to the real struggles faced by women in their day-to-day lives.[11]

However, what is also at issue here is the hegemony of Western theoretical production and the marginalization of non-Western epistemologies through the progression of colonial and postcolonial modernity. Not only metropolitan feminist theories[12] but Western theories in general continue to shape educational, political, and economic agendas and policies in "third world" contexts. The movement of theories drawing upon non-Western epistemological and cultural traditions as well is relatively negligible, and when it does occur it takes place according to the limits set by the hegemonic center.[13] This unevenness cannot be delinked from the "global hegemony of western scholarship—i.e., the production, publication, distribution, and consumption of information and ideas"[14] and the economic and political hegemony of the West with respect to the rest of the world. My point here is not to undermine what James Clifford refers to as the "ambivalent appropriations and resistances" that theories encounter in traveling from one place to another.[15] As he argues, linear paths of travel do not address adequately the multiple points of production and consumption through which theories are transformed and reproduced. Such invocations to postcolonial hybridity, however, often fail to address the larger context of the hegemony of Western theoretical production within which the movement of theories and texts takes place. This is a key concern that motivates the present intervention.

The most compelling reason to undertake this project, however, is that the displacement of "indigenous" knowledges threatens the economic and political survival of many poor "third" and "fourth world" peoples. For example, a very large percentage of people living in countries such as China, India, Thailand, and Indonesia still depend on agriculture and activities related to it for their livelihood.[16] Colonial as well as "modern" agricultural paradigms, in addition to having various other effects, have often displaced traditional agricultural knowledges, thereby endangering the cultural and economic survival of many of these people.[17] Further, as Alejandro Argumendo[18] points out, the sustenance of indigenous knowledges is also connected to the preservation of biodiversity which is crucial for the survival of "first peoples" as "cultures of the land. For Indigenous people, biodiversity means just that: the land."[19] Hence, reconstructing "indigenous theories" must be seen not as an end in itself but as an integral part of movements for ecological and economic survival.

This essay contributes to the efforts of various grassroots initiatives on

preservation of indigenous knowledges[20] and the work of relatively less
well known writers and activists such as Anil Gupta who has, in the form
of the Honeybee Collective, initiated efforts to document indigenous
knowledges and to struggle for the protection of the intellectual property
rights of poor Indian farmers.[21] Although environmental and ecological
concerns are central to the issues I am problematizing, my main focus
here is not on evaluating the environmental debate in India[22] or in
critiquing the Western ecofeminist discourse.[23] Rather, through a consideration of Shiva's work, specifically her earlier book *Staying Alive*, my
interest is in suggesting how theory which negotiates with the idioms,
modes of resistance, and struggles of the marginal can inform oppositional
feminist practice within elite institutional frameworks.[24] I focus especially
on *Staying Alive* because it is here that Shiva takes up the issue of the
displacement of women's indigenous knowledges and its link with the
marginalization of women and nature most directly. With respect to this
issue, her position in later works such as *Monocultures of the Mind*[25] and
Ecofeminism[26] is not fundamentally different from her earlier position.
While in *Staying Alive* her focus is on earlier modernization and development policies such as the Green Revolution, her later works illustrate the
perpetuation of the problem within the context of more recent international policies such as the Biodiversity Convention and the Uruguay
round of General Agreement on Tariffs and Trade (GATT) talks.

The subversion of the hierarchy between Western and non-Western
epistemological frameworks and the centrality of displaced knowledges to
the survival of the rural poor that Shiva's work suggests is, I think,
necessary to the formation of a self-reflexive and transformative pedagogy.
I begin with a brief discussion of the terms *indigenous* and *indigenous theory*
and why this project is significant at all within the metropolitan context
within which I, as a "third world" feminist, teach and write. This is
followed by a critique of Shiva's work, in particular her book *Staying Alive*.
The imprint of the two locations I inhabit most, India and the United
States, clearly overdetermine my reading of her work.

WHAT ARE INDIGENOUS THEORIES?

Within colonialist discourse, the *indigenous* has always occupied the space
of the *other*, as the subordinate term in binary relation to the terms
Western, *colonial*, or *elite*. The language of colonialism, despite its internal

contradictions and ambivalences, constructs the "other" as savage, primitive, barbaric, inert, and subhuman with a longevity matched only by the resilience of the native. Interpretations about the "other," as Edward Said argued in *Orientalism*,[27] were not disinterested representations but played a constitutive role in the enhancement of colonial power by setting up an ontological and epistemological duality between the Orient and the Occident. Describing the Manichean ordering of the colonial world, Fanon argues that for the settler, it is insufficient to restrict the place of the native physically. Instead, he is represented as "a sort of quintessence of evil."[28] "The native is declared as insensible to ethics, he represents not only the absence of values, but also the negation of values."[29] The counterhistory of modernity has shown how Western discourses of science, literature, philosophy, anthropology, and history, long considered to be authentic expressions of universal human values, functioned as forms of colonialist knowledge. Darwin's views on natural selection and the moral philosophy of Mills and Rousseau, for example, provided the inspiration for representing "non-European" peoples as embedded within nature. Ironically, however, while nature was understood as inherently passive, adversarial, and hostile to human survival, the idea of "natural" superiority over native peoples was used to conquer their lands and territories.[30] Discourses of race and culture not only accommodated themselves to the needs of a rapacious colonial mentality but also justified colonialism as a process of natural evolution and human progress.[31]

A similar account of the "indigenous" subaltern is also found in various "third world" nationalist discourses. Through the optics of Nehru's paternalistic commentary, for example, the figure of the peasant masses emerges as "ignorant," given to "passions," and needing to be "led" and "represented."[32] The marginalization of the politics of the "indigenous" subaltern is also present within dominant modes of Indian historiography. By recasting the subaltern as a subject of history and restoring him/her to his/her historical and political being, the Subaltern Studies Collective, under the editorship of Ranajit Guha, poses a formidable challenge to this genre of historical writing. While challenging the elitism and the adequacy of dominant paradigms of historiography of Indian nationalism to speak for the people, their deconstructive reading impels one to suspend the colonialist tropes within which the "indigenous" subaltern has been framed and reimagine his/her relation to dominant culture. The recent formation of the Latin American Subaltern Studies group inspired by the

South Asian group suggests how the latter's work has become a model for interventionist practice elsewhere.[33]

Discourses of modernization and development, master-narratives of the so-called postmodern period, are also constituted through reductionist tropes of identification which draw upon an earlier colonialist ideology. The bipolar metaphorics of "developed" and "underdeveloped," "modern" and "traditional," repeat the construction of difference as absence and inadequacy. Here, too, the "indigenous" is seen as lacking any agency, intellectual history, or cognitive ability. In a context where the science of development, as Ashis Nandy argues with respect to India, "has become a new reason of the state," the result not only has been to undermine what he calls "traditional" knowledges, but to justify violence against thousands of ordinary people in the name of national progress.[34]

By challenging dominant notions of the indigenous, the project of reconstructing "indigenous theories" recasts the indigenous as a subject of theory. Specifically, by the term *indigenous theory*, I refer to explanatory critical frameworks that draw upon non-Western epistemological systems that have become marginalized through the progression of Western modernity. However, since they are a product of the mutual imbrication of Western and non-Western cultural formations, they do not draw upon non-Western epistemologies exclusively. Rather, they call attention to the hybridity of social criticism, the specificity of which lies in the recognition that though there is syncreticism between different cultural formations, it is constituted through the reproduction of neocolonial hegemonies.[35] Thus, while emphasizing that there are forms of critique that are "constructed only partly within the normative structures of modernity itself,"[36] "indigenous theories" resist the intellectual division of labor which reproduces the West as the subject of theory and its others as evidence.

The articulation of "indigenous theories" must therefore be seen as a transaction between heterogenous cultural formations, epistemologies, aesthetics, ethics, and politics, and distinguished from any claim to cultural or ethnic absolutism. The issue here is not to recover the essence of any native tradition nor to propose an absolute difference between "Western" and "non-Western" theories. Neither is it to claim a unique "first world" or "third world" theory. Instead, it is to show that there are bases of criticism other than those immanent within Western epistemologies, that have been marginalized through the advance of colonial and postcolonial modernity. It is also, as I have argued and as Shiva's work shows, to emphasize that the marginalization of these epistemologies is often connected to the economic, political, and cultural survival of a vast majority of the world's poor "third" and "fourth" world peoples.

Indigenous theories provide a historical critique of relations of domination and exploitation, both at the levels of discursive and material social relations, from the perspective of the "indigenous." In addition to categories such as race, class, gender, colony, and nation, they also draw attention to questions of land and nature which are important for transforming existing relations of power within a global context. Thus, for instance, an examination of how hegemonic cultural constructions of "land" are historically tied to the material dispossession of "indigenous" people from native territories becomes a key issue for indigenous theories. By drawing upon indigenous epistemologies, they show not only how the displacement of indigenous knowledges are tied to cultural and economic exploitation, but also draw upon these knowledges to critique and transform social reality. It is important here not to romanticize the possibilities opened up by "indigenous theories," for the forms of social critique made available by them may be consistent or heterogeneous to those that are already available. There is no "indigenous theory" in general. Neither is there a monolithic politics or perspective underlying recent efforts to reconstruct indigenous knowledges. They emerge out of different social and historical experiences and deploy multiple, often contradictory social interests and struggles. Hence, when using the term *indigenous theory* one must contextualize it historically, discursively, and geopolitically and articulate the specific ways in which the term *indigenous* is claimed or contested.

One context in which the term *indigenous* is used is with respect to the transnational struggles of the world's various "first peoples." With the recent declaration of 1993 as the Year of the Indigenous People's Rights, their resistances have acquired a new international legitimacy in terms of their "collective aboriginal occupation prior to colonial settlement."[37] In many contexts, as in the case of native North America, New Zealand, Australia, Bolivia, and Guatemala, they survive as "nations within a nation" subject to internal colonization by settler governments.[38] Alternative discourses of nationalism embedded within their struggles against nuclearization, militarization, broken treaty rights, and dislocation from ancestral land pose a persistent threat to the dominant notion of nation as a "continuous narrative of national progress."[39] In the case of postcolonial

nations like India—its sixty million adivasies (the world's largest indigenous population according to the U.N. definition)—continue to be
treated as colonial subjects by the native elite. While sharing a common
history of exploitation in relation to the West, here, the "indigenous" elite
exploits the "indigenous" as subaltern. For native South Africans, self-
definition as "indigenous" is inseparable from "black as a political-class
identification."[40] Such an identification, as Andre Nicola McLaughlin
argues, grew out of their struggle against three hundred years of apartheid
and is constituted through a dialectical relationship between cultural,
social, and political class identities. "Black political-class identity promotes the united front for self-determination across racial backgrounds,
ethnicity, religion, ideology, social status, and by virtue of solidarity with
foreign oppressed groups, across nationality."[41]

The issue of positionality is central to negotiating indigenous epistemologies. Since the term *indigenous* is itself a discursive category, one
must ask, "who speaks in the name of the 'indigenous' and to what end?"
"What kind of political vision can or cannot be claimed in its name?"
"Who is denied self-definition as indigenous, by whom and why?" For
native Hawaiians, who are still struggling to be recognized by the United
Nations as "indigenous," the question is one of survival and access to
ancestral land. In her book *From a Native Daughter*, Haunani-Kay Trask[42]
shows how Western scholarship has participated in the dispossession of
native Hawaiian people by constructing myths about a "feudal" past that
are contradictory to the received oral histories of their people, but support
the dominant interests and policies of the U.S. government.[43] Prior to
the annexation of Hawaii, Trask argues, the "land—like air or sea—was
for all to use and share as their birthright. Our chiefs were stewards of
the land, they could not own or privately possess land any more than they
could sell it."[44] The evidence for this, she argues, lies in the native
language and oral traditions of their people. Yet, by choosing to ignore
this evidence, Western scholars undermined "a successful system of
shared land use with a pejorative and inaccurate Western term. Land
tenure changes instituted by Americans and in line with current Western
notions of private property were made to appear beneficial to the Hawaiians."[45]

Such changes, Trask argues, eventually displaced the natives from their
land. Once the system of private property was instituted in Hawaii, only
one percent of the land remained with the native people while the rest
was taken over to service the interests of a plantation economy. Today,

American military presence and a thriving tourist industry have not only commodified and displaced native Hawaiian culture but led to large scale militarization and nuclearization of the land, using it as dumping grounds for an avaricious private industry. It is not lack of evidence, Trask argues, but the Western scholar's unwillingness to listen to native stories and songs, which are also repositories of their histories and epistemologies, that has led to the exploitation of indigenous peoples. This can only be understood by immersing oneself within the cultural bond between the people and their *aina* (land).[46] According to her, most "first" peoples share a reciprocal relationship with the land they inhabit. "The land cannot live without the people of the land who in turn, care for their heritage, their mother. This is an essential wisdom of indigenous cultures and explains why when native peoples are destroyed, destruction of the earth proceeds immediately."[47]

Trask's critique shows that for "first peoples" the question of indigenous knowledges and practices cannot be separated from their struggle over land rights and self-determination. The imperatives for recovering indigenous knowledges in other contexts, however, do not necessarily compliment these efforts. Within India, for instance, the thrust for recovering "traditional" knowledges has predominantly come from the academic elite belonging to various political and intellectual persuasions. One tendency has been to use dominant ideologies rooted within the Hindu Sanskritic tradition to read tradition selectively while effectively silencing the cultural politics of lower caste, women, and Muslim communities.[48] Here, it is difficult to distinguish between the concern over recovering peripheralized epistemologies from the discourse of a unified and oppressive religious nationalism. In as much as these initiatives attempt to maintain the status quo instead of changing existing relations of power, they go against the grain of how I understand the term *indigenous theory*. More salutary efforts that recognize the dynamic, heterogeneous, and contested character of traditions have been directed towards protecting the intellectual property rights of peasants and tribals and conserving biodiversity.[49] Even in this context, the question of reconstructing indigenous knowledges relates to earlier debates over tradition and modernity, internal and external influences, and is the site of complex struggles over identity, difference, and social justice. Conflicting notions of national and religious identity form the necessary context within which these debates must be considered.

It is important here to digress for a moment and explain why I prefer to use the term *indigenous theory* instead of the term *third world theory* and the politics of that choice. Like the term *indigenous*, the term *third world* too resists any unified political agency. Although it shares a common political valence with the term *indigenous* in that historically speaking, both refer to imperialized formations in the West and elsewhere, the term *third world* has had a different trajectory in academic and political circles within the international context. As Shohat[50] points out, it was first used by the French media in the early 1950s to draw parallels to the French third estate, and later came to be associated with anticolonial nationalist movements of the 1950s to the 1970s and "world systems analysis" advanced by writers such as Immanuel Wallerstein[51] and Samir Amin.[52]

In a recent discussion, Aijaz Ahmad[53] points out that there are many different versions of the three worlds theory, each of which are products of different social and political imperatives within the postwar context. The notion of "third world" as representing a unified "third world" nationalism standing in opposition to Western imperialism is usually traced back to the Bandung conference, held in 1955. Ahmad rejects the idea that this gathering of selected third world leaders embroiled in various national and regional power politics was the moment when the idea of a unified third world nationalism was born. According to him, this idea was preceded by the Western media's construction of a tripartite division of the world where the term *third world* primarily referred to "militarily non-aligned nations." This version of the three worlds theory had little to do with mapping the world in terms of modes of production, that is, the idea of a capitalist "first world," a socialist "second world" and a "third world" "indissolubly linked to the containment of communism and a 'mixed' economy of the private and state capitalist sectors,"[54] which can be associated with certain nationalist versions of the three worlds theory.

Yet another variation is found in the Maoist version where the term *third world* refers to agricultural and poor countries. Here, the third world is also seen as a space of resistance against the imperial "first world" constituted by the United States and the Soviet Union. What is common to most versions of this theory, Ahmad argues, is that "nationalism has always been designated by the propagators of this term—even in the post Twentieth-Congress, Soviet versions of it—as the determinate, epochal, ideology of the third world."[55] The notion of a "transnational nationalism" is also present in many post-Cold War notions of the "third world" where nationalism is seen as grounded upon "religion, or racial difference, or presumably shared national poverties."[56]

Various theoretical limitations as well as recent political-economic changes have brought the notion of a "third world" to crisis. Critics point out that there is no monolithic first, second, or third world. Neither is there any unified third world nationalism as witnessed by the various regional rivalries between such countries as India and Pakistan, and Iran and Iraq. Relations of power and resistance are also much more diverse and dispersed than the first/third world polarity suggests. Further, given the dissolution of the Soviet Union, the emergence of United States as the world superpower, and the transnationalization of capital and labor, especially in the last decade, it is difficult to characterize the world in terms of the categories industrialized, socialist, and agricultural. The terms *first/third world* also become problematic when used in relation to the terms *developed* and *underdeveloped*, where development is understood primarily in terms of economic growth. This particular usage is not only ethnocentric because it holds the degree of development in the West as norm and measures the periphery with respect to it, but also because it overlooks historical reasons for development and underdevelopment.

Despite the ambiguity and inadequacy of the term *third world*, it still retains value in emphasizing the common economic and structural exploitation faced by many imperialized regions of the world in relation to colonialism and neocolonialism.[57] As Ella Shohat[58] points out, it also signifies a common basis for resisting neocolonialism and the hierarchical structuring of power within the global context. In the North American context, it is used by many diasporic critics, activists, and people of color as well to articulate this sense of solidarity and alliance.[59] It is in this sense of opposition against neocolonial practices that I retain my use of the term *third world* in this essay.

However, I prefer to use the term *indigenous* to problematize the marginalization of non-Western epistemologies because in addition to emphasizing the sense of structural exploitation and displacement connoted by the term *third world*, it highlights the struggles of "first peoples" which are either subsumed or made invisible by the term *third world*. One site of contestation within these struggles, as I have pointed out, is the struggle over land which is often not problematized within "third world" debates. I use the term *indigenous* also because the marginalization of indigenous knowledges through colonial modernity has been a much

longer historical process than the more recent emergence of the term
third world suggests. Finally, as Ahmad[60] points out, most usages of the
term *third world* assume nationalism to be the principal ideology through
which imperialism must be resisted.[61] This is problematic because, as
Fanon argues, the "battle against colonialism (or neo-colonialism) does
not run straight away along the lines of nationalism."[62] All relations of
power do not flow directly out of the hegemony of the West. There are
other relations of power whose specificity must be accounted for. The
struggles of various "indigenous" or "first" peoples, defining themselves
as "nations" in many instances, highlight the internal fissures that fracture
the terrain of the hegemonic nation-state, both first and third world.
Considered within this context, the term *indigenous theory* does not necessarily decenter our fixation on the term *nation* but opens up the possibility
of contesting and reimagining it.

Indigenous theories, embedded within marginalized knowledges, challenge the hegemony of Western theoretical production. As Abdul R.
JanMohamed and David Lloyd[63] have argued in relation to a "theory of
minority discourse," they provide alternative contexts of interpretation
within which difference that has been constructed as absence, lack, or
deformity can be read in more transformative and oppositional ways.[64]
Marginalized knowledges are always in danger of being selectively inter-
preted and assimilated within dominant ideologies, both within and outside of academic institutions. The cloning and patenting of human genetic
material mainly of "indigenous" peoples without even a "by-your-leave,"
by multinational biotechnology and pharmaceutical companies and the
U.S. and other Western governments working within the GATT framework of IPRs (Intellectual Property Rights), is an insidious example of
how multinational expropriation erases the difference between people and
knowledges through the process of commodification. The underlying
motives here are not those of democratization or social justice. Rather,
the idea is that "they are going to die off soon, so let us get whatever we
can." The ravenous desire, once limited to the mineral wealth of indigenous lands, now extends to the "wealth" of their bodies. Here, the theoretical articulation of displaced knowledges must be crosshatched with a
critique of capital. While pluralizing oppositional subject positions by
themselves will be inadequate in resisting cooptation, it does allow for a
reevaluation of hegemonic structures and dominant interpretations of the
indigenous/settler relation. In what follows, I look at some of the key

themes emerging out of Vandana Shiva's work. Through a critique of her text *Staying Alive*, I trace how she constructs the figure of indigenous peasant women, and the ways in which she deploys their epistemologies for the purpose of social critique. Despite its limitations, such an intervention, I argue, is necessary to restore the indigenous to her epistemological being within dominant culture.

WOMEN'S DISPOSSESSION AND EPISTEMIC DISPLACEMENT

The central focus of Shiva's[65] work is a critique of modern science and economic development from a feminist, ecological, and "third world" perspective. In her writing, she extends poignant critiques of modern agricultural and social forestry programs, resource management, reproductive technologies, dominant biodiversity conservation and regulation policies, international economic policies such as the GATT, and trade-related intellectual property rights. In doing so, she draws upon both peasant and grassroots struggles in India, and also collaborates with academic metropolitan and third world writers. In this sense, her work militates against being characterized as either strictly academic or activist.

One way to contextualize Shiva's work is to situate it within the larger history of women's activism in India, such as the various regional and issue-based women's protests like the anti-alcohol agitations since the 1960s, struggle against dowry deaths, police rape, anti-caste and tribal movements, struggle for land redistribution, demand for traditional rights to forest produce, and the left and radical women's struggles within and outside of party politics.[66] Her work however can be more closely aligned to environmental and antidevelopment activism such as bauxite mining in Orissa and Madhya Pradesh, iron ore and coal mining in the Chotanagpur plateau, the ongoing Narmada Bachao Andolan which is challenging the construction of a series of large scale dams on the Narmada river, organized protests by the villagers of Ballipal, Orissa, against the construction of a "national rocket test range which will displace 70,000 people from their fertile homeland,"[67] the Chipko struggle in Uttarkhand, and the struggle by women gas victims of the Union Carbide gas leak in Bhopal, 1984. Shiva, along with many Indian environmental critics and activists, has drawn attention to how national and international developmental policies have intersected with commercial interests to produce widespread ecological destruction and to work against the interests of local, especially rural people.[68] One of her contributions has been to draw attention to ways in which ecological destruction in third world countries has disproportionately affected rural women, and to demonstrate their centrality in grassroots environmental and peasant struggles in India, a role often ignored by dominant accounts of movements such as the "Chipko."[69]

Shiva collaborates with both metropolitan ecofeminists and third world environmental feminists to the extent that most of them emphasize the interconnection of all life, especially that between women and nature. However, in linking ecological destruction and women's marginalization with capital accumulation, Shiva's work departs from metropolitan liberal, cultural, and spiritual ecofeminists who do not extend a critique of capital.[70] In this regard, her work is more consistent with metropolitan and third world socialist environmental feminists, who have insisted upon examining the material and ideological basis linking the exploitation of women and nature. Perhaps what distinguishes Shiva's interventions from many metropolitan and even some Indian environmental feminists[71] is that she advances a specifically "third world viewpoint" which influences, as we will see, both her analysis of current ecological problems and the possibilities for social change. The unity of such a viewpoint is grounded in the structural poverty linking imperialized formations as vastly different as India, Philippines, and Peru, a structural crisis produced through their shared relation to colonialism and neocolonialism. It situates the exploitation of third world women and nature within the dynamics of global capital and critiques it from "the perspective of the exploited people and nature of the South."[72] Like the world systems theorists, Shiva understands the "world market system"[73] historically in terms of the unequal accumulation of capital, the most significant effect of which has been the polarization of the world in terms of a developed center, the "North," and an impoverished periphery, that is the "South." Her viewpoint is also constituted through the possibility of collective resistance against the North's continued economic and ecological exploitation of the South (MM, EF). Categories such as "North" and "South," as I will discuss later, are often used as monolithic and homogenous in Shiva's work.

In understanding global power relations in terms of the center/periphery model and staking out the possibility of a third worldist resistance, Shiva moves away from many metropolitan postcolonial interventions where sites of power and resistance are seen as much more dispersed and heterogeneous, involving multiple identities and subject positions. Like postcolonial theorists, she too draws attention to the historical effects of colonial relations as a significant area for analysis and intervention. Her central focus, however, is not on the politics of representation or identification with the "other" within colonial discourses and texts. Her concern, rather, is with the material basis of the exploitation of women, nature, and the "third world" brought about through the hegemony of Western science and development. In this sense, her work provides a general critique of the dominant tendency within metropolitan cultural theory which while problematizing colonialism as a cultural project has often ignored its economic and ecological dimensions.[74]

Throughout her work, Shiva emphasizes continuities rather than discontinuities between the colonial and postcolonial phases of capital accumulation. Modernization and development policies instituted in the post-independence period, she argues, are not a means for emancipating the third world, but are forms of neocolonialism. Instead of offering liberatory spaces for poor third world farmers and peasants, the recent transnationalization of capital and labor perpetuates the uneven development marking earlier colonial formations. In her essay "Decolonizing the North," she articulates three distinct but related phases through which the center lives off the periphery.

In the early phases of colonization, the white man's burden consisted of the need to "civilize" the non-white peoples of the world—this meant above all, depriving them of their resources and rights. In the later phase of colonization, the white man's burden consisted of the need to "develop" the third world, and this again involved depriving local communities of their resources and rights. We are now on the threshold of the third phase of colonization, in which the white man's burden is to protect the environment, especially the third world's environment— and this, too, involves taking control of their resources and rights. (*EF*, 264)

Shiva's *Staying Alive* can be seen as a critique of this second moment of colonization. Her analysis in later works such as *Monocultures of the Mind* and *Ecofeminism* shows how current international trade, environmental, and agricultural policies are reconstituted as imperializing practices. I will return to this later in the chapter.

In *Staying Alive*, Shiva argues that discourses of Western science and development are patriarchal, reductionist, and imperialist and have led to the current ecological crisis and the marginalization of women especially in the "third world." Following Merchant,[75] she argues that the sixteenth-century scientific revolution provided the moral and epistemic basis for the industrial revolution. This marked a fundamental shift in the dominant perception of nature from *terra mater* to a resource to be exploited (*SA*, xvii). By privileging a binary relation between man/woman, human/nature, mind/matter, "the ideology of science sanctioned the denudation of nature" and "legitimized the dependency of women and the authority of men" (*SA*, 18). Such an ideology, she argues, was well suited to the accumulation of capital. While, in the colonial era, this took place through the direct acquisition of territories, exploitation of "native" resources to support the industrial revolution in Europe and systematic slave trade, in the postindependence period this occurs in the name of modernization and economic development.[76]

That the ideology of modernization was not simply an imposition of the colonial state but was rearticulated and reappropriated by many "third world" nationalist leaders, a point Shiva (*SA*) addresses but does not adequately critique, can be clarified by considering the example of India. Within this context, the strongest support for the modernization paradigm came from Oxford-educated nationalist leaders like Nehru who believed in the thesis that Asia was once a great civilization which had decayed due to various conjunctural factors.[77] The country's present backwardness lay not in any innate cultural characteristics but in the oppressiveness of colonial rule. For Nehru, scientific values constituted *yugadharma*, that is, the "spirit of the age" or true universal human values. They were not peculiar to Western culture but were represented by it within the present historical conjuncture.[78] Science, Nehru argued, is not only applicable "to the domain of positive knowledge but the temper which it should produce goes beyond that domain."[79] As Partha Chatterjee suggests, "Within the ideological framework of mature nationalism, therefore, the path of economic development was clearly set out in terms of the 'scientific' understanding of society and history."[80]

Thus, scientific advancement, industrialization, and economic growth became synonymous with national progress. Shiva argues that belief in the ideology of progress by the newly independent "third world" nation-states universalized the Western scientific understanding of "growth," "productivity," "needs," "value," "development," and "nature," displacing local modes of perception.

The assumptions are evident: nature is unproductive, organic agriculture based on nature's cycles of renewability spells poverty, women, tribal and peasant societies embedded in nature are similarly unproductive, not because it has been demonstrated that in cooperation they produce less goods and services for needs, but because it is assumed that "production" takes place only when mediated by technologies for commodity production, even when such technologies destroy life. (*SA*, 4)

The much-celebrated "green revolution" is a particularly insidious instance of violence against peasant women and nature.[81] The primary objective of this resource and capital intensive technology is not the preservation of the balance of local ecosystems, but the maximization of agricultural products for profit. According to Shiva, it involved a fundamental reversal in the location of the subject and object of knowledge. "Nature, women and peasants were no longer seen as primary producers of food. . . . The emergence of a new breed of agricultural 'experts' with fragmented knowledge of individual components of the farm system, and a total integration of this fragmented knowledge with the market system, led to the displacement of the traditional agricultural experts—women and peasants" (*SA*, 103-4).

Traditionally, the production, selection, and use of seeds, for instance, primarily has been the domain of rural women. However, Shiva argues that with the invention of "hybrid 'miracle' seeds" by U.S.-based research institutes, control over seeds passed into the hands of multinational corporations. This occurred largely by making access to foreign aid conditional upon openness of third world markets through the U.N. Food and Agriculture Organization (FAO), and Western educated "native" agricultural experts trained in land-grant agricultural schools.[82] The complicity of the national elite to exploit the people in the name of national development within this context is not exceptional. "With international aid, third world governments were prepared to heavily subsidize prices and also to force peasant farmers to buy new seeds by linking the use of 'improved' varieties to access to agricultural credit and other inputs, including irrigation. Third world peasants did not always choose new seeds: they were often forced on them" (SA, 128). The effect has been to dislocate farmers who do not have access to government credits for food production, diminished purchasing capacity which has shown up as a surplus in food production, hierarchization of different varieties of crops as superior and inferior, loss in "genetic diversity" of crops through the replacement of mixed cropping patterns by centrally produced uniform hybrid varieties, decreased resistance to new viral diseases, and delegitimation of indigenous knowledges. It has also transformed the preexisting sexual division of labor, where women played a central role in the production of food, by decreasing the land available for the production of basic food, devaluing women's work, and increasing the amount of work they do to survive and sustain themselves. It is in this sense that, for Shiva, the modernization of agricultural practices and their integration into the global market system is patriarchal.

One way to understand how the profit motive works simultaneously to displace indigenous knowledges and construct the innocence of dominant knowledges is to consider Richard Lewontin's discussion of hybrid corn seeds. Lewontin argues that the invention of the hybrid seeds was not simply a product of scientific advancement, but a deliberate strategy by seed (and agricultural/chemical) companies to enable genetic copy protection. Hybrid corn seeds are not true breeding and lose their productivity by about thirty bushels per acre with each replanting. Thus, any farmer using these seeds must repeatedly purchase new seeds from seed corporations in order to maintain his/her productivity. To quote Lewontin,

If hybrids are really a superior method for agricultural production, then their commercial usefulness to the seed company is a side issue. The question is whether other methods of plant breeding might have worked as well or better without providing property-rights protection for the seed companies. . . . [However,] we have known the truth of the matter for the last 30 years. . . . The nature of the genes responsible for influencing corn yield is such that the alternative method of simple direct selection of high-yielding plants in each generation and the propagation of seed from those selected plants would work.[83]

Interestingly, these alternative methods are not advocated either by commercial plant breeders or even government sponsored agencies. The U.S. and Canadian agricultural experiment stations that are funded by public funds are some of the strongest proponents of the hybrid method. Lewontin concludes that "A purely commercial interest has so successfully clothed itself in the claims of pure science that those claims [of the superiority of the hybrids] are now taught as scientific gospel in university schools of agriculture."[84]

By resolving to open "third world" economies and agricultural sectors to foreign investment, to transfer control over seed production and biological materials from poor farmers to multinational corporations, and to protect their interests with the help of patent and other "intellectual property" laws, the recently concluded GATT agreement promises to intensify the ongoing cycle of violence. Shiva (*EF*) argues that the GATT agreements like the Green Revolution are also patriarchal because they intensify the displacement of third world farmers, who are primarily women, from traditional participation in food production, processing, and consumption and place these activities in the domain of multinational agribusiness corporations.[85] This is being enforced through various clauses such as patents and trade-related intellectual property rights, "market access" which forces countries "to allow import of food grain and remove all restrictions on imports and exports" (*SA*, 233), and through "shifting of subsidies from poor producers and consumers to big agribusinesses" (*SA*, 233). Shiva recalls that to some extent this has already taken place through the World Bank/IMF structural adjustment programs, carried out in the 1980s, through which various "third world" governments have been pressured into removing food subsidies "which provided cheap food for public distribution" (*SA*, 233) and liberalizing farm imports. Often this has benefited giant agribusinesses because, "despite high costs of production, U.S. corporations and the U.S. government can subsidize and fix prices" (*SA*, 234). Dumping cheap imports onto third world countries displaces small farmers and women from production into famine, since production is the primary way in which they have access to food (*SA*, 236). By formalizing, standardizing, and universalizing many of these measures, the GATT, according to Shiva, intensifies control over third world markets.

For Shiva, the recently concluded Biodiversity Convention[86] is yet another instance of the hegemony of the North over the South. In *Monocultures of the Mind*, she argues that the Convention secures the rights of multinational conglomerates to patents and intellectual property but fails to protect the rights of local communities (who have been foremost in conserving biodiversity), "to conserve and use biological diversity" (*MM*, 152). While genetic resources to be collected from participating nations in future are addressed by the Convention, there is no discussion of genetic materials which have already been obtained from various "third world" countries and are now available in botanical gardens and gene banks controlled by "Northern countries and the World Bank."[87] Instead of being compensated for biodiversity which they have nurtured over years, "third world" farmers, Shiva argues, will now have to pay royalty to biotechnology industries for modified genetic material taken from them and patented and protected through intellectual property rights. The convention therefore perpetuates a structure of exploitation characteristic of the colonial era in which biological resources were unevenly transferred "from the colonies to the centers of imperial power" (*MM*, 78). Shiva concludes that capital accumulation rather than ecological preservation and social justice is still the overriding factor underlying the North's initiatives to conserve biodiversity in the South (*MM*, 79).

For Shiva then, the political, legal, and institutional framework within which current global economic and environmental policies are being negotiated and legitimated continue to exercise an oppressive economic stranglehold on "third world" nation-states. This is done specifically through the agency of what she calls the "superstates" (*EF*, 108), that is, macrostructural international institutions such as the International Monetary Fund (IMF) and the World Bank (WB), first world nation-states, and various multinational corporations, especially agribusinesses, pharmaceutical corporations, and biotechnology industries. This concentration of economic and political power is the defining feature of the "world market system" especially in the last two phases of neocolonialism.

Shiva (*SA, EF*) rejects the dominant assumption that development naturally ameliorates women's economic situation. "Insufficient and inadequate 'participation' in 'development' was not the cause of women's increasing under-development, it was rather their enforced and asymmetric participation in it, by which they bore the costs but were excluded from the benefits, that was responsible" (*SA*, 2). Characterizing development as "maldevelopment"[88] in *Staying Alive*, she argues that it is another "source of male/female inequality" (*SA*, 5) which has exacerbated "ecological degradation and the [women's] loss of political control over nature's sustenance base" (*SA*, 2). Arguing that an ecologically sustainable alternative is "epistemologically unattainable" within the development paradigm, she suggests that one must recover the feminine principle or *prakriti*. "Feminism as ecology, and ecology as the revival of Prakriti, the source of all life, become the decentered powers of political and ecological transformation and restructuring" (*SA*, 7).

Prakriti is one of the most basic concepts within Hindu cosmology, very much in use in various Indian languages. As Shiva points out, it is used commonly by rural women in their interactions with nature. It is a multivalent concept having both religious and secular connotations. It refers to nature, the feminine creative force, primordial matter, or creation itself. It is considered to be the physical manifestation of Brahma.

One of many Hindu creation myths suggests that Brahma in his desire for a companion, divided himself into two, *purusha* (the masculine principle) and *shakti* (dynamic energy or the female principle). *Prakriti* is a manifestation of this divine play (lila). This "will-to-become many (Bahu Syam-Prajayera) is her creative impulse and through this impulse, she creates the diversity of living forms in nature" (*SA*, 39). Many Hindu goddesses such as Radha, Durga, Laksmi, Parvati, Ganga, and Sarasvati are understood as synonymous with *prakriti* which symbolizes their creative impulse. Brown[89] points out that in the earlier Samkhya school, *prakriti* was understood as *pradhana* (first principle of material existence) and was neither male nor female in gender. Eventually, it acquired feminine connotations through its association with the notion of *jagad-yoni* (womb of the world). Although it is feminine in gender, *prakriti* is commonly used to characterize the creative force in men, women, animals, and objects. Hence, it is not assumed to be simply located in the female body. Nature as *prakriti* is not understood in terms of the dualistic subject/object relation. Neither is it assumed to be a resource to be "developed" or exploited. Rather, it is endowed with life and assumed to be a manifestation of the sacred.[90]

Shiva's (SA) argument is that the notion of *prakriti* embedded within the worldviews of rural Indian women involved in the Chipko movement poses a challenge to the objectification of women and nature inherent within Western science and modern development projects. Briefly, the Chipko struggle started in the early 1970s in the hills of Uttarkhand in northern India. According to Vimla Bahuguna, one of the activists in the struggle, the movement "began against certain contractors who were cutting down certain valuable trees for the sale of badminton rackets and other luxury goods."[91] Since the trees were essential for the daily survival of the people of the region, the women decided to cling to them to ward off the contractors. The idea for doing so, Vimla Bahuguna argues, "came from all of us."[92] The women continued their struggle having realized that deforestation in the region had also led to soil erosion and landslides, which had taken many lives. The movement was decentered and took place in many different parts of Gharwal and Kumaon. It was led by various local women such as Sarla Behn, Vimla Bahuguna, Radha Bhatt, and Gaura Devi, and men such as Sunderlal Bahuguna, Chandi Prasad Bhatt, Ghanshyam Raturi, and Dhoom Singh Negi. It was almost after a decade-long struggle that the felling of trees for commercial purposes was banned by the Indian Government.[93] Shiva argues that by producing primarily for sustenance rather than profit maximization, the women involved in the Chipko movement propose a "feminist ideology that transcends gender, and a political practice that is humanly inclusive, they are challenging patriarchy's ideological claim to universalism not with another universalizing tendency, but with diversity, and they are challenging the dominant concept of power with the notion of power as nonviolence" (*SA*, xviii).

By casting the struggles of the Chipko activists as "simultaneously ecological and feminist" (*SA*, 18), Shiva wants a feminism without "gender." A "gender-based" ideology according to her, is one in which gender relations are organized around the normativeness of man, and where masculinity and femininity are taken to be biologically determined. The essential superiority of man provides the justification for domination over women and nature (*SA*, 49). What is problematic however, as I will discuss shortly, is her argument that Western critiques of the modernization paradigm have all been "gender-based." These responses which call for a "masculinization" and a "feminization of the world"[94] are inadequate because both have retained the dualistic association of men with violence and activity, and women with nonviolence and passivity. Instead, she (*SA*, 52) proposes "a third concept," a "trans-gender" ideology which grounds itself in a feminism where gender is not conceived in terms of a dichotomy between men and women, and where women are not considered solely in their relation to men as norm. Her discussion proceeds as follows.

In this non-gender based philosophy the feminine principle is not exclusively embodied in women, but is the principle of activity and creativity in nature, women and men. One cannot really distinguish the masculine from the feminine, person from nature, Purusha from Prakriti. Though distinct, they remain inseparable in dialectical unity, as two aspects of one being. The recovery of the feminine principle is thus associated with the non-patriarchal, non-gendered category of creative non-violence, or "creative power in peaceful form" as Tagore stated in his prayer to the tree. (*SA*, 52)

Shiva's assumption is that despite their material dispossession, rural third world women engaged in ecological struggles for survival are not intellectually colonized. Instead, she regards them as "leaders in creating new intellectual ecological paradigms" (*SA*, 46) both because of their experience of dispossession and direct understanding of the interdependence of human life and nature.

For Shiva, although an alternative epistemology is necessary for the survival of "third world" women and nature, it is not the only realm at which transformative social and ecological change needs to be brought about. Changes in economic practices brought about through initiatives taken at the level of macrostructural international institutions are also essential. In *Monocultures of the Mind*, for instance, she argues that a sustainable and just policy towards conserving biodiversity implies discontinuing aid, subsidies, and public support for destroying ecosystems where biodiversity thrives. "Since the drive for this destruction comes from international aid and financing, the beginning for stopping biodiversity destruction has to be made at that level. In parallel, support needs to be given to ways of life and systems of production that are made on the conservation of diversity and which have been marginalized by the dominant pattern of development" (*MM*, 88).

Further, she argues that organized struggle is required not only at the local and global levels, but also at the national level. To quote,

After centuries of the gene rich South having contributed biological resources freely to the North, third world governments are no longer willing to have biological wealth taken for free and sold back at exorbitant prices to the third world as "improved' seeds and packaged drugs. From the third world viewpoint, it is considered highly unjust that the South's biodiversity be treated as the "common heritage of mankind," and the return flow of biological commodities be patented, priced and treated as private property of northern corporations. (*MM*, 90-91)

While there may be some legitimacy in imagining a unified "third world" opposition to "first world bio-imperialism" (*MM*, 78), this constitutes a rather depoliticizing move for Shiva. She not only fails to examine the contradictions that constitute the so-called third world viewpoint but equates it with the agency of "third world governments." This mystifies the complicity of the latter in the current transfer of biodiversity from the South to the North. Third world governments are made to stand in for the will of the people as a whole, the assumption being that there is no contestation between various third world government policies and their people, and every member of the "third world" is united in his/her opposition to the "first world." A more adequate strategy of resistance would ground itself not in the indefensible unity of a monolithic third world but in its differences, contradictions, and ambivalences in terms of their modes of production, relative position within the hierarchically structured global economic system, history, sociocultural formation, form of state or government, and so on.

For Shiva, decolonization in the North and South are linked. It involves demythologizing the notion of dependency of the South on the North. In fact, she argues, "in the 1980s, the South's poor countries have been massive exporters of capital. The net transfer of resources from South to North is U.S. $50 billion per year" (*EF*, 271). In addition, the North must be made accountable to the use of science and technology, especially biotechnology in its relation to the South. One aspect of this is the way in which intellectual property rights are being enforced within the framework of the Uruguay round of GATT talks. According to Shiva, "If the stricter intellectual property regime demanded by the U.S. takes shape, the transfer of these extra funds from poor to rich countries would exacerbate the current debt crisis of the South ten times over" (*EF*, 275). Instead of unproblematically assuming that science and technology can cure ecological problems, Shiva suggests that we must question the "consumption patterns of the industrialized countries which are responsible for most of the environmental destruction" (*EF*, 278).

READING INDIGENOUS WOMEN'S STRUGGLES

From the perspective of theorizing feminist politics, Shiva's analysis is both problematic and enabling. By rejecting the category "gender" based on a limited definition of it, she forecloses its potential for challenging women's oppression. Her position in fact dehistoricizes the advances made by the politicization of the term both in the reconstruction of dominant knowledges and in the creation of a legitimate social space for feminist activity. Shiva is right in assuming that the notion of biological determinism still persists in metropolitan critiques of the domination of women and nature. Many radical ecofeminists, for instance, assume that "biologically based domination of women by men is the root cause of oppression"[95] and celebrate women's association with nature as a source of female power. However, in assuming that there have been only two kinds of responses to what she calls "gender-ideology," Shiva ignores a broad spectrum of "first world" feminist critiques of patriarchy and the domination of nature. In this, she presents a rather dated view of metropolitan feminist scholarship and collapses the differences between a wide range of often contradictory histories, subject positions, and projects. Feminism, both as a discursive formation and as lived practice and struggle, is a highly contested terrain. There is little consensus over "What is feminism?" "What is the project of feminism?" "Who is the subject of feminism?" "What is the relationship between women and nature?" "What should be the basis of solidarity between women?" or "What constitutes effective social change?" Even though mainstream feminist scholarship in the United States may not have moved away from conceiving the subject of feminist theory primarily in relation to white men,[96] it has to a large extent moved away from the assumption that gender is biologically determined. Shiva ignores this shift.

In trying to account for relations other than those between men and women which might contribute to women's dispossession, Shiva's position is similar to black feminists and feminists of color both within and outside of the metropolitan context who have argued for a "simultaneity of oppression."[97] Writing from India, feminist historians Sangari and Vaid, for example, argue that "patriarchies are not, . . . we believe, systems either predating or superadded to class and caste but intrinsic to the very formation of, and changes within these categories."[98] According to them, gender difference is not a simple relation between men and women, but is "both structuring and structured by a wide set of social relations."[99] Where Shiva differs from Sangari and Vaid is in seeing women's oppression primarily as an effect of class relations and in linking it to the marginalization of their epistemologies and ecological destruction.

As the discussion in the previous section shows, Shiva situates the exploitation of rural third world women within the dynamics of global capital. Here "globalism as defined in the perspective of the capitalist patriarchy, means only the global reach of capital to embrace all the world's resources and markets. The instruments for achieving freedom for capital are simultaneously instruments for creating unfreedom for local communities" (*EF*, 109). Although Shiva rightly recognizes the extent to which multinational capital has reterritorialized the global economy and the economic and political power exerted by what she calls the "super-states," the problem here is that women's exploitation and the destruction of nature become primarily effects of capital flows. Throughout her work, patriarchal eurocentric capital becomes the final determinant in all instances of third world women's exploitation. Such an approach fails to account for the specificity of patriarchal relations and assumes the particular ways in which class articulates with other forms of sociality such as caste, ethnicity, or nation in different sociohistorical contexts to be pregiven. Although Shiva[100] recognizes how the profit motive works at the local level, an extended discussion of this level of determination is also neglected.[101] As a result, she often valorizes the local over the global and ignores the hybrid, often contradictory ways in which privilege penetrates local cultural, economic, and political practices. These problems can be attributed to a binary way of characterizing global relations of power in terms of a center/periphery model to which the exploitation of third world women and nature are ultimately reducible.

It is important here to consider the role played by "nation-states" in Shiva's theorization of feminist politics. Though the terms *nation-state* and *national elite* remain relatively unproblematized in her work, these agencies are seen as participating in the exploitation of rural third world women. In *Staying Alive*, Shiva criticizes the national elite for "master-mind[ing] the exploitation [of rural third world women and farmers] on grounds of national interest and growing GNPs" in the postindependence era. In a later essay titled "Masculinization of the Motherland," she argues that in the first few decades after independence, which is also the second phase of colonialism for her, the function of the state was to provide services to its citizens and "protect" them from foreign domination. However, in the third phase of colonialism, the new role of the state "has become the provider of natural resources, of basic and essential services, concessions, infrastructure and patent protection for TNCs, and to protect them from people's demands for labor rights, health, environment, and human rights" (*EF,* 109). This transformation according to her has been precipitated through changes in global capital flows.

Once again, the effectivity of the nation-states is reduced to global economic flows. Shiva treats the term "nation-state" as an economic and political unit while neglecting the various cultural and discursive forces at work in the imagination of the nation space.[102] There is no discussion, for instance, of how the nation-state remains hegemonic in the Gramscian sense, despite its transformed and exploitative role. Through which signifying practices are national identity and attachment reconstructed? What are the boundaries between the state and the nation as a whole, especially since she often sees the relationship between the two as antagonistic and contested? By ignoring these issues, Shiva reduces the field of ideological struggle within which the nation-state acquires its legitimacy to a one-dimensional play between national and international capital. Elsewhere, she calls upon "Governments of the South" to "stand behind their peoples and their biodiversity" if they are to protect their sovereignty and control over biodiversity from the "economic powers in the North" (*MM,* 92).

Shiva's critique of the exploitation of rural third world women within the dynamics of global capital, therefore, cannot be seen as a call for theorizing feminist politics outside of a nationalist framework.[103] Instead, her project is to transform the exploitative conditions within which third world women live by demanding a reconstruction of the nation space.

In casting rural and peasant Indian women as subjects of history, actively struggling to change their means of existence, Shiva makes an advance over many metropolitan feminist analyses of "third world women" which see them as victims or mere objects of discourse and history.[104] Her position also departs from the intellectual ethnocentrism of traditional modernization paradigms which sought to explain the "backwardness" of "traditional" societies in terms of the irrational beliefs, values, and character traits of their members.[105] However, Shiva often uses the term *third world women* as a monolithic construct and uses it interchangeably with the term *rural Indian women*. This amounts to "discursively coloniz[ing] the material and historical heterogeneities of the lives of women in the third world, thereby producing/re-presenting a composite, singular 'third world woman.' "[106] Further, Shiva (*SA*) tends to romanticize rural Indian women by virtue of their oppression. The assumption that rural women have been intellectually uncolonized and only materially disempowered is problematic for it assumes the presence of subjectivity outside of its constitution through specific discursive practices and processes of historical change. Such a formulation also assumes a mind/body dualism, as if one could undergo historical change without the other. Poststructuralist and postcolonial writers have done much to undermine the notion of a unified subject consciousness, by historicizing it and insisting "that it is irreducibly discursive."[107]

Following Spivak,[108] Rey Chow[109] has criticized the Western intellectual's impulse to invest the "native" with an authentic subjectivity. She argues:

As we challenge a dominant discourse by "resurrecting" the victimized voice/self of the native with our readings—and such is the impulse behind many "new historical" accounts—we step, far too quickly, into the otherwise silent and invisible place of the native and turn ourselves into living agents/witnesses for her. This process, in which we become visible, also neutralizes the untranslatability of the native's experience and the history of that untranslatability. . . . Rather than saying that the native has already spoken because the dominant hegemonic discourse is split/hybrid/different from itself, and rather than restoring her to her "authentic" context, we should argue that it is the native's silence which is the most important clue to her displacement.[110]

Although Chow's critique of "positivistic forms of identification" with the "other" is specifically addressed to the Western intellectual, many of her concerns illuminate the limits of Shiva's position as speaking subject. Inasmuch as Shiva, a "native" intellectual writing about other "natives," does not sufficiently differentiate between her own location as an educated, middle-class woman and that of the poor rural and peasant women she writes about, she renders herself transparent. Although she points out (*SA*, 67) that she has been inspired by her interaction with the Chipko women, her own relation to the peasant women remains virtually invisible throughout the text. In this, she appears to suggest an identity between herself and them and becomes an agent/witness for them. The presumed continuity between her own discourse and that of the peasant women flattens differences in language, class, education, socialization, and sexualization. The authenticity of their discourse and the difficulty of translating it into hers is left unproblematized. The reader, for example, is led to believe that the Chipko women see themselves as "creating a feminist ideology that transcends gender" (*SA*, xviii), without any indication that they perceive themselves as feminists.

The problem with Shiva's analysis is not that she fails to assign the oppressed women any enunciative position but that she does not adequately historicize their enunciations. No account is given as to how the significance of the term prakriti may have changed over time, how it has articulated unevenly with different social and material practices, or how, in many instances, ecological destruction may have taken place despite the belief in nature as *prakriti*. One may recall here, A. K. Ramanujan's[111] discussion of the Indian experience of modernity. He argues, "When Indians learn, quite expertly, modern science, business, or technology, they 'compartmentalize' these interests . . . ; the new ways of thought and behavior do not replace, but live along with older 'religious' ways. Computers and typewriters receive ayudhapuja ('worship of weapons') as weapons of war did once. The 'modern' the context-free, becomes one more context, though it is not easy to contain."[112]

If Ramanujan is right, then one must distinguish between the accommodation of *prakriti* within the larger context of progress and economic development and the politicization of *prakriti* as a paradigm for social change. This difference is lost in Shiva's text. A nuanced discussion of her own location and how she reached the conclusions about the way in which the Chipko women interpret *prakriti* would have enormously helped her critique. Further, though Shiva acknowledges that discourses of science and development are not "class, culture and gender-neutral,"[113] they are presented as monolithic and noncontradictory. In proposing a feminism without "gender" and rearticulating *prakriti* as a feminist and ecological paradigm, Shiva's relation to metropolitan discourses remains contradictory. While associating herself with feminism, a discourse that has historically emerged in the West, she identifies herself with the project of women's emancipation, though as Madhu Kishwar[114] points out, one need not be a "feminist" in order to struggle for women's equality. On the other hand, by wanting to cast it as a "trans-gender ideology," Shiva departs from one of its key terms "gender." Can one have a feminism without "gender," understood specifically in terms of sexual/biological difference? From Shiva's perspective, one must in order to establish an ecologically conscious feminism. The term *gender*, in her view, merely repeats the master discourse without disabling it. Although her categorical rejection of the term as I have argued is problematic, what emerges from her analysis is a theory of feminism which goes beyond "gender" as a category for analyzing social inequalities. At the very least, it displaces the centrality of the "body in sexuality"[115] from the term *gender* and provides an interactional strategy of reformulating it. Here, gender becomes a site not merely for resisting sexual repression but for registering cultural, economic, ecological, and epistemic displacement as well. In this, her work provides a substantive advance over feminisms that privilege the category of gender over other forms of social oppression.

THEORY'S BASIS IN THE MARGINAL

Despite these ambiguities, what is most persuasive about Shiva's analysis is her commitment to articulate an alternative to the development paradigm from the epistemologies of displaced rural men and women. Their worldview, which is mediated by her own interpretive, linguistic, and political strategies, is key to her analysis. By engaging and extending their idioms, she validates and makes visible an oppositional theoretical framework emergent within their struggle for survival. Inasmuch as Shiva draws upon the work of various metropolitan and third world writers as well as upon the epistemologies of rural Indian women, her critique cannot be situated exclusively within any singular tradition. However, while mediating various critical cultural paradigms, the notion of a transgender feminist ideology is articulated from the way in which *prakriti* is mobilized by the Chipko activists, that is as a lived critique of commercial and modern forestry programs.

In arguing that "the recovery of the feminine principle is a response to multiple dominations and deprivations not just of women, but also of nature and non-western cultures" (*SA*, 53), Shiva's attempts to articulate an "indigenous" critique of imperialism and the exploitation of women and nature. Here, it is important that *prakriti* is not an archaic concept that can only be defended on the basis of scriptural accuracy, but thrives in many rituals, practices, and Indian languages. Within Shiva's feminist and ecological framework, it is rearticulated and politicized. Inasmuch as it is located not just within the female body but persists in all living beings, it suggests a different form of engagement with the other, not as "other" to oneself but as continuous with oneself. In this sense, it provides a critique of binary constructions of human/nature, man/woman, and reconstructs difference such that the survival of nature is constitutive of one's own survival. Such a notion of nature is an advance over the concept of nature available within dominant development paradigms where it is perceived as "raw material" and a "resource to be exploited." Shiva's feminism without "gender" also critiques dominant development models by problematizing one of its key terms, namely *development*. From her perspective, development is seen not as "infinite economic growth" but in terms of production for sustenance. This notion, she argues is drawn from the epistemologies of the Chipko activists who "have challenged the western concept of economics as production of profits and capital accumulation with their own concept of economics as production of sustenance and needs satisfaction" (*SA*, xvii). These alternatives for Shiva are crucial not only in changing the systems of representation through which we relate to social reality but also in transforming hegemonic structures of national and international economic, political, and legal practices. This suggests how the scope of living traditions and epistemologies can be broadened into theory, criticism, and political action. It is this strategy of transacting between local traditions and social crisis which Shiva recuperates from the struggles of the Chipko men and women, that allows me to read in her work the articulation of an indigenous theory.

Reading *Staying Alive* symptomatically, one could infer that feminism without "gender" is not an abstract academic activity disengaged from the realities of the indigenous female subaltern. Rather, it is constructed out of the idioms mobilized within indigenous women's popular struggles. In Shiva's text, rural third world women appear as "leaders in creating new intellectual ecological paradigms" (SA, 46). Here, the native's speech, understood as semiotically and ideologically constituted, becomes the most important clue to her exploitation. In speaking, rural peasant women assume a cultural authority usually not accorded to the indigenous as subaltern. This forms the specificity of Shiva's engagement with the "indigenous."

In Gramsci's[116] terms, the Chipko women can be seen as *organic* intellectuals[117] in the sense that they are involved in organizing and mobilizing themselves and the people in their community according to a new intellectual, cultural, and political vision. By seeing them as having a more complex understanding of local forestry and agriculture than university-trained agricultural experts (*traditional* intellectuals in Gramsci's sense), Shiva opens up the possibility of rearticulating the links between the two, a rearticulation which, for Gramsci, is key to the formation of a resistant counterhegemony.[118] The assumption that rural third world women serve the function of being intellectuals within their communities, therefore, becomes central to transforming the relations of power that underlie official forestry and agricultural practices, challenging women's exploitation, and resisting ecological devastation.

From my perspective, feminism without "gender" constitutes an indigenous theory because it shows how the displacement of rural Indian women's epistemologies are tied to their material exploitation, and tries to use those epistemologies, however problematically, to critique and transform social reality. By casting the "indigenous" peasant woman as a subject of epistemology, Shiva's feminism without "gender" also contests the hegemony of Western theoretical production by subverting the binary equivalence between West as theory and East as evidence that dominant theoretical paradigms have often assumed. In Shiva's critique, the distinction between "indigenous" as "first peoples" and "indigenous" as the rural, subaltern, third world men and women is not made. However, the particular issue of the link between indigenous knowledges and economic and ecological survival that Shiva problematizes is often common to both these constituencies. If indigenous theories are to challenge and disrupt existing relations of power, the term *indigenous* must be adequately historicized and contextualized geopolitically. As I have argued, there is no "indigenous theory" in general. Indigenous theories emerge from different social, economic, and cultural contexts and are not unified through any singular politics. The specific alternatives they provide depend upon which "indigenous" tradition one is talking about, who is doing the theorizing, with what tools, from what perspective, context, and location, and so on.

Metropolitan theories, as I argued earlier, play an important role in molding educational, political, and economic agendas in "third world" contexts. As Shiva's work demonstrates, the implementation of the science of development in the service of the state and modern capital is directly connected to the delegitimation of indigenous epistemologies and material dispossession of women living in the backward zones of capitalism. The question for the third world "diasporic" academic feminist, inhabiting the privileged site of the metropolitan university, is how can she mobilize her own site of enunciation, engage her audience, and effectively intervene within the specific relations of power she inhabits?[119]

This is not the place where the specificities of the historic spaces she occupies can be elaborated. Clearly, it is heterogeneous to the social space occupied by "native" third world academic feminists and is far removed from the socioeconomic realities of indigenous subaltern women. An interrogation of one's own privileges and constraints including those of speaking in elite discourses is necessary in order not to romanticize one's abilities to bring about social change. The challenge is to find ways of using one's privileges to create oppositional consciousness within the spaces one inhabits.[120] These spaces, as Shiva's work shows, are not entirely unrelated to those in which indigenous subaltern women live. Disrupting the hegemony of metropolitan theories is one mode of intervention. Oppositional critical consciousness, especially that which occurs within the privileged site of the university, by itself cannot guarantee social change but it does allow "us" to imagine possibilities of doing so. In the very least, it makes assimilation of the marginal into dominant culture a more contested process.

NOTES

I would like to thank Ajay, Ian Angus, Chandra Talpade Mohanty, R. Radhakrishnan, Shakuntala Rao, and the readers of *Genders* for their encouragement and comments on earlier versions of this essay.

1. Chandra Talpade Mohanty, "Under Western Eyes: Feminist Scholarship and Colonial Discourses," in Chandra Talpade Mohanty, Ann Russo, and Lourdes Torres, eds., *Third World Women and the Politics of Feminism* (Bloomington: Indiana University Press, 1991), 51.

2. The terms *indigenous* and *indigenous theory* are discussed in detail in the next section. As I explain later in the chapter, I do not assume that the term *indigenous theory* is a monolithic construct which is equivalent to the terms *third world* or *non-Western* theory. Neither do I want to suggest a binary opposition between the terms *indigenous theory* and *first world theory*.

3. For various debates around the problematic of theory, see Homi Bhabha, "The Commitment to Theory," *New Formations* 5 (1988): 5-23; Judith Butler and Joan W. Scott, "Introduction," in Butler and Scott eds., *Feminists Theorize the Political* (New York: Routledge, 1992); Barbara Christian, "The Race for Theory," *Cultural Critique* 6 (Fall 1987): 335-45; James Clifford, "Notes on Theory and Travel," *Inscriptions* 5 (1989): 177-88; Vivek Dhareshwar, "Toward a Narrative Epistemology of the Postcolonial Predicament," *Inscriptions* 5 (1989): 135-57; Teresa Ebert, "Ludic Feminism, the Body, Performance, and Labor: Bringing Materialism Back into Feminist Cultural Studies," *Cultural Critique* 23 (Winter 1992-1993): 5-50; Henry Louis Gates, Jr., "Introduction: Writing 'Race' and the Difference It Makes," in Henry Louis Gates, Jr., ed., *"Race," Writing, and Difference* (Chicago: University of Chicago Press, 1986); Inderpal Grewal and Caren Kaplan, "Introduction: Transnational Feminist Practices and Questions of Postmodernity," in Grewal and Kaplan, eds., *Scattered Hegemonies* (Minneapolis: University of Minnesota Press, 1994), 1-33; Madhu Kishwar, "Why I Do Not Call Myself a Feminist," *Manushi* (1990): 2-8; Edward Said, "Traveling Theories," in *The World, the Text, and the Critic* (Cambridge: Harvard University Press, 1983), 226-47; Gayatri Spivak, "Explanation and Culture: Marginalia," in *In Other Worlds* (New York: Routledge, 1988), 103-17.

4. Teresa L. Ebert, "Ludic Feminism, the Body, Performance, and Labor: Bringing Materialism Back into Feminist Cultural Studies," *Cultural Critique* 23 (Winter 1992-1993): 12.

5. Ibid. 17.

6. Ibid. 15.

7. Ibid. 13.

8. Vandana Shiva, *Staying Alive: Women, Ecology, and Development* (Atlantic Highlands, N.J.: Zed Books, 1989). Further references to this work will be included parenthetically as (*SA*) in the text.

9. The term *prakriti* refers to nature, the feminine creative force or primordial matter within Hindu cosmology. This concept is discussed in detail later in the chapter.

10. Nancy Hartsock, "Rethinking Modernism: Minority vs. Majority Theories," *Cultural Critique* (Fall 1987): 187-206.

11. See also bell hooks, "Postmodern Blackness," in *Yearning* (Boston: South End Press, 1990), 23-31.

12. See Patricia Uberoi, "Some Reflections on Teaching the Sociology of

Gender," *Samya Sakti* IV and V (1989-90): 279-89, and Madhu Kishwar, "Why I Do Not Call Myself a Feminist," *Manushi* 61 (1990): 2-8.

13. See P. Pillai, "Reinterpreting the Margins of Theory," Ph.D. diss., University of Massachusetts at Amherst (1993), and R. Radhakrishnan, "Cultural Theory and the Politics of Location," in D. Dworkin and L. Roman, eds., *Views Beyond the Border Country* (New York: Routledge, 1993).

14. Mohanty, 55.

15. James Clifford, "Notes on Travel and Theory," *Inscriptions* 5 (1989): 184.

16. See M. N. Buch, *Environmental Consciousness and Urban Planning* (New Delhi: Orient Longman, 1993).

17. See, for instance, D. M. Waren, D. Brokensha, and L. J. Slikkerveer, eds., *Indigenous Knowledge Systems: The Cultural Dimensions of Development* (London: Kegan Paul, 1993).

18. Alejandro Argumendo, "The Convention on Biological Diversity," *Abya Yala News* 8 (Fall 1994): 30-32.

19. Ibid., 30.

20. See, for instance, the work of the Indigenous People's Biodiversity Network, Ontario, Canada and The Abya Yala Fund, Oakland, Cal. For a discussion of biodiversity and human rights issues with respect to indigenous peoples, see Andrew Gray, "The Impact of Biodiversity Conservation on Indigenous Peoples," in Vandana Shiva, ed., *Biodiversity* (Atlantic Highlands, N.J.: Zed Books, 1991).

21. See contributions to the journal *Honeybee*, edited by Anil Gupta, Indian Institute of Management, Ahmedabad, India.

22. See Bina Agarwal's "The Gender and Environment Debate: Lessons from India," *Feminist Studies* (Spring 1992): 119-58, and M. Gadgil and R. Guha, *This Fissured Land: An Ecological History of India* (Berkeley: University of California Press, 1993). See also notes 68 and 69.

23. For a broad and often contradictory range of perspectives within metropolitan ecofeminism, see Carol J. Adams, ed., *Ecofeminism and the Sacred* (New York: Continuum, 1993); Irene Diamond, *Fertile Ground: Women, Earth, and the Limits of Control* (Boston: Beacon Press, 1994); Irene Diamond and Gloria Orenstein, eds., *Reweaving the World: The Emergence of Ecofeminism* (San Francisco: Sierra Club Books, 1990); Mary Mellor, *Breaking the Boundaries: Towards a Feminist Green Socialism* (London: Virago Press, 1992); Carolyn Merchant, *The Death of Nature* (San Francisco: Harper and Row, 1980); and Carolyn Merchant, *Radical Ecology* (New York: Routledge, 1992).

24. V. Shiva, J. Bandhopadhyay, and N. D. Jayal, "Afforestation in India: Problems and Strategies," in *Ambio* 4 (1985); V. Shiva, *Staying Alive: Women, Ecology and Development* (Atlantic Highlands, N.J.: Zed Books, 1989); V. Shiva, "Reductionist Science as Epistemological Violence," in Ashis Nandy, ed., *Science, Hegemony and Violence: A Requiem for Modernity* (New Delhi: Oxford University Press, 1990), 232-56; V. Shiva, *The Violence of the Green Revolution* (Atlantic Highlands, N.J.: Zed Books, 1991); V. Shiva, *Monocultures of the Mind: Perspectives on Biodiversity and Biotechnology* (Atlantic Highlands, N.J.: Zed Books, 1993); Maria Mies and Vandana Shiva, *Ecofeminism* (Atlantic Highlands, N.J.: Zed Books, 1993);

V. Shiva, "Biodiversity and Intellectual Property Rights," in *The Case against Free Trade: GATT, NAFTA, and the Globalization of Corporate Power* (San Francisco: Earth Island Press; Berkeley: North Atlantic Books, 1993), 108-20; V. Shiva, ed., *Close to Home* (Philadelphia: New Society Publishers, 1994).

25. Further references to *Monocultures of the Mind* will be included parenthetically as (*MM*) in the text.

26. Further references to *Ecofeminism* will be included parenthetically as (*EF*) in the text.

27. Edward Said, *Orientalism* (New York: Vintage Books, 1978).

28. Frantz Fanon, *The Wretched of the Earth* (New York: Grove Press, 1963), 41.

29. Ibid., 41.

30. D. Spurr, *The Rhetoric of the Empire* (Durham, N.C.: Duke University Press, 1993).

31. Ibid.

32. Jawaharlal Nehru, *The Discovery of India* (New Delhi: Oxford University Press, 1985).

33. See their "Founding Statement" in *Boundary 2* 20 (1993): 3.

34. A. Nandy, "Introduction: Science as a Reason of State," in A. Nandy, ed., *Science, Hegemony, and Violence* (New Delhi: Oxford University Press, 1990), 10.

35. Here I have greatly benefited from Ella Shohat's discussion of "post-colonial" hybridity in "Notes on the 'Post-Colonial,' " *Social Text* 31/32 (1992): 99-113, and also from Paul Gilroy's critique of modernity from the perspective of the black diaspora in *The Black Atlantic: Modernity and Double Consciousness* (Cambridge: Cambridge University Press, 1993).

36. Gilroy, *The Black Atlantic*.

37. See the *Universal Declaration on the Rights of Indigenous People*, United Nations, Draft.

38. See, for example, Ward Churchill, *The Struggle for the Land* (Monroe, Me.: Common Courage Press, 1993); and *Fantasies of the Master Race* (Monroe, Me.: Common Courage Press, 1992).

39. H. Bhabha, "Introduction: Narrating the Nation," in H. Bhabha, ed., *Nation and Narration* (New York: Routledge, 1990), 1.

40. Andre Nicola McLaughlin, "Black Women, Identity, and the Quest for Humanhood and Wholeness: Wild Women in the Whirlwind," in Joanne Braxton and Andre Nicola McLaughlin, eds., *Wild Women in the Whirlwind* (New Brunswick, N.J.: Rutgers University Press, 1990), 153.

41. Ibid., 156.

42. Haunani-Kay Trask, *From a Native Daughter: Colonialism and Sovereignty in Hawaii* (Monroe, Me.: Common Courage Press, 1993).

43. For a detailed historical account of changes in the land tenure system in Hawaii through colonialism, see Lilikala Kame'eleihiwa's *Native Land and Foreign Desires: Pehea La E Pono Ai* (Honolulu: Bishop Museum Press, 1992).

44. Trask, *From a Native Daughter*, 150.

45. Ibid., 150.

46. Ibid., 80.

47. Ibid., 82.

48. N. Venugopal Rao, "Learning from a Legacy: How and What?" *Economic and Political Weekly* (Feb. 1994): 288-89.

49. In addition to the work of the Honeybee collective, the work done by the Gene Campaign, undertaken by activist Suman Sahay, is noteworthy. See, for instance, the Manifesto of the Gene Campaign, available at the Gene Campaign Office, Green Park, New Delhi, India.

50. E. Shohat, "Notes on the 'Post-Colonial.' "

51. I. Wallerstein, *The Modern World-System: Capitalist Agriculture and the Origin of the European World Economy in the Sixteenth Century* (New York: Academic Press, 1974).

52. Samir Amin, *Eurocentrism*, trans. R. Moore (New York: Monthly Review Press, 1989). Here, Amin understands the "world-system" historically in terms of the unequal accumulation of capital which has resulted in the polarization of the world into a developed "center" and an impoverished "periphery." Contradictions along lines of race, for instance, are seen as effects the "principal contradiction" engendered through the eurocentric expansion of capital. This imperialist dimension of capitalism, Amin argues, must be considered central to any socialist critique of global culture.

53. Aijaz Ahmad, *In Theory: Classes, Nations, Literatures* (New York: Verso, 1992).

54. Ibid., 307.

55. Ibid., 307.

56. Ibid., 310.

57. One could provide many economic indicators here such as the massive debt crisis faced by most third world countries, the relative growth in GNP between first and third world countries since the 1960s, relative increase in poverty levels, pervasiveness of malnutrition and hunger, relative energy consumption in relation to size of population, and so forth.

58. E. Shohat, "Notes on the 'Post-Colonial.'"

59. Ibid.

60. Ahmad, *In Theory*, 101.

61. There are some exceptions. For instance, this is not necessarily true of the way in which the term *third world* is deployed by various peoples of color within the North American context.

62. Fanon, *The Wretched of the Earth*, 148.

63. Abdul R. JanMohamed, and David Lloyd, "Introduction: Toward a Theory of Minority Discourse," *Cultural Critique* (Fall 1987): 8.

64. Both terms *indigenous theory* and *theory of minority discourse* problematize the marginalization of "non-Western" cultures. However, I prefer the former because within many contexts such as India, what is at issue with respect to debates around the term *indigenous* are not only "minority" concerns but also concerns of a vast majority of people. In this sense, while problematizing the issue of marginalization historically, the term *indigenous* resists being ghettoized with only minority issues.

In other contexts such as in North America, while problematizing minority concerns, it also helps to foreground the specificity of "first peoples" struggles whose concerns are not identical to those of "minority" cultures.

65. Shiva is currently the Director of the Research Foundation for Science, Technology, and Natural Resource Policy, Dehradun. She is a physicist by training and an environmental activist who gained international recognition with her participation in various international forums on environmental policy and regulation and especially with the publication of her book *Staying Alive*. She is also a member of the Third World Network.

66. See Radha Kumar, *The History of Doing: An Illustrated Account of Movements for Women's Rights and Feminism in India 1800-1990* (New Delhi: Kali for Women, 1993), for a detailed discussion of women's struggles in India from the nineteenth to the twentieth century.

67. Shiva, *Close to Home*, 101.

68. The literature here is rich, extensive, and represents a wide range of positions. For a selected reading, see Bina Agarwal, *Cold Hearts and Barren Slopes: The Woodfuel Crisis in the Third World* (New Delhi: Allied Publishers and Institute of Economic Growth, 1986); Tariq Banuri and Frederique Apffel Marglin, eds., *Who Will Save the Forests?: Knowledge, Power and Environmental Destruction* (Atlantic Highlands, N.J.: Zed Books, 1993); Madhav Gadgil and Ramachandra Guha, *This Fissured Land: An Ecological History of India* (Berkeley: University of California Press, 1993); Ramachandra Guha, ed., *Social Ecology* (New Delhi: Oxford University Press, 1994); P. Leelakrishnan, *Law and Environment* (Lucknow: Eastern Book Company, 1992); Winnin Pereira, *Tending the Earth: Traditional Sustainable Agriculture in India* (Bombay: Earthcare Books, 1993); Enakshi Ganguly Thukral, ed., *Big Dams, Displaced People* (New Delhi: Sage Publications, 1992); Raajen Singh, *Dams and Other Major Projects: Impact on and Response of Indigenous People* (Hong Kong: CCA-URM, 1988).

69. Again, Shiva is not alone in pointing out the specificity of women's exploitation in relation to the destruction of nature. See, for instance, Bina Agarwal, "The Gender and Environment Debate: Lessons from India," *Feminist Studies* 18, no. 1 (Spring 1992): 119-58; Anil Agarwal, "An Indian Environmentalist's Credo," in Ramachandra Guha, ed., *Social Ecology* (New Delhi: Oxford University Press, 1994), 346-84; Anil Agarwal and Anita Anand, "Ask the Women Who Do the Work," in *The New Scientist* 4 (November 1982); Malini Chand Sheth, "Indian Women in Defense of Forests," in *Women and the Environmental Crisis, Report on Workshop on Women, Environment, and Development*, Nairobi (July 1985).

70. An extensive comparison between metropolitan ecofeminists and third world environmental feminists is beyond the scope of this chapter. See Bina Agarwal, "The Gender and Environment Debate," for a brief discussion of this issue. For a typological discussion of metropolitan ecofeminism, see Carolyn Merchant, "Ecofeminism and Feminist Theory" and *Radical Ecology*.

71. For instance, Indian feminist environmentalist Bina Agarwal, in "The Gender and Environment Debate," provides a more complex analysis of the local and national interests underlying the marginalization of rural Indian women but

does not situate her critique within a global context, nor does she cast her viewpoint as necessarily third worldist.

72. Maria Mies and Vandana Shiva, *Ecofeminism*, 1.

73. Ibid.

74. Gayatri Spivak's work is an exception here. Questions of development and ecology, though marginalized in her earlier work, are addressed in her later work. See, for instance, her essay, "Responsibility," *Boundary 2* 21 (Fall 1994): 19-64.

75. See Carolyn Merchant's *The Death of Nature: Women, Ecology, and the Scientific Revolution* (New York: Harper and Row, 1980). Unlike Shiva, Merchant does not talk about colonialism in her analysis.

76. See also Clive Ponting, *A Green History of the World* (New York: Penguin, 1991) and Wolfgang Sachs, *The Development Dictionary* (Atlantic Highlands, N.J.: Zed Books, 1992).

77. See P. Chatterjee, *Nationalist Thought and the Colonial World—A Derivative Discourse* (Atlantic Highlands, N.J.: Zed Books, 1986), and J. Nehru, *The Discovery of India* (New Delhi: Oxford University Press, 1985).

78. P. Chatterjee, *Nationalist Thought and the Colonial World*, 138.

79. J. Nehru, *The Discovery of India*, 512-13.

80. P. Chatterjee, *Nationalist Thought and the Colonial World*, 144.

81. The Green Revolution refers to the structural transformation of third world agriculture, initiated in the 1960s, through the introduction of modern technologies and capital intensive farming methods, developed and supported by industrialized countries, international funding agencies, and first world research institutions. While the ostensible purpose of this project was to wipe out hunger and malnutrition in the third world, decrease poverty and unemployment, impede the popularity of communism, and bring about world peace, critics such as Ernest Feder, in *Perverse Development* (Quezon City, Philippines: Foundation for Nationalist Studies, 1983), argue that the underlying purpose was to expand markets for agricultural commodities produced by first world multinational corporations. Although it increased productivity of certain crops in the short term, the Green Revolution has had disastrous environmental, economic, and social effects, in terms of displacing small farmers, prioritizing commercial rather than subsistence farming, encouraging centralized ownership and control, and so forth, in most of the countries where it has been enforced. In addition to Shiva's *The Violence of the Green Revolution*, see Ali M. S. Fatemi, "The Green Revolution: An Appraisal," *Monthly Review* (June 1972): 116-20; Ed Oasa, *The International Rice Research Institute and the Green Revolution: A Case Study on the Politics of Science*, Ph.D. diss., University of Hawaii, Honolulu; Andrew Pearce, *Seeds of Plenty, Seeds of Want: Social and Ecological Implications of the Green Revolution*, (Oxford: Oxford University Press, 1981).

82. R. C. Lewontin, *Biology as Ideology: The Doctrine of DNA* (New York: Harper Perennial, 1992).

83. Ibid., 56.

84. Ibid., 57.

85. Although Shiva talks about GATT primarily in terms of agricultural prac-

tices (which have until recently not been part of the GATT framework) and intellectual property rights, the GATT framework addresses various other issues such as tariffs, nontariff measures, textiles and clothing, tropical products, and so forth. See Chakravarthi Raghavan, *Recolonization: GATT, the Uruguay Round and the Third World* (Penang, Malaysia: Third World Network, 1991).

86. The Convention text was signed by 154 participating countries during the UNCED summit in Rio de Janeiro, June 1992, and became effective in December 1993. For an extended version of the text, see *MM*.

87. See *MM*, 154. These materials have been collected from various third world regions by different WB and IMF funded agricultural research institutions. One example is the International Bureau for Plant Genetic Resources (IBPGR) which is run by the Consultative Group on International Agricultural Research (CGIAR), launched by the World Bank in 1970.

88. Shiva's critique of development is similar to the positions of many other researchers. For a recent exposition, see Bruce Rich, *Mortgaging the Earth: The World Bank, Environmental Impoverishment, and the Crisis of Development* (Boston: Beacon Press, 1994).

89. C. M. Brown, "The Theology of Radha in the Puranas," in J. S. Hawley and D. M. Wulff, eds., *The Divine Consort* (Boston: Beacon Press, 1982), 65.

90. Donna Haraway's (1992) rewriting of Western concepts of nature in "The Promises of Monsters: A Regenerative Politics for Inappropriate/d Others," in Lawrence Grossberg, Cary Nelson, and Paula Treichler, eds., *Cultural Studies* (New York: Routledge, 1992), 295-337, is relevant here. Like Shiva, she argues against the objectification and commodification of nature and the construction of nature as "other" in the discourses of colonialism and modern science. Haraway rearticulates nature as a common place—"locations that are widely shared, inescapably local, worldly, enspirited" (296) and as discursively constituted. Nature, she argues, "is not given but made as both fiction and fact" (297). This involves recasting discourses of science and technology as culturally constructed and reimagining both humans and nonhumans as agents of nature (297).

91. Vimla Bahuguna, "A Woman with Rocklike Determination," interviewed by Madhu Kishwar, *Manushi* 70 (May-June 1992): 12-21.

92. Ibid., 18.

93. While writers such as Ramachandra Guha (1993) have referred to "Chipko" as a peasant movement and placed it within the context of protests against commercial forestry dating back to the mid-nineteenth century in the Uttarkhand region, others such as Shiva have called it an "ecological and feminist movement" (*SA*, 76). Disputing such claims, Sunderlal Bahuguna, one of the best-known activists within the movement, argues that "Some have called Chipko a preservation movement, some call it a peasant's movement, and so on. They try to fit it into their political ideology. Many books have been written on the movement, but very few have been able to understand the spirit of the movement." See Sunderlal Bahuguna, "Sunderlal Bahuguna's Crusade," interviewed by Madhu Kishwar, *Manushi* 70 (May-June 1992): 10. Shiva's description of the movement as "feminist" will be problematized later in the essay.

94. See *SA*, 52. Shiva is respectively referring to Simone de Beauvoir and Marcuse here.

95. Yenestra King, "Healing the Wounds: Feminism, Ecology, and the Nature/Culture Dualism," in Irene Diamond and Gloria Orenstein, eds., *Healing the Wounds* (San Francisco: Sierra Club Books, 1990), 109.

96. Norma Alarcon, "The Theoretical Subject(s) of *This Bridge Called My Back* and Anglo-American Feminism," in Gloria Anzaldua, ed., *Making Face, Making Soul* (San Francisco: Aunt Lute Foundation, 1990), 356-69.

97. See, for instance, Barbara Smith, ed., *Home Girls: A Black Feminist Anthology* (New York: Kitchen Table Press, 1983); Cherrie Moraga and Gloria Anzaldua, *This Bridge Called My Back* (New York: Kitchen Table Press, 1983).

98. K. Sangari and S. Vaid, "Recasting Women: An Introduction," in K. Sangari and S. Vaid, eds., *Recasting Women* (New Brunswick, N.J.: Rutgers University Press, 1990), 1.

99. Ibid., 3.

100. See *Staying Alive, The Violence of the Green Revolution*, and *Ecofeminism*.

101. See Bina Agarwal's critique of Shiva in "The Gender and Environmental Debate."

102. See Benedict Anderson, *Imagined Communities* (New York: Verso, 1983), and Homi Bhabha, ed., *Nation and Narration*.

103. See Inderpal Grewal and Caren Kaplan, eds., *Scattered Hegemonies* (Minneapolis: University of Minnesota Press, 1994), for an interesting theorization of feminist practices within a transnational frame.

104. See C. Mohanty, "Under Western Eyes: Feminist Scholarship and Colonial Discourses," 51-80. For a particularly fascinating account of the reconstitution of women's political agency within communal politics in India, see Tanika Sarkar's "Women's Agency within Authoritarian Communalism: The Rashtrasevika Samiti and Ramjanmabhoomi," in Gyanendra Pandey, ed., *Hindus and Others* (New Delhi: Penguin Books, 1993).

105. See Everett Rogers, ed., *Communication and Development: Critical Perspectives* (London: Sage Publications, 1976).

106. C. Mohanty, "Under Western Eyes," 53.

107. Gayatri Spivak, "Subaltern Studies: Deconstructing Historiography," in R. Guha and G. Spivak, eds., *Selected Subaltern Studies* (New York: Oxford University Press, 1988), 3-32. Her reading of subaltern consciousness is particularly relevant here.

108. Gayatri Spivak, "Can the Subaltern Speak?" in C. Nelson and L. Grossberg, eds., *Marxism and the Interpretation of Culture* (Urbana: University of Illinois Press, 1988), 271-313.

109. Rey Chow, *Writing Diaspora* (Minneapolis: University of Minnesota Press, 1993).

110. Ibid., 38.

111. A. K. Ramanujan, "Is There an Indian Way of Thinking? An Informal Essay," *Contributions to Indian Sociology* 23 (1989): 41-58.

112. Ibid., 57.

113. *SA*, xvi.

114. Madhu Kishwar, "Why I Do Not Call Myself a Feminist," *Manushi* 61 (1990): 2-8.

115. Veena Das, "Gender Studies, Cross-Cultural Comparison, and the Colonial Organization of Knowledge," *Berkshire Review* (1986): 74.

116. Antonio Gramsci, *Selections from the Prison Notebooks* (New York: International Publishers, 1971).

117. For Gramsci (ibid., 9), "all men are intellectuals" in the sense that everyone constructs a specific vision of the world. But only some people serve the function of being intellectuals in any society. Gramsci distinguishes between two types of intellectuals: organic intellectuals, members of an "essential social group" which "give it homogeneity and an awareness of its own function not only in the economic but also in the social and political fields" (5), and traditional intellectuals, "categories of intellectuals already in existence and which seemed indeed to represent an historical continuity uninterrupted even by the most complicated and radical changes in the political and social forms" (7). While the latter category includes teachers, priests, philosophers, and the like, the former category includes intellectuals exercising intellectual and moral leadership within any fundamental social group within a social formation.

118. See "Antonio Gramsci," in T. Bennett, G. Martin, C. Mercer, and J. Woollacott, eds., *Culture, Ideology and Social Process* (London: Open University Press, 1981), 191-218.

119. See Mary E. John's "Postcolonial Feminists in the Western Intellectual Field: Anthropologists and Native Informants," *Inscriptions* 5 (1989): 49-73.

120. See Chandra Talpade Mohanty's "On Race and Voice: Challenges for Liberal Education in the 1990s," *Cultural Critique* 14, (Winter 1989-1990): 179-208.

EIGHT

Charming Men, Charming History

Joseph Litvak

Recounting the history of the relations between "history" and the novel as those genres are deployed in eighteenth-century conduct books, Nancy Armstrong has identified a significant realignment at the end of the century. Up until then, history—more precisely, an insistently psychologizing *reading* of history—is prescribed by conduct book authors as a kind of prophylaxis against the dangerously seductive effects of fiction on the female mind. Armstrong cites a typical exhortation to "Use no Monstrous, Unnatural, or Preposterous Fictions to divert her with, but either ingenious fables, or real histories."[1] If the protectors (and producers) of the new feminized middle-class subject thus seem to cast the novel in the role of a ruinous aristocratic rake, they do not hesitate to censure it at the same time as an alarmingly effective conduit for the vulgarity of lowlife. In the intertwined eighteenth-century projects of class and gender construction, novels and romances figure as historiography's doubly demonic other: so much is at stake ideologically, and so great is the anxiety aroused by fiction, that it must be phobically overdetermined as at once too high and too low, as both emblem and agent of the promiscuous erasure of social boundaries. In the last decade of the century, however—the decade in which Jane Austen began and wrote most of *Northanger Abbey*—"a sudden shift of categories can be observed. . . . [O]ne finds abundant evidence to suggest that the classification of fiction had suddenly become more sophisticated."[2] Although anticipated, as Armstrong shows, by developments earlier in the century, this shift of categories—whereby, not just in conduct books but in novels themselves, novels and histories start to look more alike than different—is an index of the large-scale cultural

248

reorganization delineated in Armstrong's revisionist version of the rise of the novel, her story of how it became respectable, its contradictory stigmatization in the eighteenth century giving way dramatically to its refashioning and mobilization as a privileged instrument of middle-class hegemony in the nineteenth century.

Located (though somewhat problematically) at Armstrong's turning point, *Northanger Abbey* recapitulates the process up to and including that point: if history and the novel appear as antitheses in Chapter 5, by Chapter 14 their relationship has somehow become one of mutual supple-mentarity.[3] And while "history" is never again referred to explicitly, I will argue that it persists covertly throughout the rest of the narrative, at once as what can be taken urbanely to go without saying, and as a mildly nagging unanswered question, thereby rendering even more "sophisti-cated" its sustained interplay with its novelistic counterpart. In the pro-cess, moreover, I want to consider the unanswered—indeed, mostly un-asked—question of "sophistication" itself: that is, of its role in the formation of what, in our gender-minded histories of the novel, we are often too quick to homogenize as "middle-class identity."

Tellingly, Armstrong herself has to qualify Austen's enterprise as the construction of a "middle-class *aristocracy*."[4] It would be easy enough, of course, to dismiss Austen as the polished product of the transition from a less firmly *embourgeoisé* eighteenth century (and Regency) to nineteenth-century culture "proper." Indeed, Austen's works, despite the energetic deidealizing efforts of generations of anti-Janeite critics, continue to sig-nify an embarrassingly anachronistic gentility—anachronistic, that is, even in relation to nineteenth-century fiction. But I would suggest that, insofar as the sophisticated classification of fiction and history in a novel like *Northanger Abbey* works to classify—to class—both its heroine and its reader *in terms of* sophistication, Austen in fact foreshadows the deter-minative indeterminacy that, well into the Victorian regime of domestic-ity and interiority, keeps marking the nineteenth-century novelistic sub-ject, whose "bourgeois" constitution can't quite seem to take place without leaving certain telltale "aristocratic" residues.[5] Articulating "his-tory" with "sophistication"—an issue whose class politics, as we shall see, are inextricable from a complex gender politics—this essay will pose a question about more recent history as well, asking what we are doing when we do sophisticated historical readings of literary texts, readings that allow us to satisfy both our refined professorial taste for difficulty and difference and our newer, lustier appetite for the beefy world outside the academy.[6]

"FROM" PARANOIA "TO" SOPHISTICATION

Readers of *Northanger Abbey*—and of the body of criticism around it—know that the high-profile metacommentary in the book is not about the novel and history but about the novel and Gothic romances. It is generally understood that Austen offers not a debunking, rationalistic parody of works like Radcliffe's *Mysteries of Udolpho* but rather a streamlined, modernized—in short, a sophisticated—Gothicism that follows in their footsteps. In different ways, numerous critics have made the case that Catherine Morland's progress toward "a more sophisticated use of cultural forms" constitutes an education in dialectics, whereby realism evolves as a refinement upon rather than a denial of Gothic.[7] In the novel's paradigmatic phrase, "The anxieties of common life beg[in] soon to succeed to the alarms of romance" (203). Even the long passage in which Catherine displays her new sophistication by condescending to the author she had once naïvely adored can be read, as one critic puts it, as representing "a complex admission rather than rejection of the Gothic":[8]

Charming as were all Mrs. Radcliffe's works, and charming even as were the works of all her imitators, it was not in them perhaps that human nature, at least in the midland counties of England, was to be looked for. Of the Alps and Pyrenees, with their pine forests and their vices, they might give a faithful delineation; and Italy, Switzerland, and the South of France, might be as fruitful in horrors as they were represented. Catherine dared not doubt beyond her own country, and even of that, if hard pressed, would have yielded the northern and western extremities. But in the central part of England there was surely some security for the existence even of a wife not beloved, in the laws of the land, and the manners of the age. Murder was not tolerated, servants were not slaves, and neither poison nor sleeping potions to be procured, like rhubarb, from every druggist. (202)

Although this xenophobia might seem to have domestic reassurance as its intended effect, the apparent non sequitur, "Catherine dared not doubt beyond her own country," gives one pause. After all, if the passage opposes English law and order to Continental viciousness, the line should read: "Catherine dared not doubt *within* her own country." But as the passage continues, we discover that, far from marginalizing the motives for the Gothic, its tendentious narrowing from geocultural "extremities" to a figural linkage of middles and centers with the putative virtues of English moderation actually enables a tightening of the Gothic screw. Exemplifying the perversity of paranoia, the passage moves from a presumably calming invocation of the median and the middling to the disconcertingly paradoxical conclusion that this stable middle ground in fact supplies a basis for nothing so much as intensified suspicion:

Among the Alps and Pyrenees, perhaps, there were no mixed characters. There, such as were not as spotless as an angel, might have the dispositions of a fiend. But in England it was not so; among the English, she believed, in their hearts and habits, there was a general though unequal mixture of good and bad. Upon this conviction, she would not be surprised if even in Henry and Eleanor Tilney, some slight imperfection might hereafter appear; and upon this conviction she need not fear to acknowledge some actual specks in the character of their father, who, though cleared from the grossly injurious suspicions which she must ever blush to have entertained, she did believe, upon serious consideration, to be not perfectly amiable. (202)

Having gone from geographical middleness to cultural moderation, the passage proceeds from cultural moderation to psychological mixture. Thus rehearsing its own representational logic, "realism" makes the (bad) dream of female Gothic paranoia come true: where Catherine was just paranoid before, now she recognizes that she really has something to be paranoid about.[9] As though to provide her—and us—with further reassurance of the need for anxiety, the narrative goes on to confirm with a vengeance her belief that General Tilney is "not perfectly amiable": a few chapters later, after all, he kicks her out of his house because he discovers that she isn't as rich as he had thought, and because he's afraid that she's after his fortune. But even before this climactic reinscription of the Gothic, the narrative has managed to cast the permanent shadow of a doubt. Catherine "would not be surprised if even in Henry and Eleanor Tilney, some slight imperfection might hereafter appear," if only for the reason that Henry at least, as many critics have observed, has been exhibiting such "imperfections" from the outset, revealing himself, to the suspicious gaze, not as Gothic hero to his father's Gothic villain, but as the practitioner of a more systematically euphemized, more suavely generalized, and thus more conveniently misrecognizable male sadism than that directed against Catherine by his rather too anxiously and ineptly malevolent parent.

That Catherine does misrecognize Henry's sadism—that she takes his elaborate sarcasms and insults, for instance, as manifestations of a charm even more seductive than that of "Mrs. Radcliffe's works"—accounts for why the novel's paranoid or Gothic realism seems much less paradoxical than my framing of it. In other words, because Catherine's education necessarily assumes the diachronic form of a linear narrative, of a female *Bildungsroman* that is also a heterosexualizing "love story," she seems not to descend from a relatively abstract and innocuous paranoia to a more concrete and insidious one, but rather to ascend from paranoia *tout court* toward something more epistemologically legitimate and more socially desirable, something that the novel, in promoting (and in promoting Catherine to) "a more sophisticated use of cultural forms," signally invests in the "lover-mentor" Henry himself—that something, of course, is sophistication *as* a cultural form, as a class-specific, and thus, as we shall see, gender-marked, style or disposition.[10]

Catherine's refined paranoia depends heavily on a thematics and an imagery of middleness, and though this middleness gets mapped along national and regional axes, the resulting symbolic cartography also inscribes an allegory of *class*. Since the socially middling can be defined only in relation to the extremes it is always having to avoid, Catherine's realistic paranoia could be traced to the disciplinary system that, as critics have shown, keeps the normative, implicitly feminized middle-class subject of the nineteenth-century novel in line by keeping that subject fluctuating between, but never quite reaching, opposite "extremities," uncertain about *where* the lines that would define its normative status have been drawn.[11] In the liberal police state that is realism's utopia, nothing succeeds like anxiety in maintaining not just the suspense but also the suspension of both novel-reader and novel-character, especially when the latter *is* a novel-reader, as in *Northanger Abbey*. But if middle-classing them means keeping them up in the air, hovering uneasily between lowlife and high society, they must also, given the strong teleologies that impel nineteenth-century narratives, seem to be on the move, going places, up and coming, even if only on the intellectual and ethical scale that a novel like *Great Expectations* would have us substitute for a social and economic one. (Pip may end up having to lower his expectations, but in renouncing the "bad" sophistication of snobbery, he accedes to the "good" sophistication of a quasi-authorial narrative privilege.) As a result, what *Northanger Abbey* and its successors disclose is an odd asymmetry in the formation of their middle-class protagonists, those essentially labile desiring subjects whose middleness, as John Kucich has suggested with regard to Trollope, is always slightly off-center, tilted sometimes toward the lower end of the social order but gravitating (or levitating) more often than not toward the upper echelons.[12] At least in nineteenth-century fiction, it would seem, it is the "middle-class aristocracy," that hybrid, centrifugal, exogamous, overachieving, self-displacing social trope, that you have always with you.

The (self-)decentering or asymmetry of Catherine Morland, for example, can be discerned in the mechanics of the novel's final explanations and resolutions: while John Thorpe's socially anxious misrepresentations of her family's economic position precipitate both her hyperbolic rise and her equally hypobolic fall in General Tilney's estimation, thereby enabling her "true" status to be fixed at some presumptive midpoint between the false extremities of wealth and need, of *having* more land and *wanting* more land, that determination is what in the end compels the General to consent to her *marrying* more land—namely, his son's—than her middle-class father owns. Figuring the "more" of middle-class culture, which keeps pushing it, as though by some indomitable inner law, some Cinderella instinct, toward alliances and identifications with its "aristocratic" other, the "more" built into this middle-class heroine consists in the way she exceeds herself merely by *becoming* herself—that is, by getting ranked accurately in the social hierarchy (thanks to the intervention, not coincidentally, of a viscount and a viscountess), so that she can advance, via marriage with Henry Tilney, from the lower to the upper gentry.

What I am trying to describe here is a process in the novel whereby refinement as particularization, as in the "realistic" psychology of mixed character and the "bourgeois" ethos of moderation, seems inevitably to upgrade itself by tending toward refinement as "aristocratic" style.[13] Or, in terms put into productive analytic play by Pierre Bourdieu in his sociology of aesthetics: the act of *making* distinctions comes to *confer* distinction on the one who is making them; the classifier classifies herself, showing by means of her classifications that, in vulgar parlance, she has class, proving in her own person that, as is "only natural," class will out.[14] Teaching her how to make distinctions, Catherine's course in refined Gothicism prepares her to become distinguished, to attain a condition in which, someday, in her life after the novel's close, she might seem to have left Gothicism—even refined Gothicism—behind. At the beginning of the novel, she is "in training for a [Gothic] heroine" (39); at the end, she is in training, with her husband as tutor, for assimilation into the elite culture that he embodies. Were we to project that training beyond the limit of the novel, we would have to imagine that her refined Gothic paranoia will ultimately refine itself to the point where, though it may retain the *form* of Gothic paranoia, it will no longer *look* Gothic or paranoid, so successful will its sublimation have been.

The trouble with Gothic, the reason why it has to produce its own *Aufhebung*, derives from its very centrality to Catherine's aesthetic education. It centers her—middle-classes her—but as a result of its own too-conspicuous fluctuation between extremities. And in thus centering her, it proves itself lacking in that extra quantum of energy that will simultaneously *de*center her: it is too antithetical and therefore too symmetrical to give Catherine the precisely calculated boost, the hydraulic lift, that she needs to reach the *off-center* center of the *upper-middle* social register. However realistically middling and mixed a perspective her Gothic curriculum may ultimately secure, it leaves too many traces, in the process, of its own spectacular, promiscuous shuttle between the poles of its aristocratic subject matter and highly artificial conventions, on the one hand, and its irrecuperably vulgar social reputation and distinctive (but undistinguished) corporeal effects, on the other. Notwithstanding Austen's famous spirited defense of her sister-novelists, including her Gothic forerunners, in Chapter 5, her heavily ironic emphasis on Gothic fiction's absent referential ground (Catherine's Gothic future is in doubt because "There was not one lord in the neighbourhood; no—not even a baronet" [40]), as well as the metonymic taint that no amount of palimpsestic revision can ever quite obliterate once the gold-digging, social-climbing Isabella Thorpe has gotten her hands on *The Mysteries of Udolpho*, indicate the need for some other, less visibly contradictory, more discreetly upscale literary paradigm through which to chart her heroine's progress.

In other words, despite the legitimating shift of categories noted by Armstrong, *Northanger Abbey*, at any rate, still evinces the necessity of living down the bad press that the novel as genre had received in the preceding century, and that the social and aesthetic extremism of the Gothic novel in particular seems destined to reactivate. This, of course, is history's cue to reenter the discussion. For if the classification of fiction becomes more sophisticated in Austen's time, and if the novel's cultural stock rises concomitantly, those changes have a great deal to do with the move whereby novels take historiography as their model. It is well known,

of course, that fictional narratives had modelled themselves on and even
called themselves histories before the end of the eighteenth century;
what is significant about the shift in question, however, is precisely the
sophistication with which that generic self-definition was negotiated.[15] In
this historical framework, Scott would be the obvious canonical name to
invoke. But while Austen could hardly be classified as a "historical novel-
ist," a work like *Northanger Abbey*, I would suggest, improves its class
standing considerably by enlisting history as its secret partner, enacting a
sophisticated reclassification of *itself*.

I want to signal the distinctively understated presence of this "history,"
or of this "historicism," alongside or within the novel's more aggressive
thematization of the Gothic—as, for instance, in Henry's speech to Catherine, where he reproaches her for indulging in the sort of Gothicizing
fantasy for which he has in fact set her up:

Dear Miss Morland, consider the dreadful nature of the suspicions you have
entertained. What have you been judging from? Remember the country and the
age in which we live. Remember that we are English, that we are Christians.
Consult your own understanding, your own sense of the probable, your own
observation of what is passing around you—Does our education prepare us for
such atrocities? Do our laws connive at them? Could they be perpetrated without
being known, in a country like this, where social and literary intercourse is on
such a footing; where every man is surrounded by a neighbourhood of voluntary
spies, and where roads and newspapers lay every thing open? Dearest Miss Morland, what ideas have you been admitting? (199-200)

Sounding for all the world like a Foucauldian new historicist *avant la
lettre*—not only does the ubiquitous existence of informal networks of
"voluntary spies" evoke the generalized panopticism of modern culture,
but "social *and* literary intercourse" constitutes that panopticism's disciplinary lining—Henry provides Catherine with the perverse model for
her transformation of the supposedly reassuring discourse of enlightened
reason into grounds for redoubled paranoia. Except that, when he speaks
the language of paranoia, it doesn't seem so much like a discreditably
female (if justified) paranoia ("Dearest Miss Morland, what ideas have you
been admitting?") as like a seductively urbane, indeed, imperturbably
male, rhetoric of authority.

The point is not to reduce Foucauldian self-consciousness to a mere
psychopathology. Where the term "paranoia" is ordinarily applied diag-
nostically and/or disparagingly, I am using it here—inspired by feminist

revisions and revaluations of female paranoia—in such a way as to problematize the familiar distinction between legitimate, male knowledges and
illegitimate, female ones, to demonstrate the surprising continuity between a relatively privileged discourse of historicist "truth-telling" and a
relatively unprivileged one of novelistic, or novelistically induced, "delu-
sion."[16] To demonstrate this continuity is to uncover one of the most
ingenious mechanisms of this novel's marriage plot, which is to say, its
narrative of upward mobility. In marrying Henry, that is, Catherine marries his "sophistication"; but since his "sophistication" is structurally similar to her "naïveté," the marriage happily combines something old with
something new. Nothing less than a social coup on the part of the
heroine, it somehow seems "natural" as well. And this impression of
naturalness is helped, as we shall see, by the fact that, while sophistication
is initially represented by a man, it unfolds as a class style characterized
by a less rigorous policing of gendered tastes than Catherine has known
in her polarized milieu: the world into which she ascends includes sophisticated women as well as sophisticated men. Though "Dearest Miss Morland" puts up for now with Henry's male condescension, its resemblance
to what it condescends to already offers her the hope (however illusory)
that to join him in matrimony would be to join him in his urbane
superiority.

Having mastered his paranoia in the sense of having perfected it, at
any rate, Henry may seem instead to have mastered it in the sense of
having triumphed over it. Far from supplanting Gothic paranoia, historicist sophistication merely renders even more systematic what is already an
obsessively and defensively systematizing activity in the first place.[17] But
in showing Catherine an underlying connection between paranoia and
sophistication, Henry also shows her how to progress from the former to
the latter; he shows her how one can seem to rise above Gothicism *by
means of* Gothicism. His lesson, in short, promotes history as Gothicism
disciplined.

"FROM" THE NOVEL "TO" HISTORY

If *Northanger Abbey* takes pains to stage its relationship with Gothic
fiction, its inscription of history, I have been suggesting, is no less conse-
quential for being less ostentatious—which is to say, more Austenian.
Indeed, the strategic importance of that inscription resides precisely in its

subtlety, in the quiet good taste with which it is performed—with which, indeed, the name of the author is virtually synonymous. I have pointed out the implicit functioning of "history" in more noticeably Gothic-centered passages; but even where its name does comes up, it behaves, one might say, like a gentleman, never parading its attractions or pushing its own claims at the obvious expense of other literary or artistic forms.

Admittedly, the novel's first reference to history, which occurs in the context of Austen's defense of the novel in Chapter 5, is not particularly honorific. If she allows history-writing to preserve a certain air of tedious gentility amid the Grub Street jumble to which she consigns it, her apparent revenge on the literary class structure nevertheless has the general effect of subjecting history not just to a declassification but to a not-so-subtle *déclassement*. By Chapter 14, however—in what is almost but not quite the middle of the book, in what constitutes its slightly lopsided centerpiece—Austen appears to have felt a certain compunction about what she might fear has looked like an unseemly display of resentment, for in this later chapter she intimates a *re*classification of history that reaffirms its upper-middle status. It is as though, rehearsing in miniature the development of the novel as a genre, the author had herself reenacted the progress from its terrible childhood through its rebellious adolescence to its reasonable maturity, where, finally on an equal footing with its literary progenitors, it can come to terms both with its own history and with history itself. Thus, when Catherine, Henry, and his sister, Eleanor, discuss *The Mysteries of Udolpho*, Eleanor asks Catherine:

"You are fond of that kind of reading?"
    "To say the truth, I do not much like any other."
    "Indeed!"
    "That is, I can read poetry and plays, and things of that sort, and do not dislike travels. But history, real solemn history, I cannot be interested in. Can you?"
    "Yes, I am fond of history."
    "I wish I were too. I read it a little as a duty, but it tells me nothing that does not either vex or weary me. The quarrels of popes and kings, with wars or pestilences, in every page; the men all so good for nothing, and hardly any women at all—it is very tiresome: and yet I often think it odd that it should be so dull, for a great deal of it must be invention. The speeches that are put into the heroes' mouths, their thoughts and designs—the chief of all this must be invention, and invention is what delights me in other books." (123)

This passage makes clear that, while Catherine may be anti-intellectual, she is hardly unintelligent. Her lower-middle-brow naïveté, in fact, furnishes her with an alibi for the rather sophisticated feminist critique of traditional history that she broaches here, and that Austen seems obliquely to endorse a couple of pages later in her ironic aside about the social and political advantages of female "ignorance." While this passage thus provokes a sympathetic recognition in many contemporary readers, it also calls up—just as grippingly—the sense of panic familiar to some academic critics in the face of the current imperative always to historicize.[18] A feminist critique of patriarchal history, of course, need not signify antihistoricism; many feminisms are also sophisticated historicisms, and many antihistoricisms are also antifeminisms, or at least nonfeminisms. What I would emphasize as valuably feminist in Catherine's skepticism toward history is her recognition of, and resistance to, the compulsory character of the historicism with which she is faced, a historicism that itself *means* sophistication. Especially in the current critical context, where the virtue of historicizing has almost acquired the status of an orthodoxy, and where the failure to historicize (or to honor the most familiar historical paradigms) can still be alleged humiliatingly against certain feminist as well as, for instance, many gay, lesbian, and queer (including Foucault-inspired) critical practices, Catherine's resistance, however anxious, however easily overcome, usefully suggests a sophisticatedly naïve reading of sophistication itself—that is, of the "sophistication" that, bearing down on its objects with all the coercive pressure of such values as maturity, responsibility, and discipline, necessarily asserts itself over a literariness associated with immaturity, irresponsibility, and (mere) pleasure, so that to be a (merely) literary literary critic, one who fails to locate the literary work in its proper historical setting, is simply, or simple-mindedly, to refuse to join the ranks of the grown-ups.[19] Which is why Catherine's resistance is hard for her (and for some of us) to sustain, why, to the well-read, well-bred Eleanor's cool acknowledgment that she is "fond of history," we may find ourselves responding, with Catherine, "I wish I were too."

Yet there is another kind of sophistication implicit in Catherine's complaint about "history, real solemn history," and in the next paragraph, the novel unpacks it in such a way as to offer the lure of a more *literary* history than the one we wish we were fond of. Picking up on Catherine's insight into history's "invention" or fictionality, Eleanor comments:

Historians, you think ... are not happy in their flights of fancy. They display imagination without raising interest. I am fond of history—and am very well contented to take the false with the true. In the principal facts they have sources of intelligence in former histories and records, which may be as much depended on, I conclude, as any thing that does not actually pass under one's own observation; and as for the little embellishments you speak of, they are embellishments, and I like them as such. (123-24)

Just as Henry shows Catherine how to refine Gothic paranoia as historical discipline, so Eleanor opens up for her a passage from fiction to history, *by way of* fiction. For history, as Henry also illustrates, is not the opposite of fiction but fiction in a particularly displaced form: in place of the "dull" history of which Catherine complained, the Tilneys offer her a *new* historicism, one that, claiming all the authority and distinction of a discipline, also affords the compensatory "embellishments" of the un-discipline known as the literary.[20] Eleanor's worldliness vis-à-vis the referential status of historiography in no way disrupts her confidence in her access *to* the world, the world with which historiography presents her: she professes herself "very well contented to take the false with the true," untroubled by her recognition that the difference between them may be undecidable. To be sophisticated about history, Eleanor's example shows, is not just to know that history is a kind of fiction: it is to know that and *not make a big deal out of it.* Liking what she gets, if not exactly getting what she likes, the sophisticated reader of history knows how to convert her boredom into a virtue.

That the normative interpretation of history is mediated here by Eleanor, moreover, is not lost on Catherine: "You are fond of history!—and so are Mr. Allen and my father; and I have two brothers who do not dislike it. So many instances within my small circle of friends is remarkable" (124). Although the fondness for history on the part of the Morland men might seem to diminish its cultural cachet, what is most "remarkable" is that Eleanor's fondness for it helps make a difference between the upper-middle class and the merely middle-middle class. In the class fraction represented by the Morlands, that is, history is what fathers and brothers "do not dislike"; in the class fraction represented by the Tilneys, a taste for history is found in women as well as in men (Henry wastes no time in praising the historians' "method and style" [124]). Once this difference has been established, history can define the novel's desired class style itself, another finely regulated mixture, this time at the level of gender stereotypes. Unlike the rigid sexual division of taste in families like the Morlands, this style signifies a pseudo-equality of the sexes, whereby women consume and talk about the patriarchal texts of history with the same ease with which their brothers consume and talk about the supposedly feminine and feminizing texts of Gothic fiction. By imitating Eleanor, Catherine can get closer to Henry; she can get, that is, from a middle-class and female Gothic paranoia to an upper-middle-class historical sophistication whose definitive maleness consists precisely in the subsumptive "androgyny" of its total *comprehension*. [21]

No sooner does history get raised as a question, however, than it gets dropped as a subject. After this discussion, the Tilneys move on to such other topics as the picturesque and, not surprisingly, the insistent Gothic novel. Yet it is this very eclecticism that accounts for Eleanor and Henry's allure as embodiments of a certain privileged cultural style. Not for them the gauche pedantry of the pushing autodidact: what emanates from their conversation is not so much knowledge as the sexier mystique of *knowingness*. [22] Enfolded in their spaciously cosmopolitan discourse, the subject of history acquires much of the discreet charm with which they treat it. And while it thus may look like merely one status symbol among others in the catalogue of topics for cultivated name-dropping, we should not take its self-effacement at face value. For one thing, as I have shown, history returns implicitly in Henry's speech about the policing of England, and in Catherine's subsequent reflections on the English character. For another, once it has been put into subtextual circulation as the prescribed refinement of Gothic, it keeps suggesting itself all the more fantasmatically as the half-concealed paradigm for the novel's own discursive procedures.

This odd effect becomes most evident at the end of the novel, when Austen, blithely exposing the arbitrariness and fictionality of her narrative, does not so much undermine it as frame it in much the same way that Eleanor frames history—as a mixture of, for instance, "the false with the true." That we will be "very well contented to take" it as such, just as Eleanor takes the works of Hume and Robertson, seems indeed the author's confident expectation, so little does her ironic parabasis interfere with her concurrent rhetoric of reference. If history in general is displaced fiction that still tells the truth, then this fiction in particular may be displaced history that still has its tropes: the two forms appear finally to supplement and to frame each other, but without any of the melodrama one might associate with a certain style of deconstructive criticism. Indeed, what we have here is a case of the *un*-uncanny: what the conclusion performs most emphatically is *exemption* from anxiety. When, for instance,

Austen writes, "The anxiety, which in this state of their attachment must be the portion of Henry and Catherine, and of all who loved either, as to its final event, can hardly extend, I fear, to the bosom of my readers, who will see in the tell-tale compression of the pages before them, that we are all hastening together to perfect felicity" (246), who can get anxious about this alienation-effect? Who's afraid of Austen's "I fear"? And if we suspect that "perfect felicity" isn't *exactly* what's in store for us, we can remain "very well contented" with the suspicion itself, since our ability to entertain it, to consider it *fearlessly*, demonstrates our own sophistication, our inclusion in the charmed and charming circle that Austen's novel describes. Reading *Northanger Abbey*, we have learned not only how to be suspicious without seeming anxious, but also how to have our world without giving up our worldliness. In short, even though Austen may be too well mannered to specify the extent to which history figures in her text, it is as though we had learned how to read that text "historically."

THE MOST CHARMING YOUNG MAN IN THE WORLD

Like all good pedagogues, Austen knows that the best way to make a boring subject like history interesting is to make the students develop a crush on the teacher. Catherine Morland of course has not one but two seductive teachers in the brother-and-sister team of Henry and Eleanor Tilney, whose intricate relation to Catherine mirrors Austen's intricate courtship of the reader. In other words, if Catherine's graduation neatly coincides with the inevitable tying of the knot that cinches the marriage plot, the entanglement of desire and identification leading up to that telos can never be straightened out along exclusively heterosexual lines. The admirable Eleanor obviously functions as a role model for Catherine, but it would take a wilfully obtuse "common sense" to pretend that wanting to be like Eleanor has nothing to do with wanting Eleanor, period. Even in the 1950s, Austen criticism could bring itself to acknowledge lesbian energies in her novels, if only in the disapproving terms of a more or less popular Freudianism.

But while some Austenians have at least recognized the possibility in her novels of desire between women—on the condition, of course, that it appear under the pathologizing, moralizing rubric of, say, "narcissism"—both male and female critics, both sexists and feminists, have been notably reluctant to look at the various charming young men whose desirability drives Austen's heterosexualizing masterplot as surely as Henry Tilney, in pointed contrast to the bumptious John Thorpe, with his dubious boasts about how "[w]ell hung" (67) his gig is, drives the carriage that takes Catherine from Bath to Northanger Abbey.

> Henry drove so well,—so quietly—without making any disturbance, without parading to her, or swearing at [the horses]; so different from the only gentleman-coachman whom it was in her power to compare him with!—And then his hat sat so well, and the innumerable capes of his great coat looked so becomingly important! To be driven by him, next to being dancing with him, was certainly the greatest happiness in the world. (163)

Perhaps critics worry that repeating Catherine's gaze would land *them* in the passenger's seat, in the unglamorous subject position of an impressionable femininity. Regarding Henry—rather, refusing to regard Henry—they have chosen between two apparently antithetical but mutually reinforcing tactics: the patriarchal one of imitating his condescending wit and irony while pretending not to notice its sexual performativity, and the antipatriarchal one of registering that sexual performativity, but only as the manifestation of a somewhat abstract male chauvinism.

This scopophobia might adduce its moral justification in Austen's other novels. Judith Wilt has observed that, after *Northanger Abbey*, charm in Austen's young men (Wickham, Willoughby, Frank Churchill) begins to signify duplicity or villainy, so that, "[b]y the time of *Mansfield Park*, Henry Tilney has metamorphosed into the charming villain, Henry Crawford."[23] Where the charming Ann Radcliffe merely gets assimilated into a higher, more refined Gothicism, it is not long before the charming young man who replaces her meets with the less genteel violence of repudiation. Within Austen's fiction itself, that is, male sex appeal begins its long nineteenth-century slide toward the demonized figure of the Pretty Boy with an Ugly Problem, whose apotheosis hangs ignobly at century's end in the picture of Dorian Gray. Indeed, the story of the nineteenth-century English novel might be told as the story of how social intercourse itself stops getting embodied by the charming man and starts getting embodied either by the disgusting man (Uriah Heep in *David Copperfield*, Slope in *Barchester Towers*, Casaubon in *Middlemarch*) or by the equally disgusting, because theatrically bewitching, woman (Becky Sharp in *Vanity Fair*, Alcharisi in *Daniel Deronda*), and of how, faced with this hideous progeny, all we can do is follow the lead of the rebarbatively "plain" heroes and heroines of Charlotte Brontë, as they retreat from social existence in general into an intensively psychologized, protosuburban paradise.[24]

Limiting our scope to the Austen canon itself, we might ask: how do we get from attractive Henry Tilney to repulsive Mr. Collins, from an image of the social as an object of desire to an image of the social as an object of disgust, as the site of what I have referred to in a reading of *Pride and Prejudice* as a "nauseating vicariousness"?[25] Is male charm in *Northanger Abbey* already somehow contaminated, already inhabited, à la Dorian Gray, by its phobogenic opposite? Just what *makes* a man charming, according to this novel, and just what would make his charm vulnerable to self-subversion? Henry's charm, at any rate, is announced from the moment of his introduction to Catherine in the pump-room at Bath:

> The master of ceremonies introduced to her a very gentlemanlike young man as a partner;—his name was Tilney. He seemed to be about four or five and twenty, was rather tall, had a pleasing countenance, a very intelligent and lively eye, and, if not quite handsome, was very near it. His address was good and Catherine felt herself in high luck.... He talked with fluency and spirit—and there was an archness and pleasantry in his manner which interested, though it was hardly understood by her. (47)

What does it mean to be "not quite handsome" but "very near it"? What exactly separates "handsome" from "very near handsome"? That Austen withholds this crucial information—as though it were *not* crucial information, as though everyone knew the difference but no one cared—and that she seems to qualify and evade Henry's attractiveness even as she asserts it, might suggest that she already has reservations about male charm. And if we were to seek a plausible reason for these reservations, we wouldn't have to look much further than the "archness and pleasantry," which even Catherine, "fear[ing] ... that [Henry] indulged himself a little too much with the foibles of others" (50), isn't too bedazzled to recognize as precursors of the *Schadenfreude* with which he will soon treat her.

But is it the aggressivity of archness that gives Austen pause? As its etymology reminds us, "archness" is the rhetorical prerogative of those at the top of the social hier*arch*y, those who command the authority to articulate that hierarchy in the first place. If "charm," as Bourdieu has argued, "designate[s] the power, which certain people have, to impose their own self-image as the objective and collective image of their body and being; to persuade others, as in love or faith, to abdicate their generic power of objectification and delegate it to the person who should be its object, who thereby becomes an absolute subject, without an exterior (being his own Other), fully justified in existing, legitimated," then, precisely to the extent that it foreshadows his more elaborated sadism, Henry's archness not only *constitutes* his charm, but constitutes it as the novel's proudest achievement: the historicist sophistication that objectifies the would-be objectifying surveillance of a whole "neighbourhood of voluntary spies," and that thus transforms paranoia into panopticism.[26]

Yet there remain in the novel other traces of an anticharismatic tendency that can't be explained away quite so easily. Henry's inability to do more than *approximate* handsomeness resonates strikingly, for example, with Austen's arch refusal, in the novel's final chapter, to let us see "the most charming young man in the world" (247), as she tantalizingly refers to the wealthy peer who shows up like a deus ex machina to marry Eleanor and thus enable General Tilney to consent to the marriage of Henry and Catherine as well. Austen's excuse that "the rules of composition forbid the introduction of a character not connected with my fable" (247), and her mocking assurance that, despite this interdiction, "the most charming young man in the world is instantly before the imagination of us all" (247), though in themselves charming instances of self-conscious fictiveness, may not be quite charming enough to satisfy readers who, still wondering about "not quite handsome," want to *see*, not just imagine, the character she is keeping from us, and who want to know why she is doing so. Why can the novel tolerate only one charming young man, and why does even he have to fall slightly short of the charms we desire for him?

Unpersuaded that "too much" charm can get to be as boring as, say, history before it became literary, we might hypothesize that the problem with *two* charming young men is rather one of excessive excitement: this doubling raises the specter of social intercourse as uncontrolled and uncontrollable imitation. "The problem, perceived by many commentators on eighteenth-century mores," Jerome Christensen has written, "was usually associated with the 'present rage of imitating the manners of high life [which] hath spread itself so far among the gentlefolks of lower life, that in a few years we shall probably have no common folk at all.' "[27]

Though it maintains a strict quota system in order to regulate mimetic desire between men, *Northanger Abbey* does represent one rather disturbing case of cross-gender desire and identification between "the gentlefolks of lower life" and the "high life" for which they yearn. The example of Isabella Thorpe shows that, much as the novel needs Henry's charm to stimulate the desire of the middle class for the "aristocracy," it also needs to guard against the danger of stimulating *too much* desire— that is to say, of producing an overidentification that would end up blurring the line between middle-class women and "aristocratic" men. When Henry is described as "forming his features into a set smile, . . . affectedly softening his voice" and speaking "with a simpering air" (47), the narrative has little trouble absorbing these potentially discrediting mannerisms into the general "fluency and spirit" (47) required of the "very gentlemanlike young man." When a similar theatricality shows up in a character like Isabella Thorpe, however, the narrative isn't so tolerant. In Isabella, affectation bespeaks not social distinction but a fatal vulgarity and inauthenticity. The contrast between her and Eleanor is decisive:

Miss Tilney had a good figure, a pretty face, and a very agreeable countenance; and her air, though it had not all the decided pretension, the resolute stilishness of Miss Thorpe's, had more real elegance. Her manners shewed good sense and good breeding; they were neither shy, nor affectedly open; and she seemed capable of being young, attractive, and at a ball, without wanting to fix the attention of every man near her, and without exaggerated feelings of extatic delight or inconceivable vexation on every little trifling occurrence. (76)

But where Eleanor's defense of history serves indirectly to recommend her brother's "historical" practice, underscoring the superiority of the class style he thereby embodies, here her mediation has the rather embarrassing effect of bringing out—by disavowing—the *resemblance* between Henry's style and Isabella's mere "stilishness." Though Eleanor is interposed as a screen or a buffer against any awareness of such slippage across class lines, it is clear not only what Isabella's "pretension" is pretending to, but also that this "pretension" comes a bit too close to the more accomplished "affectation," to the more artfully opaque "archness and pleasantry," that are its models. (Isabella's confession to Catherine that "[s]he had long suspected the [Tilneys] to be very high" [139]—that is, haughty—bespeaks more poignantly her envious aspiration to that height.) And when the same chapter that contains a warning that "Dress is a frivolous distinction, and excessive solicitude about it often destroys its own aim" (92) also features an extended discussion of dancing as a metaphor for marriage, in which Henry's rhetorical conceits are all too visibly dressed to kill, we can see how his example might make it difficult to distinguish between good distinction and its "frivolous" perversion.

Undeniably, the force of the passage in which Catherine contrasts Eleanor with Isabella, and indeed much of the appeal of the first half of the novel itself, derive from a powerful fantasy of legibility at the heart of Austen's fiction as a whole: the fantasy that, at least in reading one's acquaintances, one *doesn't* have "to take the false with the true," since one can learn to distinguish reliably between those with genuine class and those who are merely vulgar *poseurs*—between the Tilneys and the Thorpes of the world. Culminating almost ritually in the heroine's embrace by the former, and in the equally gratifying exposure and expulsion of the latter, the fantasy's power consists in large part in its implicit flattery of the reader, whom it congratulates for *having* the distinction necessary to *make* distinctions, for setting herself apart from the upstarts by whose pretentious impostures she might otherwise have been taken in—or, worse, in whose pretentious fantasies she might otherwise have had to recognize her own.[28] If the novel makes its heroine a reader, it even more delightfully makes its reader a heroine.

Fully committed to the punitive, projective logic that accounts for so much of the pleasure of the "realistic" text, *Northanger Abbey* indeed sees to it, for example, that Isabella gets what's coming to her, finding herself abandoned by the "fashionable" (141) Captain Tilney just as she had abandoned Catherine's brother. If the target audience for this revenge plot consists of the multitude of the socially insecure (that is to say, of the middle class), the annoying Isabella obviously makes an irresistible target herself, but where "target" means "scapegoat." The social insecurity—the destabilizing of the class structure—that her "pretension" threatens to effect, however, is ultimately traceable not to her undisciplined desire, but rather to the advertising campaign whose function it is to incite that desire in the first place. Though her transgression obviously consists in not knowing her place, what induces that libidinal errancy, that grotesque imitative identification, is the spectacle of the charming young man, the sex symbol who, what Isabella wants to be even more than to have, figures as the object of her affections. Isabella may pursue the irresponsible *Frederick* Tilney, but the eroticized class style that she is after finds its fullest embodiment in the novel in his supposedly good younger brother.

Showcasing Henry as the object of a desire that is not limited to Catherine, the novel risks setting in motion a general imitativeness whose effect would be to erase the distinctions it has so painstakingly drawn—and to implicate itself in the social promiscuity for which fiction in general had been denounced throughout the previous century. One of Isabella's most obnoxious traits is her arch way of attributing archness to others; eventually, she even has the rhetorically unadventurous Catherine pretending to the "arch penetration" (132) with which Isabella charges her. As though fancying herself (to pun badly on the name of James's noble heroine) a sort of Isabella Archer, she brazenly lays claim to a supercilious rhetoric that not only links her obscenely with Henry but also calls Henry's identity into question; in imitating him, she makes him seem to imitate her. Here, as throughout Austen's fiction, the arriviste's aping of "the manners of high life" furnishes her with one of her favorite and most egregious examples of social interaction as nauseating vicariousness. What could be more disgusting than the vulgarian's pretentious emulation of the sophisticate? Only the resulting undifferentiation, which announces itself under the sign of a second, perhaps even more disturbing vicariousness: the vicariousness, strategically thematized by Jacques Derrida in a reading of the disgusting in Kant's aesthetics, in which imitation takes place not just between people but between parts of the same body.[29]

As when, in the following passage, Henry Tilney's hair "imitates" his penis: "The Mysteries of Udolpho, when I had once begun it, I could not lay down again;—I remember finishing it in two days—my hair standing on end the whole time" (121). Catherine expects all men to be like the boorish John Thorpe, who is as vulgarly contemptuous of novels as she is vulgarly enamored of them, but Henry's interest in Gothic fiction looks forward to the appropriative hipness of a certain opportunistic style of "male feminism." Impressing his interlocutors with the arresting (if proverbial) image of his "hair standing on end the whole time," he stages his petrification (or castration) in the paradoxical, apotropaic mode of erection.[30] Indeed, Henry disarmingly, that is, aggressively, installs himself in the space of novelized "femininity," all the better to engage in a menacing display of cultural capital as phallic privilege. Affirming his superior command of Gothic fiction, he warns Catherine:

Do not imagine that you can cope with me in a knowledge of Julias and Louisas. If we proceed to particulars, and engage in the never-ceasing inquiry of "Have you read this?" and "Have you read that?" I shall soon leave you as far behind me as—what shall I say—I want an appropriate simile;—as far as your friend Emily herself left poor Valancourt when she went with her aunt into Italy. Consider how many years I have had the start of you. I had entered on my studies at Oxford, while you were a good little girl working your sampler at home! (122)

But Henry's "feminism" may not be entirely distinguishable from his "feminization": it may not be reducible, that is, to the sort of power play that characterizes patriarchy with a baby face. Though his cute receptivity to Gothic novels rectifies itself as a defensively offensive stiffness, his reference to his "studies at Oxford," in addition to casting him in the subordinate role of The Student, evokes the whole constricting network of family ties in which he must play the other, less escapable subordinate role of The Younger Son—a role that, as he lets slip in a startlingly fratricidal fantasy a few pages later, he has every reason to resent. For while Catherine was "a good little girl working [her] sampler at home," Henry was, and must remain, a good little boy—perhaps, since he'll have to cede the title of most charming young man, the best little boy in the world. But he's charming enough, and could easily be added to the company of the charming young men in Austen's novels of whom Sandra M. Gilbert and Susan Gubar observe: "Willoughby, Wickham, Frank Churchill, and Mr. Elliott are eminently agreeable because they are self-changers, self-shapers. In many respects they are attractive to the heroines because somehow they act as doubles: younger men who must learn to please, narcissists, they experience traditionally 'feminine' powerlessness and they are therefore especially interested in becoming the creators of themselves."[31]

Where Bourdieu describes charm's characteristic *effects*, Gilbert and Gubar provide it with a *genealogy*, so that the traditionally "masculine" power of the charming (or absolute) subject, which masquerades as pure cause, gets demystified as itself an effect: an effect of "traditionally 'feminine' powerlessness," a peculiar afterglow of the anxious rhetorical performance perhaps best exemplified, in our time and idiom, by the abused child struggling to survive the dysfunctional family. That many abused or "merely" dominated children grow up to be "self-changers," "self-shapers," and even self-creators (less honorifically: "narcissists"), may thus signify not so much triumph over the familial reign of terror as continuing subjection to it. Where Henry's charming "archness and pleasantry" initially seemed to define charm in general as a *supersocial* disposition—not just the social disposition par excellence, but the social disposition that panoptically rules over and thereby *transcends* the social—now, while pleasantry emerges as an almost Pavlovian reflex forcibly instilled in those "who must learn to please," archness begins to resemble a professional deformation, a curvature of the tongue imposed upon those who can't enjoy the rewards, or who can't afford the risks, of straight talk.

Henry isn't exactly an abused child, but if Catherine begins to sense that General Tilney "seemed always a check upon his children's spirits" (163), she soon learns, through painful firsthand experience, that his "parental tyranny" extends beyond mere oppressiveness (248). Henry of course finally rebels against this tyranny; yet his rebellion, and his consequent proposal of marriage to Catherine, seem to entail a curious stylistic change. Expressing his "embarrassment on his father's account" (239) through a gratifying profusion of "blushes" and other "pitiable" somatic signs, Henry seems almost to have been assigned a new class body: the charming, easy body of the "aristocrat" seems to have been replaced by the awkward, self-conscious body of the petit bourgeois.[32] For a moment, it appears not that Cinderella is ascending to the level of Prince Charming but that he is descending to hers, and that their union heralds not a bold reentry into the symbolic order but a panicky exit from it.

If this humbling of Henry doesn't entirely divest him of his "aristocratic" charm, it furnishes one more piece of evidence that, even in *Northanger Abbey*, the homophobic aversion therapy of nineteenth-century fiction is already being prepared. Even here, where so much effort goes into making the (presumptively female) reader mad about the boy, we can see intimations of the dreary cultural project thanks to which the charming young man will cease to be engrossing and become merely gross. *Northanger Abbey*, moreover, intimates the logic of this revulsion, showing how charm itself implies not only the archcommentator's arch penetration of the social text but also his inscription in that text, and thus the possibility of his penetration by others. Just as the most charming young man in the world gets linked, through his servant, with the "washing-bills" Catherine misidentifies in her Gothic wishfulness, and thus with dirty linen, so Henry threatens to reveal the nauseating versatility of the body in charm.

What disconcerts Austen, and a whole novelistic tradition after her, is a sense that upper-middle-class sophistication, the very stock in trade of nineteenth-century fiction in general, might turn every upper-middle-class male body into that nauseating body. Indeed, as the style of the middle-class aristocracy becomes increasingly associated with the style of what John Kucich has called the antibourgeois intellectual elite—or with the style of what Bourdieu calls the dominated fraction of the dominant class—men like Henry Tilney become increasingly troubling for their "perverse" combination of cockiness with complaisance, of cosmopolitanism as mastery with cosmopolitanism as marginality. In order to save upper-middle-class men for the upper-middle-class and would-be upper-middle-class women whose fate it is to love them, Austen begins remodelling the former along the virile, though rather charmless, lines of, say, Darcy—making them more like lawyers or businessmen than like literature professors—and annexes the remaining sophistication as the legitimate function only of a relatively disembodied female authorship, and not of a relatively embodied male characterhood. As the charming young man sinks into villainy, and as his dirty linen expands itself as the general sleaze that ultimately defines him, the archness and pleasantry that he also leaves behind become the property of Jane Austen herself. If her gender permits her to let down the hair that previously stood on end, and to develop Henry's archness and pleasantry into the "irony" and "wit" for which she is famous, it is because "irony" and "wit" are the names we must give to resentment and sarcasm to find them charming—that is, to misrecognize the violence of a social order that, barring women from the exercise of power, grants them the authority of a "style" that can only keep biting the hand that doesn't feed it.[33]

NOTES

1. Nancy Armstrong, *Desire and Domestic Fiction: A Political History of the Novel* (New York: Oxford University Press, 1987), 106. For a discussion of the "preposterous" in eighteenth-century fiction (and in a wide range of other texts and contexts), see Lee Edelman, "Seeing Things: Representation, the Scene of Surveillance, and the Spectacle of Gay Male Sex," in *Homographesis: Essays in Gay Literary and Cultural Theory* (New York: Routledge, 1994), 173-91.

2. Armstrong, *Desire*, 106.

3. Although the novel was published posthumously in 1817, Anne Ehrenpreis cites Austen's sister Cassandra as claiming that it was "written about the years 98 and 99." Ehrenpreis also notes that a version of the novel may have been "drafted as early as 1794," and that, according to the author's "Advertisement," the work was "finished in the year 1803." See Ehrenpreis's Introduction to her edition of Jane Austen, *Northanger Abbey* (Harmondsworth: Penguin, 1972), 9-10. Further references to this work will be included parenthetically in the text.

4. Armstrong, *Desire*, 160 (emphasis added).

5. For an example of the framing of Austen as transitional, see Raymond Williams, *The English Novel: From Dickens to Lawrence* (New York: Oxford University Press, 1970), 61. See the second chapter of my *Caught in the Act: Theatricality in the Nineteenth-Century English Novel* (Berkeley: University of California Press, 1992), esp. pp. 27-29, for a critique of the opposition between Austenian "worldliness" and Brontëan interiority. For an astute and suggestive account of the pro-

duction of a certain middle-class sophistication in Trollope, see John Kucich, "Transgression in Trollope: Dishonesty and the Antibourgeois Elite," *ELH* 56 (1989): 593-618. Kucich's argument has provided much of the inspiration for the present essay, as well as for the longer project of which it is a part. On the curious variability of views about Austen's class position, see Claudia L. Johnson, *Jane Austen: Women, Politics, and the Novel* (Chicago: University of Chicago Press, 1988), xviii. An extensive discussion of class, gender, and ideology in Austen may be found in Mary Poovey, *The Proper Lady and the Woman Writer: Ideology as Style in the Works of Mary Wollstonecraft, Mary Shelley, and Jane Austen* (Chicago: University of Chicago Press, 1984).

6. This reference to "professorial taste" is perhaps the first signal of the considerable influence, throughout the present essay, of Pierre Bourdieu's *Distinction: A Social Critique of the Judgment of Taste*, trans. Richard Nice (Cambridge: Harvard University Press, 1984). In some sense, my comments on "history" here represent an extension of certain themes broached in my "Back to the Future: A Review-Article on the New Historicism, Deconstruction, and Nineteenth-Century Fiction," *Texas Studies in Literature and Language* 30 (Spring 1988): 120-49. Since I wrote that article, my thinking about the politics of the new historicism has been affected importantly by Alan Liu, "The Power of Formalism: The New Historicism," *ELH* 56 (Winter 1989): 721-71, and by Stanley Fish, "Commentary: The Young and the Restless," in H. Aram Veeser, ed., *The New Historicism* (New York: Routledge, 1989), 303-16.

7. Avrom Fleishman, "The Socialization of Catherine Morland," *ELH* 41 (1974): 666. For other versions of this "dialectical" reading, see, for example: Sandra M. Gilbert and Susan Gubar, *The Madwoman in the Attic: The Woman Writer and the Nineteenth-Century Literary Imagination* (New Haven: Yale University Press, 1979), 128-45; Johnson, *Jane Austen*, 28-48; George Levine, *The Realistic Imagination: English Fiction from Frankenstein to Lady Chatterley* (Chicago: University of Chicago Press, 1981); Judith Wilt, *Ghosts of the Gothic: Austen, Eliot, and Lawrence* (Princeton: Princeton University Press, 1980), 121-72.

8. Wilt, *Ghosts*, 127.

9. On the link between realism and "the complexity of human character," see Fleishman, "Socialization," 664.

10. "Lover-mentor" comes from Wilt, *Ghosts*, 147.

11. I have in mind, for example, the essays on *Bleak House* and *David Copperfield* in D. A. Miller, *The Novel and the Police* (Berkeley: University of California Press, 1988). On the complex relationships between the middling and the extreme in the constitution of middle-class identity, see Peter Stallybrass and Allon White, *The Politics and Poetics of Transgression* (Ithaca: Cornell University Press, 1986).

12. I am drawing here upon Kucich's demonstration of how in Trollope middle-class moral norms are "rotated slightly upwards in the social scale" (598), as well as upon his insights into the formation of a middle-class elite, which "depends on a conviction . . . of the transcendent fluidity of its social and moral identity" (615). When General Tilney calculatingly "admires the elasticity of [Catherine's] walk, which corresponded exactly with the spirit of her dancing"

(118), what he *mis*calculates is the extent to which this "elasticity" prefigures the (upper-)middle-class "fluidity" that Kucich uncovers in Trollope.

13. My thinking about refinement, especially later in this essay, takes inspiration from some dense, rich paragraphs in Jerome Christensen, *Practicing Enlightenment: Hume and the Formation of a Literary Career* (Madison: University of Wisconsin Press, 1987), 115-16. For example: "If refinement is what makes the economy go, vicious luxury is what erases the bounds between a restricted economy and one generalized beyond any reason. Refinement's globalism is theoretically unchecked, its processive aggrandizement potentially and radically diseconomic" (116).

14. For example: "Taste classifies, and it classifies the classifier. Social subjects, classified by their classifications, distinguish themselves by the distinctions they make, between the beautiful and the ugly, the distinguished and the vulgar, in which their position in the objective classifications is expressed or betrayed" (Bourdieu, *Distinction*, 6).

15. There is an extensive critical literature about the relations between the novel and historiography before, during, and after the nineteenth century. For a classic deconstructive treatment of these relations, see J. Hillis Miller, "Narrative and History," *ELH* 41 (Fall 1974): 455-76.

16. On female paranoia, see, for example, Mary Ann Doane, *The Desire to Desire: The Woman's Film of the 1940s* (Bloomington: Indiana University Press, 1987). I return to this work in note 21.

17. Much new-historicist writing is explicitly antitheoretical, but if such theorists as Freud and Lacan are right about the affinity between theory and paranoia, the dissimulated paranoia of the new historicism may itself dissimulate certain stubborn theoretical residues. For a cannily Foucauldian reading of *Northanger Abbey*, see Paul Morrison, "Enclosed in Openness: *Northanger Abbey* and the Domestic Carceral," *Texas Studies in Literature and Language* 33 (Spring 1991): 1-23. Where Morrison tends to posit his reading over and against Henry Tilney's naïveté, I am suggesting that Henry is himself already a Foucauldian, and that he is teaching Catherine how to become one.

18. I allude here to the slogan, "Always historicize!," with which Fredric Jameson begins *The Political Unconscious: Narrative as a Socially Symbolic Act* (Ithaca: Cornell University Press, 1981), 9. Though current, this imperative isn't exactly new. Almost twenty years ago, Paul de Man disdainfully remarked that behind the then-resurgent pressure to historicize "stands a highly respectable moral imperative that strives to reconcile the internal, formal, private structures of literary language with their external, referential, and public effects" (*Allegories of Reading: Figural Language in Rousseau, Nietzsche, Rilke, and Proust* [New Haven: Yale University Press, 1979], 3). That de Man evades the historical imperative in favor of an even more "rigorous" (if also, or therefore, more "unreliable") critical practice (19) perhaps suggests one of the differences between his stance and the present essay's vis-à-vis historicism.

19. I am not arguing, in a totalizing fashion, that feminist and gay critics who invest in historicism thereby inevitably become complicit in their own oppression.

Nor would it be difficult to cite examples of the oppressiveness of various formal-isms. My point is that the historicist imperative, *as an imperative*, can exercise a normalizing function that precludes many of the pleasures, aptitudes, and in-sights—call them "literary," for now—that a lot of feminist and gay critics might well be reluctant to renounce. Though a sophisticated (or "new") historicism significantly mitigates some of the more rebarbative features of history as a *discipline*—and though Foucault's sophisticated gayness, for example, no doubt has much to do with the sex appeal of the new historicism, or at least with the charm it exerted in the 1980s—sophistication has normalizing, disciplinary implications of its own. (On the problematic overdetermination of charm, see the third section of this essay.)

20. On the similarities between history, as described by Catherine, and Gothic fiction, see Wilt, *Ghosts*, 130.

21. On the way in which "the whole set of socially constituted differences between the sexes tends to weaken as one moves up the social hierarchy," see Bourdieu, *Distinction*, 382-83. Though the literature on female paranoia necessar-ily works with, or within, psychoanalytic paradigms that do not explicitly address questions of class, I have found provocative Mary Ann Doane's comment on how, in certain Gothic-influenced "woman's films," "the mixture effected by a marriage between two different classes produces horror and paranoia" (*Desire to Desire*, 173). In light of this comment, Doane's characterization of female paranoia as simultaneously a foreclosure of the paternal, a hyperbolization of the paternal, and a fear of the maternal (*Desire to Desire*, 145) could be opened up into an analysis of the cross-class dynamics of *Northanger Abbey*, where Catherine Mor-land's paranoid *social* desire gets played out in relation to the symbolic positions occupied not only by her own parents, but by General Tilney as a father figure, by Henry Tilney as an "androgynous" compromise between the paternal and the maternal, by Eleanor Tilney as an idealized version of the self, and so on.

22. See Bourdieu, *Distinction*, 329: "But above all, the autodidact, a victim by default of the effects of educational entitlement, is ignorant of the right to be ignorant that is conferred by certificates of knowledge, and it would no doubt be futile to seek elsewhere than in the manner in which it is affirmed the difference between the forced eclecticism of this culture, picked up in the course of unguided reading and accidental encounters, and the elective eclecticism of aesthetes who use the mixing of genres and the subversion of hierarchies as an opportunity to manifest their all-powerful aesthetic disposition."

23. Wilt, *Ghosts*, 151.

24. This is not to say, of course, that male charm is unambiguously valorized in fiction before the nineteenth-century; in a discussion of an earlier version of this essay, one respondent cited the character of Lovelace in *Clarissa* as a notable counterinstance, and others could no doubt be adduced. Much as I value this kind of sophisticated historicist suspicion, I persist in the "naïve" historicist belief that one of the ways in which Austen's novels enjoy a peculiarly indicative relation to both eighteenth- and nineteenth-century fiction is in registering as acutely as they do the effects of a changing sex/gender/class system. A fuller consideration of this

system would locate Austen's charming young men vis-à-vis such other increasingly problematic male figures as the rake, the fop, the dandy, and the gentleman. On this context, see, for example, Regenia Gagnier, *Idylls of the Marketplace: Oscar Wilde and the Victorian Public* (Stanford: Stanford University Press, 1986), and Ellen Moers, *The Dandy: Brummell to Beerbohm* (Lincoln: University of Nebraska Press, 1978).

25. Joseph Litvak, "Delicacy and Disgust, Mourning and Melancholia, Privilege and Perversity: *Pride and Prejudice*," *qui parle* 6 (Fall/Winter 1992): 41.

26. Bourdieu, *Distinction*, 208.

27. Christensen, *Practicing*, 118 n.

28. This fantasy of social identification anticipates the imaginary structure D. A. Miller sees as typical of Victorian fiction in general: "an affective schema as adolescent as the protagonists who command our attention therein: those whom we love struggle with those whom we hate, against a background of those to whom we are largely indifferent" (Miller, *Novel*, 132).

29. Jacques Derrida, "Economimesis," trans. Richard Klein, *Diacritics* 11 (Summer 1981): 3-25.

30. On this mechanism, see Sigmund Freud, "Medusa's Head," in *The Standard Edition of the Complete Psychological Works*, trans. James Strachey (London: The Hogarth Press, 1991), vol. 18, 273-74, and Neil Hertz, "Medusa's Head: Male Hysteria under Political Pressure," in *The End of the Line: Essays on Psychoanalysis and the Sublime* (New York: Columbia University Press, 1985), 161-91.

31. Gilbert and Gubar, *Madwoman*, 167.

32. See Bourdieu, *Distinction*, 207-8.

33. This perspective on Austen's "style" owes much to D. A. Miller, "Austen's Attitude," *The Yale Journal of Criticism* 8 (1995): 1-5.

Contributors

JENNIFER DEVERE BRODY teaches in the English department at the University of California, Riverside. Her work has appeared in *Callaloo, American Quarterly*, and most recently in *Unnatural Acts: Theorizing the Performative*. She is completing a book on hybrids and hybridity in Victorian discourse.

EILEEN CLEERE is a Ph.D. candidate at Rice University. Her dissertation, "'The Shape of Uncles': Capitalism, Affections, and the Cultural Construction of the Victorian Family," was awarded a 1995 Woodrow Wilson Women's Studies Fellowship. The project examines the intersecting discourses of nineteenth-century economic history and family sentiment.

BRIDGET ELLIOTT teaches nineteenth- and twentieth-century art history at the University of Western Ontario. She has recently coauthored *Women Artists and Writers: Modernist (Im)positionings* with Jo-Ann Wallace and is currently working on a study of visual representations of late-nineteenth-century British music-hall entertainment.

ROSEMARY HENNESSY teaches postmodern cultural critique, feminist theory, and gay and lesbian studies in the English department of the University of Albany, SUNY. She has written *Materialist Feminism and the Politics of Discourse* and edited, with Chrys Ingraham, *Materialist/Marxist Feminism: A Reader*. She has also written on queer theory and lesbian feminism. Her current book project deals with the historical materiality of new sexual economies.

275

BETTY JOSEPH is Assistant Professor of English at Rice University. Her book in progress on feminism and imperialism explores how strategies of reading for 'woman' can transform literary histories and narrativizations of colonialism.

JOSEPH LITVAK, Associate Professor of English at Bowdoin College, is the author of *Caught in the Act: Theatricality in the Nineteenth-Century English Novel,* and of essays on sexuality and pedagogy. He is currently completing a book-length study of the politics of sophistication from Jane Austen to cultural studies.

LAURA LYONS is an Assistant Professor at the University of Hawaii. She is currently working on a book-length project titled "Writing in Trouble: Protest and the Cultural Politics of Irish Nationalism."

POONAM PILLAI teaches Cultural Studies in the Department of Communication, Ohio State University, Columbus, Ohio. She is also associate faculty at the Division of Comparative Studies and the Program in Women's Studies at Ohio State University. Currently, she is visiting scholar at the Pembroke Center, Brown University. Her present research focuses on feminism and transnational media practices.

Guidelines for Prospective Contributors

Genders welcomes essays on art, literature, media, photography, film, and social theory. We are especially interested in essays that address theoretical issues relating sexuality and gender to social, political, racial, economic, or stylistic concerns.

All essays that are considered for publication are sent to board members for review. Your name is not included on the manuscript in this process. A decision on the essay is usually reached in about four months. Essays are grouped for publication only after the manuscript has been accepted.

We require that we have first right to any manuscript that we consider and that we have first publication of any manuscript that we accept. We will not consider any manuscript that is already under consideration with another publication or that has already been published.

The recommended length for essays is twenty-five pages of double-spaced text. Essays must be printed in letter-quality type. Quotations in languages other than English must be accompanied by translations. Photocopies of illustrations are sufficient for initial review, but authors should be prepared to supply originals upon request.

Place the title of the essay and your name, address, and telephone number on a separate sheet at the front of the essay. You are welcome to include relevant information about yourself or the essay in a letter to the editor, but please be advised that institutional affiliation does not affect editorial policy. Since the majority of the manuscripts that we receive are photocopies, we do not routinely return submissions. However, if you would like your copy returned, please enclose a self-addressed, stamped envelope.

To submit an essay for consideration, send *three* legible copies to:

Thomas Foster
Genders
Department of English
Ballantine Hall 442
Indiana University
Bloomington, IN 46405